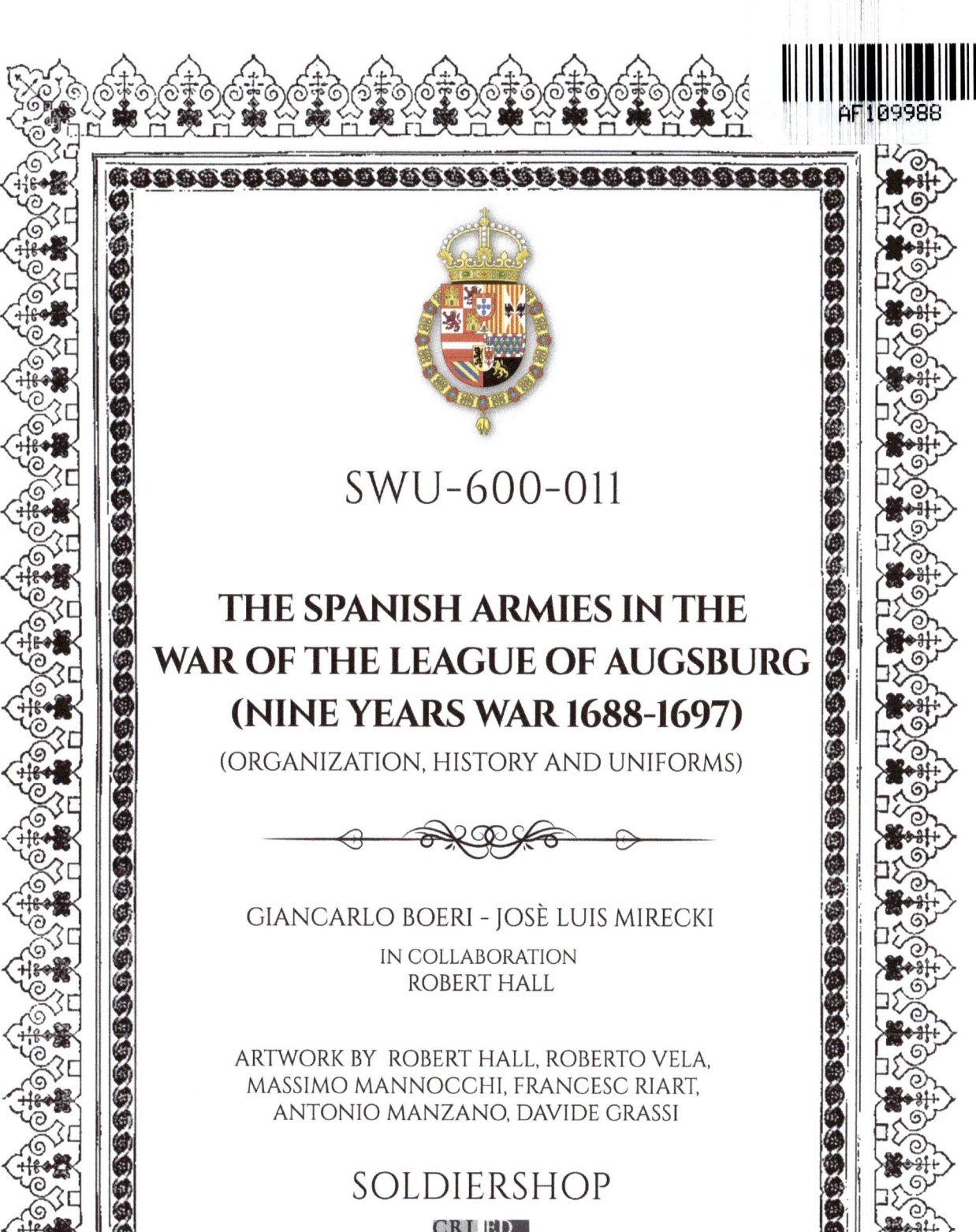

SWU-600-011

THE SPANISH ARMIES IN THE WAR OF THE LEAGUE OF AUGSBURG (NINE YEARS WAR 1688-1697)

(ORGANIZATION, HISTORY AND UNIFORMS)

GIANCARLO BOERI - JOSÈ LUIS MIRECKI

IN COLLABORATION
ROBERT HALL

ARTWORK BY ROBERT HALL, ROBERTO VELA,
MASSIMO MANNOCCHI, FRANCESC RIART,
ANTONIO MANZANO, DAVIDE GRASSI

SOLDIERSHOP

AUTHORS

Giancarlo Boeri (b. Sanremo, 1944) holds a degree in Physics but has been devoted since childhood to the study of military history and iconography of the 17th and 18th centuries. Over the years, he has meticulously researched all aspects of the armies of pre-unification Italian states, as well as the Spanish, French, and other Western European armies of the 17th and 18th centuries, establishing himself as a leading authority in the field. He has authored numerous articles and books, both independently and in collaboration with other scholars in Italy and abroad. Notable among his works is a multi-volume series on the Bourbon army from the French Revolution to the end of the Kingdom of Naples (1789–1861), published by the Historical Office of the Italian Army General Staff. Additionally, he has produced significant works on the uniforms of pre-unification Italian navies and a series of monographs (in both Italian and English) on the Savoyard, Spanish, French, and Austrian Imperial armies during the 17th and 18th centuries. For Soldiershop, in collaboration with Paolo Giacomone Piana and Roberto Vela, he has co-authored several key works, including the volumes on the War of Sardinia and Sicily (1717–1720), focusing on the Savoyard, Spanish, and Austrian armies; two studies on the Papal Army in 1708–1709 (covering the War of Comacchio and Ferrara); a three-part series on the French army in Italy during the War of Polish Succession —the first in a planned collection on the armies involved in that conflict in Italy. Recently the volumes on the Battle of Cassano (1705) and Savoyard Cavalry during the 1692 campaign against the French. Boeri's scholarship combines rigorous archival research with a deep understanding of military organization, uniforms, and tactics, making his contributions indispensable for historians and enthusiasts of early modern European warfare

José Luis Mirecki (Madrid 1958) Retired infantry lieutenant and military historian. Co-author with Giancarlo Boeri of *Spanish Armies in the War of the League of Augsburg* (The Pike & Shot Society, 2011); *Los Tercios de Carlos II durante la Guerra de los Nueve Años 1689–1697* (La espada y la pluma, 2006). With the late José Palau Cuñat, he published *Rocroi, cuando la honra española se pagaba con sangre* (Actas, 2016). For Soldiershop, he contributed to the volume on the War of Sardinia and Sicily (1717–1720) focusing on the Spanish army. His current research examines Philip V's attempts to reclaim the empire between 1715 and 1746.

Robert Hall (Belfast, 1947) Irish historian now based in Germany, recognized as one of the world's foremost experts on the armies of The War of the League of Augsburg (1688–1697) abd the War of the Spanish Succession (1701–1714). A skilled and prolific illustrator, he has authored (both independently and collaboratively) numerous works, including *Uniforms and Flags of the French Army under Louis XIV, 1688–1714* (multi-volume series on infantry, cavalry, dragoons, artillery, and militia); *Uniforms and Flags of the Imperial Austrian Army 1683–1720; Flags and Uniforms of the Dutch Army, 1685–1715. Vol. 1: Cavalry, Dragoons, Artillery & Subsidy Regiments. Vol. 2: Infantry, and the Army of the Principality of Liège.* Most of these were published by The Pike and Shot Society between 2004 and 2014.

Roberto Vela, (b. Acqui Terme, 1952) A passionate military historian with expertise in local history, heraldry, and 17th–18th century uniforms and weaponry, he has dedicated himself to iconographic research and the creation of illustrations for numerous publications. His work has appeared in journals such as the *Bollettino dell'Accademia di San Marciano*. For decades, he has collaborated with Giancarlo Boeri on historical publications, actively contributing to research and the production of the aforementioned works. His detailed artwork and archival investigations have been instrumental in reconstructing the visual history of early modern European warfare.

Acknowledgments

The authors would like to express their special thanks for the contributions received over time from Francesc Riart, Espino Lopez, Antonio Rodriguez, Etienne Rooms, Guglielmo Peirce, Luis Sorando Muzas, Antonio Manzano Lahoz, Carlos Belloso Martin, and Isabel Aguirre. In addition, they would like to acknowledge the contribution made by Josè Palau. Special thanks go to Robert Hall for reviewing the English text, providing additional information, and editing the initial draft of the illustrations, interpreting the dry archive data. Similar thanks go to Paolo Giacomone Piana for reviewing the texts and providing relevant contributions.

PUBLISHING'S NOTE

© Luca Cristini Editore 2025, Tutti i diritti riservati. Nessuna parte del testo o della grafica di questo sito può essere riprodotta o trasmessa in qualsiasi forma o con qualsiasi mezzo, elettronico o meccanico, incluso le fotocopie, la trasmissione facsimile, la registrazione, il riadattamento o l'uso di qualsiasi sistema di immagazzinamento e recupero di informazioni, senza il permesso scritto dell'editore. L'editore rimane tuttavia a disposizione per gli eventuali aventi diritto per tutte le fonti iconografiche dubbie o non identificate. Il nome soldiershop, come quello delle nostre collane è trademark © della Luca Cristini Editore.

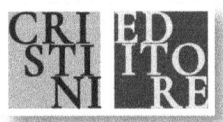

THE SPANISH ARMIES IN THE WAR OF THE LEAGUE OF AUGSBURG (NINE YEARS WAR 1688-1697)
(ORGANIZATION, HISTORY AND UNIFORMS)

By Giancarlo Boeri, Josè Luis Mirecki, with Robert Hall

Plates by Robert Hall, Roberto Vela, Massimo Mannocchi, Francesc Riart, Antonio Manzano, Davide Grassi.
Editing: Luca Cristini Editore per i tipi di Soldiershop. June 2025 Cover and DTP by L.S. Cristini.
ISBN code: 9791255892274

PREFACE

This book does not aim to explore all aspects of the reign of Charles II (Carlos II), the last Habsburg (*Austrias*) king of Spain, nor does it delve into the complexities of the Spanish state machinery—still partly rooted in medieval traditions and rife with court intrigues and personal rivalries, which flourished due to the monarch's weak character and significantly influenced the conduct of military campaigns.

Instead, its focus is on providing an overview of the composition of this Monarchy's armies—using the plural because each constituent kingdom, province, or principality maintained its own forces, militias, and budget, despite continuous osmosis between territories. Each region was governed by a viceroy or governor (appointed by the king), who also served as captain-general (supreme military commander) of the forces operating there. However, strategic decisions and partial funding depended on the Crown, which exercised control through various Councils—the most influential for military affairs being the Council of War, where factional clashes and intrigues played out. Only royal orders could authorize troop transfers between territories when necessary.

The study is confined to the War of the League of Augsburg (Nine Years' War, 1688–1697), which marked the close of the 17th century. For Spain, the conflict was defined by the siege and fall of Barcelona in 1697, its decisive conclusion. Geographically, coverage is limited to Europe and the Mediterranean basin.

Where possible, we reconstructed the succession of *maestres de campo* (field masters) and colonels leading military formations—a crucial detail for tracing campaigns, as most historical sources mention only their names or titles at a given time.

A deliberate emphasis, rarely addressed adequately in past works, reflects the authors' commitment to iconographic and material history of uniforms and flags.

This volume is a fully revised, corrected in some details, and expanded version of the English-language edition of *"The Spanish Armies in the War of the League of Augburg (Nine Years War 1688-1697)"* (Revised Edition) **Boeri, GianCarlo; Mirecki Quintero, José Luis; Palau Cuñat, José**. The Pike and Shot Society London, 2011. New chapters and additional elements enhance the original research, offering a more comprehensive resource.

ABBREVIATIONS

A.G.S.	**Archivo General de Simancas**	
	S.P. = Secretarias Provinciales	
	C.M.C. = Contaduria Mayor de Cuentas	
A.S.Mi.	**Archivio di Stato di Milano**	
	P.A. Parte Antica	
A.A.Vat.	**Archivio Apostolico Vaticano**	
A.C.A.	**Archivo Corona de Aragon**	
A.G.R.	**Archives Generaux du Royaume (Bruxelles)**	
A.N.	**Archives Nationaux (Paris)**	
A.S.Na.	**Archivio di Stato di Napoli**	
A.S.Pa.	**Archivio di Stato di Palermo**	
A.S.To.	**Archivio di Stato di Torino**	
	Sez.I Mat.Mil.	Sezione I, Materie Militari
A.H.N.	**Archivo Historico Nacional (Madrid)**	
B.C. A.H.	**Biblioteca de Catalunya** Arxiu Històric de l'Hospital de la Santa Creu i Sant Pau	
B.N.M.	**Biblioteca Nacional de Madrid**	
B.S.N.P.	**Biblioteca Società Napoletana di Storia Patria**	

▲ *King Charles II of Spain on horseback (Luca Giordano, Prado Madrid).*

INTRODUCTION

As it is well known, comprehensive documentation on the state of the Spanish armies at the end of the 17th century remains scarce. The primary—and indispensable—reference is Serafín de Soto y Montes, Conde de Clonard's *Historia orgánica de las armas de infantería y caballería española*, written and published in the 1850's. This monumental work (spanning sixteen volumes) was based on meticulous research, yet it was inevitably constrained by the technical limitations of its time, as the author lacked access to archives from other territories of the the Spanish Crown's empire—particularly the Italian states and the Spanish Netherlands- and later-discovered sources, such as those in Madrid's *Archivo Histórico Nacional*, were unavailable to him. A further limitation is that the *Historia Orgánica* focused almost exclusively on units still extant in the 19th century or those with direct institutional continuity. Many formations that had disbanded—and whose records were lost or forgotten—were omitted.

In more recent years, several groundbreaking studies have significantly advanced our understanding of Spain's military organization during the reign of Charles II. Among the most notable works are Antonio Espino López, *Catalunya durante el reinado de Carlos II. Política y guerra en la frontera catalana (1679-1697)* (PhD thesis, Universitat Autònoma de Barcelona, 1999) – A detailed examination of Catalonia's military and political struggles; Etienne Rooms, *De Organisatie van de Troepen van de Spaans-Habsburgse Monarchie in de Zuidelijke Nederlanden* (Royal Military Academy, Brussels, 1999; published by the Musée Royal de l'Armée, 2003) – A crucial study on the Spanish Army in the Southern Netherlands; Davide Maffi, *La Cittadella in Armi. Esercito, società e finanza nella Lombardia di Carlo II (1660-1700)* Franco Angeli, Milan, 2010, and *Los últimos tercios. El Ejército de Carlos II* Desperta Ferro, Madrid, 2020. – essential works on Lombardy's military structure and the late Habsburg army; Antonio Rodríguez Hernández, *España, Flandes y la Guerra de Devolución (1667-1668)* (Ministry of Defense, Madrid, 2007) and *Los Tercios de Flandes* (2015) – Key contributions on Spanish forces in Flanders; F. Xavier Hernández & Francesc Riart, *Soldats, Guerrers i Combatents dels Països Catalans* and *Els Exèrcits de Catalunya (1713-1714)* (Rafael Dalmau, Barcelona, 2007–2014) – though focused on the War of Spanish Succession, these works provide valuable insights into earlier Catalan military formations.

These studies, alongside archival discoveries, have filled critical gaps left by earlier historiography, particularly regarding regional armies and financial-military interactions. Spanish provincial archives, which contain valuable information, remain to be fully explored, especially for the corps that were formed and/or served in those provinces, and whose maintenance and equipment costs weighed on the finances of that given province.

The army of Charles II of Spain was a multinational force, reflecting the diverse territories of the Spanish Empire in Europe. The number of troops fluctuated significantly during his reign, though estimates suggest that at times it exceeded 100,000 men under arms. The largest contingent was stationed in Flanders, which maintained around 40,000 troops until the late 17th century, followed by the Army of Lombardy (approximately 20,000 soldiers) and the Army of Catalonia (roughly 15,000).

As it has been noted before, over the past two decades a new generation of researchers has produced a wealth of well-documented studies on different aspects of Spanish military history across the monarchy's territories — including its multiethnic composition — during the 17th and 18th centuries. Most of these works are listed in the bibliography (any omissions are unintentional and due to the authors' oversight). Key contributions include the publications by the Spanish Ministry of Defense, which has published many of these studies in its journals and monographs. To be praised the digitization efforts by Spanish archives, particularly PARES (*Portal de Archivos Españoles*), which continues to upload previously inaccessible original documents from the same Archives; and the National Library of Madrid (*Biblioteca Nacional de España*), which has digitized rare manuscripts and printed texts, greatly facilitating research.

The second half of the 17th century is universally regarded as a particularly bleak period across all European territories formerly under Spanish rule - including Spain itself, the Southern Netherlands (Belgium/Flanders), and Italian dominions (Naples, Milan, Sicily, Sardinia). This era witnessed two parallel crises that profoundly impacted European affairs: The Spanish Empire experienced a rapid deterioration from its position as continental hegemon, suffering the permanent loss of the northern Netherlands, which became the independent Dutch Republic, strategic territories first occupied then formally ceded to France through treaties, a domino effect of territorial retreats across Europe. A perfect

▲ *Queen Maria Anna of Spain, daughter of the Palatinate-Neuburg, on horseback (Luca Giordano, Prado Museum, Madrid).*

storm of interconnected crises: Collapsing state finances and trade networks, Population decline from warfare and plague. Paralysis of governance under Charles II's weak rule.

This dual collapse created a power vacuum that reshaped European geopolitics, as France emerged ascendant while Spanish territories struggled with decaying infrastructure, military overextension and local rebellions against Madrid's authority. The period's legacy remains etched in historical memory as the definitive end of Spain's "Golden Age" and a cautionary tale of imperial overreach meeting systemic failure. Contemporary accounts from across Europe's courts uniformly describe Spain's trajectory during these decades with a mixture of pity and geopolitical opportunism.

Even Spanish military historians until recent times have long treated this period[1] with surprising neglect — summarized in just a few pages by authorities like Serafín de Soto y Montes, Conde de Clonard[2]. The oversight is even more glaring in other nations, where the battlefield exploits and strategic innovations of Burgundians, Walloons, Flemish, Italians, Irish, and Spaniards who rose to prominence under Habsburg banners have faded into obscurity.

Furthermore, for Italy and Belgium, it must be considered that in current opinion the entire period in which the kings of Spain were also lords of those territories is regarded with annoyance and almost with shame, equating the dominion of the Spanish monarchy to a colonial dominion and the subjection to a monarch not born in those territories as an abdication of a dignity and of a "national" pride. In reality, the experiences gained by the various military subjects had a European dimension, particularly in Flanders and Milan, where representatives of many different countries and cultures met ... Up until almost the time of the French Revolution, the profession of arms was experienced and practiced as a trade, frequently not linked to dynastic or national loyalty, but only to the salary and commitment of the "professional"; there was a difference between the concept of nationality as belonging to a cultural community rather than a racial one and citizenship or subjection to a dynasty or a (feudal) lord, a feudal culture and dominion that ended only with Napoleon[3].

A definitely negative flaw of the system was represented by the bad government of the Viceroys, Governors and Councils of Spain, to which was added not infrequently the excessive arrogance of the Castilians, which led over time to uprisings in Portugal and Catalonia repeatedly, in Naples in 1647-1648, in Sicily in 1647, up to the revolt and war of Messina 1674-1678. In the capital of the Empire, in the Court of Madrid there was a clash between the pro-French faction and the pro-Habsburg faction (which led shortly after the death of Charles II to the secession of the Catalans in favor of the Austrian pretender to the throne of Spain); furthermore there was also a tendency to abandon Flanders, too expensive and demanding for the available resources [proposals to exchange it with Rossellon] and to concentrate attention on the possessions of the Mediterranean. The never-ending economic and administrative problem proved to be a dominant factor in the military crisis (too great a dependence on American remittances for many decades to come), territorial cessions that brought as a consequence a decrease in the population on which to rely to raise troops, taxes and natural resources to maintain and sustain them, with the paradox of an increasing recourse to foreign and auxiliary troops, with new financial outlays to be able to pay them and therefore impoverishment of the treasury and the country.

During this period, the problem of the Spanish armies was that the attitude of the military leaders was always defensive (except for the years 1670 in Catalonia) and in Piedmont (1692), and the lack of preparation of the various units to operate together; the chain of command was not always clear: generals were often inexperienced or unsuitable and quarrelsome, and capacity and initiative were rarely rewarded. The competition between nationalities certainly did not help resolve the difficulties.

---

1 For further reading on this subject, see **Luis Antonio Ribot García**'s seminal contribution in *Historia de España*, Vol. XXVIII (Madrid, 1993).

2 **Serafín de Soto y Montes, Conde de Clonard**, summarizes the reign of Charles II in his *Historia orgánica de las armas de infantería y caballería española* with these words : *"Philip IV was succeeded by Charles II, whose reign began under the gloomiest auspices (1665). A four-year-old prince and a regency composed of individuals chosen more for their social or political rank than for their wisdom or merit now held supreme authority in our nation—a weak, heterogeneous authority, exposed to the clashes of pride, the conflicts of ambition, or the apathy of selfishness. The only figure who might have served as a unifying force, a lever for good, and a check on court intrigues was the widowed Queen Mariana of Austria... What future could Spain expect under such inexperienced hands, when it emerged from Philip IV's rule externally diminished, internally weakened, its greatness reduced to a historical memory, and its prosperity to a fragile façade? Thus, under Charles II, Spain reached the extremes of decadence. Had it not vanished from the map of nations, as other great ancient states did, it was only because its constitution was fortunately homogeneous, and the blows of fortune could not sunder what nature had indissolubly united.* **Let us traverse this ill-fated period as swiftly as possible***.*" And so, in just over twenty pages, Clonard dispatches thirty-five years of continuous warfare—in a 16-volume, thousands-page work! Truly his later volumes detail individual regiments' battle histories during this era, but these accounts remain isolated vignettes, rarely contextualized within broader strategic or political developments.

3 See also **John A. Lynn** "*The Wars of Louis XIV*" Longman 1998.

The general officers were not always up to the task, also due to a lack of command experience over many combined units, in any case, with a poor tendency to take initiatives and risks, especially on Spanish soil, a sign also of paralysis and interference between the different factions operating at the Court. There was much quarrelling, and frequent "petty" disputes between commanders. In any case, it should also be noted how the scarce financial resources undermined the operational capabilities of the Spanish armies, as it was impossible to maintain high numbers of soldiers under arms due to the inability to pay them regularly; as soon as an emergency ended, as many troops as possible were dismissed, particularly the cavalry was dismounted, and the remaining troops were kept in fixed garrisons because a field army was too costly. Large unit manoeuvres were never carried out, and thus the commanders of the Spanish armies almost never had experience in managing complex operations. This is evidenced by the fact that in small unit clashes, the Spaniards were certainly not inferior to their perennial enemies, the French, often gaining the immediate advantage, while in the conduct of campaigns, large battlefield battles, and sieges, the logistical and organizational superiority (and often the numbers) of the French almost always resulted in a favorable outcome of the latters. Even when the Allied coalition could field numbers of troops and resources comparable to or even greater than those of France (as on the fronts of the Low Countries and, partially, in northern Italy), it took a long time for those troops to operate together (and for a shared objective), and, above all, for the various generals in charge of the subordinate units (divided by jealousy, rivalries, and personal and nationalist interests). In fact, only after several years of war, that of the League of Augsburg and then more so in the War of Spanish Succession, did the anti-French coalition manage to find greater coherence and unified command and develop the ability and habit of operating together, which allowed them to face the French and often push them back.

▲ *Iberian Peninsula. Detail of the Principality of Catalonia (Graphic design by R. Hall).*

THE ARMIES OF THE KING OF SPAIN

The armies of the king of Spain, after the conclusion of wars of Portugal (1668), of Messine (1678) and those practically continuous in Flanders (the last episode the siege of Luxembourg in 1684) , were reduced in Europe to only three operational corps, that is to say the army of the Principality of Catalonia, the one of the Spanish Low-Countries (Flanders) and the army of the State of Milan, not counting the garrisons of the possessions in Northern Africa. In the other territories, kingdoms and provinces, there were garrisons with a reduced number of veteran troops and some units of militia. The kingdoms in Italy (Naples, Sicily) disposed each of a tercio[4] of Spanish infantry as a fixed garrison, which in Naples and in Sicily could reach over 4,000 men, but very few other troops and some Guards and escort units (excluding Militia). In Sardinia there were only a few free companies besidees a tiny company of guard of halbardiers and a large Militia force on horse and on foot[5]. All these territories were expected to contribute in men and in kind to the military effort of the Monarchy if a situation of war erupted on any front. and Sardinia

The infantry comprised Spanish, Italian and Walloon *tercios* (all composed of subjects of the king of Spain), some weak *tercios* of Irish[6], English and Scottish infantry and a certain number of German regiments, that were raised by a «capitulation» in the German and northern Europe principalities. The *tercio* was a group of infantry companies, equivalent to a regiment in other countries, but the individual companies enjoyed greater administrative autonomy. The same difference, as we will see, existed between a *trozo de cavallos* and a cavalry regiment.

The *tercios* had a variable number of companies (10-16), each commanded by a Captain and an Ensign (*Alferez*) with their servants (2 and 1 respectively), a sergeant and some corporals (*cabo de esquadra* or, simply, *cabo*). The number of private soldiers could vary from 30-40 up to 200[7]. A certain number of these could be *reformed* officers and sergeants (at half or one third of pay. In this way the Spanish army had at disposal under the arms officers and n.c.o.'s that could easily be recalled to a superior duty and direct recruits never been at arms). Corporals and grenadiers were chosen among the privates, for their abilities or their physical aspect, with an addition to their pay. Often in the companies there was also a soldier who had the task of carrying the colour of the company (called *abanderado* in Spanish; the ensign no longer had this task and was just the second commissioned officer of the company). The *tercios* staff was formed by the Maestro de Campo (equivalent to a Colonel), a Sergeant Major (Major), a Drum Major, a Chaplain, a surgeon and a physician, a secretary and in the *tercios* in Italy 8 halebardiers for personal guard of the maestro de campo. The major difference from the regiments was that there were no lieutenants (of the maestro de campo or of the captains) and there was a greater autonomy of the companies.

It was a tradition of the Spanish military organisation to have young nobles attached as volunteers (*ventureros*) to the regular units, that served nominally as private soldiers at their own expenses, often carrying a pike, as this was considered the weapon of excellence and distinction.

According to the regulations in force (dated 1632), to become an infantry *maestro de campo* an officer had to have served for a not insignificant number of years, having passed through the various ranks of the hierarchical ladder and having been at least captain of a horse company (with rare exceptions linked to individual merit or more often to the importance and influence of the family of origin).

Each operational army had a composition of units of all the above nationalities. In addition, if the situation demanded it, the Crown "rented" existing regiments from the Empire or some German princes, generally for the duration of

---

4 There is a long debate about the origin of the name "tercio" [in Spanish "one third"]. It is largely accepted by many authors that the term was originated for the infantry units that garrisoned Italian possessions. We bring a new contribution to the discussion here. The Venetian ambassador in Naples in 1597, Girolamo Ramuzio, noted that in those times the Spanish infantry that was in Italy, had been divided in three parts: the *tercio* [third] of Lombardy (Milan), the *tercio* of Naples and the *tercio* of Sicily; and since then these units became known by the term "*tercio*". **"Corrispondenze Diplomatiche Veneziane da Napoli" Istituto Italiano per gli Studi Filosofici Napoli 1992 ...**
5 A *Tercio de Cerdeña* (Sardinia) existed briefly in 1564-1568.
6 Due to a transcription error about its name the tercio of *Olalla* (v. IRSP18) it has been logtime confused with an Irish *tercio O'Lulla*, never existed.
7 When dealing with strength of units one should not forget that during the season of the "campaign" the number of men diminished because of losses due to illness, deaths, capture by enemy, but mostly desertion, the real plague of armies of the time, especially in the Spanish armies as regular salaries were not warranted. Thus a unit that at the beginning of the season (March-April) was generally at full strength could be half or even less after the summer.

the war. The officers could advance their careers only within their national regiments (excluding German regiments in the direct pay of Spain where the officers were appointed directly by the king or the Viceroy and could be subjects of the Crown, and national Spaniards that could command corps from any nationality). Commissions for officers were generally referred to the king (always in the case of natural Spanish formations) upon proposal of the Captain General of an army; for other nationalities sometimes the Governor General or Viceroy could give a temporary commission, to be confirmed later by Madrid; German regiments fell normally under the authority of the Governor General or the Viceroy of the single territories.

Within the cavalry there was a similar rule. Only the three operational armies had units of line cavalry (grouped in *trozos*[8] in Spain, in *tercios* and German regiments in Flanders, in *trozos* and free companies in Milan), and of dragoons (*tercios* in Spain and Flanders and a regiment in Milan).

Excluding the *tercios* of Naples and Sicily, the remaining *tercios* of Spanish infantry were generally formed by 500-600 to 1,000 men, distributed in companies of 50 soldiers on the average. Cavalry companies had a force of 30-40 troopers, with the exception of the guards that had approximately double the force. After 1685 companies of grenadiers were introduced into the infantry formations.

The highest person in charge of royal authority in a given territory was either the Viceroy or the Governor of the kingdom or the state, who also held the office of Captain General of the military forces stationed in that territory, and it was on him that responsibility for government fell, both in civil and military matters. Although he had ample autonomy both to fulfil civil responsibilities and to direct the army, he was nevertheless obliged to carry out the orders that came from the king, at the suggestion of the state and war councils. When the political and military conditions of the territory became complicated and it became necessary to solve civil problems that required the full attention of the captain-general, a governor of arms was appointed to direct strictly military operations, while the captain-general, as viceroy or governor, concentrated on civil matters. The governor of arms was subject to the same limitations in command as the captain-general, having to apply directives from the court (it should also be noted that very often this office was not held).

The supreme command of the army from a strictly operational point of view was the maestro de campo-general. He was subordinate to the captain-general and, where appropriate, to the governor of the arms, so that, on many occasions, his opinions of a technical nature had to be sacrificed to instructions and orders issued without taking into account the reality of the war situation. For the transmission and execution of his orders, he relied on a number of maestros de campo-lieutenant-generals, generally Spanish, who in some cases could also be of another nationality.

Thus each of the operational armies was subject to the orders of the Captain General, who was assisted by a Governor General of Arms (who, when appointed, assumed the direction of the military organisation) and a Maestro de Campo General (who also had command over the entire infantry), a General of Cavalry with his Lieutenant-Generals (who commanded the cavalry and dragoons), a Captain General of Artillery and some Sergeant-Generals of Battle (who commanded the infantry, practically the equivalent of Brigadiers in other armies). This sequence also represented the line of command within the army and was very similar to that existing in the Habsburg-Austrian army.

Artillery had its own Captain General in each army, with his lieutenants and adjutants, and he was responsible for everything related to that weapon, in which, in addition to the train (for the country army), military engineers were included. The graduation of General of Artillery of a given army or territory was also created to give a higher rank to certain governors of the strong places and if they were present on the battlefield, seniority in the licence determined their command rank in relation to other counterparts. The various squares had a square command, which according to importance was entrusted to a general officer, or higher, down to the level of junior officers for those of lesser importance.

If a sudden need of troops arose on a particular front, the Council of War in Madrid could decide (=recommend to the Sovereign who issued a Royal order) to move some units from an army or a front to another one, or require Viceroys or Governors General to levy units or recruits in order to reinforce the weaker points of the Spanish military machine.

Formally, the (military) ordinance of Philip IV of 8 June 1632 was still in force, which was heavily based on those of 1611 and 1598, and was the only general regulation governing the organisation of armies, and was clearly obsolete by the end of the century, and therefore in fact almost useless.

---

8 The *trozo* was a group of cavalry companies, equivalent to a regiment in other countries. The *trozo*, under the orders of a Commissary General, did not have a Lieutenant or a Major (Sergeant-Major) but just the captains of the single companies. It is also noteworthy that in old Spanish texts the formations of cavalry are called *battalions* and those of infantry *squadrons*.

In the following we shall present the composition of the three operational armies of Catalonia, Flanders and Milan and those garrisoned in Naples and Sicily. The infantry *tercios* and regiments were generally known by the name of the maestro de campo; for this reason we will in the following try to supply the succession of them at the head of each unit during the period of our interest, remembering that the same man could be at the head of different units at short intervals (generally proceeding from a "younger" to an "older" one). Most of the reports of the time simply refer to the name of the maestro de campo when describing the unit. This was not the case of the cavalry in Catalonia, where the *trozos* of cavalry were called by their denomination, but in Flanders once more mounted units were designated by the name of the maestro de campo or colonel.

The list we provide does not include all the units created and been in existence, but only those that significantly participated in military operations. In compiling the succession of maestros de campo and colonels, we have used all available (and found) sources: the works and notes of *Clonard*, bills and patents or other contemporary sources, such as gazettes and notices, and finally, the service records that the soldiers of the Spanish monarchy compiled when requesting a promotion or a reward (and the data reported are not always accurate). There are some discrepancies between the "classical" sources (*Clonard*) and other original ones (archives and contemporary testimonies), and there are still numerous gaps to be filled and some uncertainties, even on the part of the authors of this essay, sometimes originating from the uncertain spelling of names, which could vary considerably, and the use of different titles [*count of ... marquis of ...*] for the same person at different times.

Principality of Catalonia

Viceroy and Captain General

1687-1688 D. Juan Tomas Enriquez de Cabrera, conde de Melgar (since 1691 Almirante de Castilla) y duque de Medina de Rioseco

1689-1690 D. Carlos Gurrea de Aragon y Borja, duque de Villahermosa

1690-1693 D. Juan Alonso Perez de Guzman el Bueno, Duque de Medina-Sidonia y (1690) de Medina de las Torres

1694 D. Juan Manuel Lopez Pacheco Acuña Giron y Portocarrero, Duque de Escalona Marques de Villena

1694-1696 D. Francisco Antonio de Agurto, Marques de Gastañaga

1696-1697 D. Francisco de Velasco, conde de Melgar

1697-1698 D. Diego Hurtado de Mendoza y Sandoval, Conde de la Corzana

1698-1701 Georg Landgraf von Hessen-Darmstadt

The duke of Villahermosa, appointed Viceroy of the Principality in December 1688, made as his first commitment the recognition of the army's positions, and he sent horrified letters to Madrid after his first reconnaissance of the military situation. In mid-February 1689, he stayed for three days in Girona, the main barrier of the Principality against the French invasion, discovering that it was in the most miserable state one could imagine, lacking everything, as were the other strongholds of the Principality: *artillery everywhere was dismantled. The lack of people was notorious, with a total absence of precautions and defense... to the point that soldiers were begging in the streets, and all the strongholds lacked straw to feed the horses.*

A part of the problem of defending Catalonia was represented by the scarce availability of men. The Catalan contribution to the royal line army consisted of providing one *tercio* of infantry of 500 men, paid by the

▲ *D. Carlos Gurrea de Aragon y Borja, duque de Villahermosa.*

city of Barcelona, and another *tercio* of 400 at the expense of the Deputation; in reality, these troops would be joined by the numerous squads of militia, especially the *Miquelets*, who supported the action of the line army with guerrilla warfare, a tactic that suited them extremely well, by which they inflicted continuous and substantial losses on the occupying enemy troops. In case of necessity, these numbers were increased: in 1693, for example, the city of Barcelona maintained two *tercios* in the field, totaling 1,400 men, and the Deputation of Catalonia had increased its *tercio* to 600 men. In addition to these, the Government could count on a *tercio* recruited and financed by the Kingdom of Aragon; for its part, the Kingdom and the city of Valencia contributed with another corps of about 500 men. All the other infantry soldiers present in the Principality were dependent on the Crown of Castile (the 5 so-called provincial *tercios*, whose theoretical strength should have been 1,000 men each), or in any case paid by the royal treasury, including the German regiments and the *tercios* of Neapolitan, Milanese, and Walloon infantry.

INFANTRY
Spanish Infantry

At the beginning of the War of the League of Augsburg (1688) the Spanish infantry of the army of the Principality of Catalonia had - as the constituting nucleus - five standing *tercios*, called Provincials [the only veteran Spanish infantry

▲ Luis de la Cerda Duque de Medina Celi by J.F.Voet Prado, Madrid, Spain.

troops on Spanish soil], which, as Clonard recalls, were created by royal decree in 1664], which carried the names of the provinces (belonging to the crown of Castile) that payed for their subsistence; these *tercios* were also known by the colours of their dress (and/or by the names of their maestro de campo)[9] :

- **IRSP01** *Toledo* (or *Azules viejos*)[10]
- **IRSP02** *Burgos y Valladolid* (or *Amarillos viejos*)[11]
- **IRSP03** *Cordova* (or *Verdes viejos*)[12]
- **IRSP04** *Sevilla* (or *Morados viejos*)[13]
- **IRSP05** *Madrid* (or *Colorados viejos*)[14]

---

9 It is here proposed an indexed number for identifying the units : IRYYxx, where IR means Infantry Regiment (tercios are regarded as regiments), YY gives the nationality (Spanish. Italian, Walloon, German [Aleman] etc) of the unit, xx the number of the order of appearance in our list, not the seniority of the unit, which would have involved too many other considerations and details.
10 In 1707 it became the regiment of **Toledo**. Succession of maestros de campo: (1682) *D. Manrique de Noroña* (1691) *D. Juan Claros de Guzman* [He exchanged this *tercio* for the one he had been appointed to in Flanders leaving it to the conde de Peñarrubia by a royal decree of 31st December 1692] (1692) *D. Gaspar Ramirez de Arellano y Pantoja*, 1st **Count of Peñarubia** (1694) *D. Diego de Alarcon* (1704) *D. Melchor de Montes y Vigil*.
11 It became in 1707 the regiment of **Guadalajara**. Maestro de Campo: (1677) D. Antonio Serrano, (1689) D. Pedro Tolesano y Velasco, (1695) D. Fernando Davila Bravo de Laguna, (1699) D. Jaoquin Fernandez Portocarrero Moscoso Osorio, Marques de Almenara (1699).
12 In 1707 it became regiment of **Cordova**, and in 1718 **España**. Maestro de Campo : (1682) D. Carlos de Eguia, (1691) D. Juan Vasquez de Acuña, (october 1694) D. Esteban de Olalla (1698) D. Francisco de Luna y Carcamo (1701) D. Diego Andres Davila Paceco.
13 At the time with the term **morado** it was meant a very dark shade of blue. In 1707 it became regiment of **Castilla**. Maestro de Campo : (1685) D. Thomas de los Cobos y Luna, (1695) D. Francisco Antonio Diaz Pimienta (1703) D. Juan Isidro Padilla y Rojas (1705) D. Manuel de Orleáns, conde de Charny.
14 It was considered the most ancient *tercio* of the army. In 1707 it became regiment of **Sevilla**. Maestro de Campo : (1658) D. Martin de Guzmán y Cárdenas (1684) D. Joseph Creel de la Hoz, (1691) D. Francisco Antonio Ibañez de Peralta, (1697) D. Juan Antonio Ibañez Ibero (1703) D. Jacinto de Pozobueno y Bellver.

Nominally the five provincial tercios were 1,000 men strong.

Soon after the war exploded in 1691 a new *tercio* was formed with levies offered by the different towns of Castilla, that was called **tercio de las Ciudades** (**IRSP06**), and was considered a *provincial tercio*. In 1694, when the *tercio* of Madrid was almost entirely captured by the French, it took its place within the list of the five provincial corps merging with another tercio formed by the guilds (***Gremios***) in Madrid[15].

In addition to this basic back-bone of the royal standing army, each of the territories of the Crown in Spain was supposed to supply, upon request by the King, one or more infantry *tercios* (*tercios* of **Granada**, **Aragon**, **Valencia**, **Galicia**, etc.),, that were to be maintained by that territory throughout the war campaign; usually this procedure was repeated each year of war and the troops were on the field for no more than 6 months (when on active campaign, then at the beginning of the bad season the *tercio* was disbanded and the men sent back to their homes till next year's campaign). Generally these *tercios* were 4-600 men strong, sometimes arriving at 1,000, while the cities of Castile provided a yearly contribution of levies (usually for companies) to make up the losses suffered by the provincial tercios or to increase their staffs. It was only after a few years from the start of hostilities that the absurdity of such a procedure was recognised and an attempt was made to keep the tercios alive in the vicinity of the areas of operation and only send new recruits from the various territories to reconstitute the strength of the units that had diminished over time for the usual various reasons (losses, illnesses and above all, desertions). The Italian and Flanders possessions acted in the same way.

Finally, the Spanish command could also dispose of the infantry assigned to the Armada, when it was not engaged in the defence of the African strongholds. The kingdom of Grenada constantly supplied two infantry *tercios*, named:

- **IRSP07** *Tercio del Casco de la Ciudad de Granada*[16], and
- **IRSP08** *Tercio de la Costa del Reyno de Granada*.[17]

The kingdom of Aragon did the same, levying an infantry *tercio* each year, called **IRSP09** *Tercio del Reino Aragon*[18], as well as did the kingdom of Valencia with its **IRSP10** *Tercio del Reyno de Valencia*[19].

Catalonia itself in case of war supplied some *tercios*: the *tercio* of the town of Barcelona (**IRSP11** *Tercio de la Ciudad de Barcelona*)[20] and the *tercio* of the Principality (**IRSP12** *Tercio de la Diputacion de Cataluña*)[21]; during the war of the Nine Years at least two more Catalan *tercios* were organised and served for some time.

The **Catalan Miquelets** (*enlisted in semi-regular units*) grew to number from about 800 to over 4,000, distributed in various squads and companies, and in 1695 they came under the command of *D. Blas de Trincheria*. Alongside them were also some disbanded companies of Fusiliers and men from the militia of the Principality.

The provinces of Navarre[22], Galicia and Estremadura supplied other units of infantry, mainly for garrison of the borders, but sometimes they were also employed in Catalonia.

In particular two out of the four *tercios* of Estremadura, one of Galicia and one from Asturias were employed in Catalonia at some stages of the war against the French.

---

15 Maestro de campo: (1690) D. Melchor de Avellaneda Sandoval, Marques de Torremayor, (1692) D. Diego del Manzano, (1694) D. Miguel Gasco y Martin.

16 It became the regiment of **Granada** in 1707. Maestro de campo: (1676) D. Diego Antonio de Viana e Hinojosa (August 1685) D. Diego Hurtado de Mendoza, conde de la Corzana (March 1689) D. Fernando Matías Arias Saavedra, barón de Voymer, (1692) D. Alonso de Granada y Barradas, (1694) D. Gonzalo Cegri y Salazar (1703) D. Pedro Arias Ozores, marques de San Miguel.

17 In 1707 it became the regiment of **la Costa** and in 1717 **Victoria**. Maestro de campo: (1688) D. Diego Hurtado de Mendoza y Sandoval, conde de la Corzana 31st December1692 Don Fernando Matías Arias Saavedra, barón de Voymer (1694) D. Antonio Colon de Portugal, conde de la Puebla de Portugal (1696) D. Diego del Campo y Vela (1697) D. Gaspar de Ocio y Mendoza December1698 D. Vicente Matías Primo Daza

18 Maestro de Campo: (1678-1691) D. Artal de Azlor, conde de Guara, (1691) D. Guillén Ramon de Moncada, marqués de Aytona, (1693) D. Geronimo Pérez de Nueros y Pueyo. Since 1691 to 1697 there was another *tercio* formed in Aragon by D. Bernardo de Abarca de Bolea y Hornes, III marques de Torres. **IRSP09bis**

19 Maestro de Campo: (1689) Marqués de Centellas, (1695) D. Joseph Ferrer, conde de Almenara.

20 Maestro de Campo: (1684) D. Joaquin de Grimau y Monserrat, (1697) Miguel Taverner, conde de Darnius.

21 Maestro de Campo: (1684) D. Juan Joaquin de Marimon, (1690) the *tercio* and its maestre de campo having being captured by the French at San Juan de las Abadesas D. Joseph Boneu, conde de la Coromina commander of the *tercio*, until 1695 when Juan de Marimon returned from captivity (1697) D. Tomas Francisco Marti de Vilanova.

22 The *tercio* of D. Diego de Salinas was levied in 1685 for the defense of Pamplona in the kingdom of Navarra. He was succeded in 1697 by D. Manuel de Toledo.

- **IRSP13** *Tercio viejo de Etremadura*[23]
- **IRSP13bis** *Tercio nuevo de Estremadura*[24]

In 1694 two additional *tercios* were created in Extremadura: that of *Diego Godoy Ponce de León, count of Valdegrana*, which never reached its full complement, (1696) *Joseph Losada*, who in the same year 1696 passed at the command of the *tercio* of *Francisco Espinola*, his own having been disbanded, and the one of (1694) D. *Juan de Zavala*, (1695) D. *Pedro González del Valle*. This *tercio* was disbanded in 1699.

- **IRSP14** *Tercio de Galicia*[25]
- **IRSP15** *Tercio del Principado de Asturias*[26].

During this period, there were some other *tercios* formed for the war by capitulation with individuals that served for short periods of time, and often merged into existing veteran units to reconstitute their ranks.

At the end of 1693, in order to renew the military effort of Spain shaken by the continuous offensive of the French, it was decided to create 10 new standing *tercios* of Spanish provincial infantry (often named after their maestros de campo or by the colour of their dress (new *blues*, new *reds*, etc.). The ten *tercios*, effectively formed at beginning of the year 1694, were thus called[27]:

- **IRSP16** *Tercio* (*nuevo*) *de Burgos*[28];
- **IRSP17** *Tercio de Valladolid*; (*Verdes nuevos*)[29];
- **IRSP18** *Tercio de Cuenca*[30];
- **IRSP19** *Tercio de Leon*; (*Amarillos nuevos*)[31];
- **IRSP20** *Tercio de Murcia*; (*Azules nuevos*)[32];
- **IRSP21** *Tercio de Sevilla* (*nuevo*)[33];
- **IRSP22** *Tercio de Gibraltar*; (*Colorados nuevos*)[34];
- **IRSP23** *Tercio de Jaen*; (silvery, *Plateados*)[35];
- **IRSP24** *Tercio de Toledo* (*nuevo*)[36];
- **IRSP25** *Tercio de Segovia*[37].

Italian Infantry

The royal army of Catalonia also included some standing Italian infantry *tercios* (Neapolitans and Milanese), named after their maestros de campo; during the war there could be other Italian units formed for the occasion.

- **IRIT01** *Italian (Neapolitan) tercio of* D. *Marino Carafa* (1685-1694) D. **Fernando Pignatelli,** 1694 **Antonio Mugiaschi,** 1696-1701 **Domenico Recco**
- **IRIT02** *Italian (Neapolitan) tercio of* D. *Francesco Serra Doria* (1691) D. **Fernando Carmignano,** (1692) D. **Antonio Mastrotuccio,** (1694) D. **Gaetano Gambacorta Prince of Macchia**[38]

---

23 Maestro de campo: (1694) D. Diego Mesia (1701) D. Marcelo Robles.
24 Maestro de campo: (1694) D. Francisco Espinola, (1696) D. Joseph de Losada.
25 Maestro de campo: (1692) D. Joseph Vélez de Cossio, (1699) D. Juan Fernández de Aguirre. The *tercio* was employed on the frontiers of Navarre till 1697, and then was at the defense of Barcelona during the great siege.
26 Maestro de campo: (1691) D. Francisco Menéndez de Avilés y Porres. The *tercio* from 1691 to 1693 was in the army of Catalonia, then, being to feeble, was sent back to its home province in order to garrison it.
27 Most of these units survived the war and were still in service at the beginning of the Spanish Succession War.
28 Maestro de campo: (1694) D. José Vélez de Guevara, (1696) D. Pedro Antonio de Lima, (1700) D. Alonso Mesia de la Cerda.
29 Maestro de campo: (1694) D. Francisco Antonio Diaz Pimienta (in 1694 passes to the **old tercio of Sevilla**), (1695) D. Francisco Domingo y Cueva, (1695) D. Thomas Vicentelo y Toledo.
30 Maestro de campo: (1694) D. Esteban de Olalla. Disbanded after the battle at the river Ter in 1694. By a mistake in the transcription of its name (*Olulla* instead of *Olalla* the *tercio* was for a long time considered by Clonard and many successive authors as an Irish *tercio* O'Lulla never existed).
31 In 1707 it became regiment of **Leon**. Maestro de campo: (1694) D. Francisco de Argüelles Celles, (1694) D. Gonzalo Cegri de Salazar, (1695) D. Manuel de Toledo y Portugal (1698) D. Joseph de Arredonda y Herreros.
32 Maestro de campo: (1694) D. Luis Fernandez Daza, (1700) D. Garcia Huidobro.
33 Maestro de campo: (1694) D. Rodrigo Venegas de Cordoba.
34 Maestros de campo: (1694) D. Gaspar de Ocio y Mendoza, (1697) D. Ambrosio Antolinez.
35 In 1707 it became regiment of **Jaén**. Maestro de campo: (1694) D. Jacinto de Espinosa, (1696) D. Juan Fernández Pedroche.
36 Maestro de campo: (1694) D. Antonio de Villaroel.
37 Maestro de campo: (1694) D. Francisco de Luna y Carcamo.
38 The *tercio* was disbanded before 1701.

- **IRIT03** *Italian (Neapolitan) tercio of* (1695) D. *Domenico Caracciolo,* (1697) D. *Giulio Pignatelli*
- **IRIT04** *Italian (Milanese) tercio of* (1695) D. *Pietro Francesco Perucca,* (1697) Marquis *Benedetto Ali*
- **IRIT04 bis** *Italian (Milanese) tercio of* (1689) D. *Luigi Sechi d'Aragona*.[39]

In 1695, a new tercio of Irish infantry arrived in Catalonia from the Milanese with the maestro de campo Count of Tirconel[40] [**IRIr02**], formed in Piedmont with prisoners and deserters from the French army of Irish nationality[41].

Walloon Infantry

At the end of the year 1694, the Council of War in Madrid, in order to reconstitute the ***old tercio of Walloon infantry of Charles Sucre*** [**IRWL01**], which had been disbanded just prior the war, demanded of the Governor of Flanders the formation of two *tercios* of Walloon infantry (and two *trozos* of cavalry) which arrived in Catalonia in the month of May 1695, each initially 1,000 men strong:

- **IRWL02** ***Walloon tercio of Lede***[42] (1694) *Jérôme-Albert, conde de Thian* (19 settembre 1694) *Jean François de Bette, marqués de Lede* (1699) *Philip Emmanuel Antoine de Bette et de Croy, Chevalier de Lede.*
- **IRWL03** ***Walloon tercio of Noyelles*** (1694) *Jean Bonaventure de Noyelles, conde de Fallais y Noyelles* (1697) *Ferdinand Jacques Ignace de Fariaux, vizconde de Maulde y Courtabamont* and (1704) D. *Juan de Camps*[43].

German Infantry

The German infantry was represented by the *old* or veteran regiment of the colonel ***Christian del Beck, Baron of Troup*** [**IRAL01** it came to Spain, during the war against Portugal, in 1661[44]] and a *new* regiment of the colonel ***Juan Simon Enriquez de Cabrera*** (**IRAL02**), formed in Milan and passed over to Catalonia at the beginning of the war in 1689[45]. These regiments were at all the major engagements of the Spanish army in Catalonia and at the defense of Barcelona in 1697. They were disbanded at the beginning of the Spanish Succession War.

In 1695, the Crown capitulated the service of two imperial infantry regiments (***Zweibrücken*** (**IRAL03**)[46] and ***Saxe-Coburg*** (**IRAL04**)[47]) and a regiment of Bavarian infantry (***Tattenbach* IRAL05**)[48]. These regiments served, from 1695 to 1701, as auxiliary troops under the command of Prince George of Darmstadt at the orders of the Viceroy, but maintained their allegiance to their princes, keeping their own flags. The auxiliary German regiments left Spanish soil for good in early 1701, after the accession to the Spanish throne of Philip V, Duke of Anjou, opposed by the Habsburgs of Austria, made units of German nationality unreliable.

In addition to these troops, all the major places and fortresses of the various provinces and kingdoms had garrisons, that could be of about ten to one hundred men, grouped into free companies, of which the Governor of the place was usually the captain.

---

39 The index of this tercio derives from the fact that it was not cited in previous editions due to the lack of documentation relating to it. Formed in Lombardy in the place of Tortona, passed in review in Voltri in July 1689 with over 1,000 men [**A.G.S. S.P. leg. 1892/41**], and sent to Catalonia in July 1689, where it was incorporated into that army [**29/06/1689** With a letter dated June 27, the Governor commands that, as Maestro di Campo *D. Luigi Secchi is to serve H.M. in the army of Catalonia with a Tercio of Lombards that has been formed for this purpose...*].
40 **Don Hugo Odonel, Conde de Tirconel**
41 In 1696 was in garrison in Tarragona with 26 officers, 23 n.c.os. and 135 privates, distributed in 6 companies. It was disbanded in 1697.
42 The *tercio* was disbanded in 1701.
43 The *tercio*, become regiment, in 1702 passed to the kingdom of Naples in order to reinforce its garrison, and in 1707 it became prisoner of war of the Austrians that had conquered the kingdom, remaining effectively dissolved.
44 From 1664 to 1683 *Colonel Adam Christobal de Hesse*. In 1683, the regiment merged with another of the same nation, commanded since 1677 by *Pierre Laurent Sordet*.
45 Since 1694 the Colonel was **Ernesto Fernando Baron de Gorcey**. The Baron de Gorcey died from a cannon ball during the siege of Barcelona and in 1698 D. *Jaime Velaz de Medrano* was appointed as the new colonel of the unit.
46 Owner **Adolph Johann Herzog v. Zweibrücken, Pfalzgraf bei Rhein [=Dupont]**; the colonel commander of the regiment was **Count Friedrich v. Löwenburg**. From 1699 to 1701, the *Zweibrücken* regiment, remaining in Catalonia, was commanded by *D. Luis Caetano de Aragon.* **Avvisi italiani di Vienna.**
47 Owner **Albrecht III Herzog von Sachsen-Coburg**; colonel commander of the regiment was Karl Sebastian Freiherr von Kratz, later replaced by Maximilian Friedrich v. Stockhorner. See for regimental history: "*Das k.u.k. 57. Infanterie-Regiment Fürst Jablonowski und die Kriege seiner Zeit „Wien 1857".*
48 Colonel **Georg Ignaz Graf v. Tattenbach**. V. **Winkler**, Leonhard "*Das kurbayerische Regiment zu Fuß Graf Tattenbach in Spanien 1695-1701*" Straub, München, 1890. Supplement-Heft zum Jahrbuch der Militärischen Gesellschaft München pro 1888-1890.

Infantry of the Armada (Marines)

The Navy (*Armada*) had at its disposal some *tercios* of infantry (4-5 during the period of our interest) employed for the garrison of the galleys and vessels and as marine infantry. They were often employed in the defence of Spanish possessions in Africa, but also in Catalonia, particularly during the siege of Barcelona in 1697 (and before during the War of Portugal):

- **IRSP26** *tercio viejo de infanteria española de la Armada real de la Mar oceano*[49],
- **IRSP27** *tercio nuevo de infanteria española de la Armada*[50]
- **IRSP28** *tercio nuevo de infanteria española de la Armada*[51]
- **IRSP29** *tercio nuevo de infanteria española de la Armada*[52]
- **IRSP30** *tercio nuevo de infanteria española de la Armada*[53]
- **IRIT05** *tercio viejo de infanteria napolitana de la Armada*[54]

Places in Northern Africa

Spain owned some fortresses in North Africa (*Plazas de soberania*): Ceuta, Melilla, Oran and Mazalquivir (Mers-el-Kebir), Larache (lost in 1689) and the small "Peñón de Vélez" and Alhucemas, the Chafarinas islands became a spanish possession in 1847. These places were kept under constant siege by Moroccans and Algerians. Maintaining possession of them responded to the precise defensive need to prevent their ports from being used by Barbary pirates, a real scourge of the Spanish and Italian coasts.

Most of these places had a small fixed garrison of free companies of infantry and some cavalry (mostly from inhabitants of the towns; there was sometimes a small contingent of regular troops, sometimes also a few Portuguese *tercios* supplied reinforcements); artillerymen and bombers were always present, but not enlisted into organic units. The basic idea was to have places well fortified and supplied with artillery; when the situation grew worse, additional troops were sent to rescue the ordinary garrison. The Armada (Fleet) was the first in line to supply reinforcements from the bases in Gibraltar and Cadiz, through its *tercios* (marine infantry), but also other veteran troops or single companies drawn from the South of Spain could be employed, even for prolonged periods in the defence of these places. Only under the new Borboun dynasty in Spain did it become possible to form fixed standing battalions in these strongholds.

Cavalry and Dragoons

The line cavalry[55] in Catalonia consisted of 7 *trozos* of Cuirassiers (= *Cavallos Corazas*, that no longer wore a cuirass and were also called light-cavalry) and a certain number of companies of Guards (of the Viceroy – that could be named either Cuirassiers or Arquebusiers or even Lances -, of the Generals of the cavalry, etc.). Each cavalry company had a captain, a lieutenant, a cornet, one or two trumpeters (and a kettle drummer in the Guards), 2 sergeants, 4 corporals and about 30-50 troopers. The companies of Guards were normally more numerous and could have as many as 100 troopers. A *trozo* was composed by 7 to 10 companies, and was under the orders of a Commissary General, who also owned a company in the *trozo*. The trozos, differently from the regiments did not have a lieutenant for the Commissary general nor a sergeant major. These units were generally 400-500 men strong. The companies of the Guards, that were at any effect fighting bodies, were those of:

- **CRSP01** *Company of Horse Cuirassiers of the Guard of the Captain General* (Viceroy);
- **CRSP02** *Company of Horse Arquebusiers of the Guard of the Captain General* (Viceroy);
- **CRSP03** *Company of Horse Cuirassiers of the Guard of the Principality of Catalonia*;

---

49   In 1707 it became regiment **Bajeles**, and in 1718 **Cordoba**; Maestro de campo: D. Bernabé Alonso de Aguilar, (1686) D. Geronimo Marin, (1695) D. Martin de Aranguren y Zavala, (1699) D. Antonio Alejandro Barrientos, (till 18th of May 1703) D. Diego Andrès Davila Pacheco, later (1707) D. Geronimo de Solis y Gante.
50   Maestro de campo: (1682) D. Pedro Fernandez de Navarrete, (1691) D. Juan Flores de Sietén y Gomez de Bedoya.
51   Maestro de campo: (1691) D. Jorge de Villalonga y Fortuny, conde de la Cueva (1705) Fernando de la Riva Herrera, Marchese di Villatorre.
52   Maestro de campo: (1690) D. Antonio Joaquin Canales (1697-1698) D. Pedro Alejandro Barrientos (1698) D. Pedro de Castro.
53   Maestro de campo: (1693) D. Martin de Aranguren y Zavala, (1695) D. Carlos San Gil y la Justicia (1703) D. Bernardino Delgado Alarcon.
54   In 1707 it became the regiment of Italian infantry of **Napoles**; Maestro de campo: D. Antonio Domenico di Dura, marquis of Polia; (1695) D. Giovanbattista Visconti, and then, in May 1703 D. Biagio Dragonetti.
55   Although the expression "line cavalry" is anachronistic (it dates back to the Napoleonic era), it is used to avoid confusion since by then there was no difference between cuirassiers and "men-at-arms", who however were still the only ones to be considered "heavy cavalry".

- **CRSP04** *Company of Horse Cuirassiers of the Guard of the Governor General of the Arms*;
- **CRSP05** *Company of Horse Cuirassiers of the Guard of the General of the Cavalry*;
- **CRSP06-07** Two *Companies of Horse Cuirassiers of the Guard of the Lieutenants-Generals of the Cavalry*.

During the campaign period there was also a small *company of Horse of the Provost General of the Army*.

The *trozos* of line Cavalry in 1689 were those of:

- **CRSP08** *Ordenes* (the Spanish Military Chivalry Order)[56],
- **CRSP09** *Rossellon*,[57]
- **CRSP10** *Milan*,[58]
- **CRSP11** *Extremadura*,[59]
- **CRSP12** *Osuna*,[60]
- **CRSP13** *Alemanes* (originally German cavalry, but during the period of the war it became composed mainly of Spaniards due to the difficulty of receiving recruits from northern Europe heavily involved in the war against the French),[61]
- **CRSP14** *Valones*.[62]

Between 1695 and 1696 the *trozo* of **Osuna** was disbanded (and some of its companies sent to the African places) and the men merged into the remaining units; in 1696 a new *trozo* of cavalry was created in Badajoz, this latter one being called **Badajoz** or **new (nuevo) Extremadura**[63] (**CRSP15**), while the existing one was also called *old (viejo) Extremadura*.

In 1695 two bodies of 10 companies each (initially 1,000 men) of Walloon cavalry arrived from Flanders, having been requested (together with two infantry *tercios*) from that Governor by the court of Madrid, and were immediately put on the foot of *trozos*, one called **Flandes**[64] (**CRWL01**) and the other one **Brabant**[65] (**CRWL02**). These *trozos*, later become regiments, survived throughout the war of the Spanish Succession, having being employed in Italy and Flanders before returning finally to Spain.

There had not been a long tradition of keeping units of dragoons in the peninsular territories of Spain. In the past, when there was the need, dragoons units were moved from Flanders or from Italy and employed for a short period in Spain. There had been a few free companies of dragoons or **horse arquebusiers** (*cavallos arcabuzeros*), as they were also called, but never maintained in existence for a long time. In Catalonia Dragoons were organised into a *tercio* only since 1676 (later called **tercio viejo de dragones DRSP01**[66]) of initially 250 men in five companies, increased during the war to over 500 in 10-12 companies. In 1695 by grouping some free companies serving in Navarre a second *tercio* was formed (**tercio nuevo de dragones DRSP02**[67]) at the beginning dismounted.

These two *tercios* disappeared from the general list of the Spanish army because, at the end of 1701, at the beginning of the War of the Spanish Succession, they were sent, along with other troops, to the Kingdom of Naples to increase the

---

56 It became in 1707 regiment of **Ordenes viejo** and in 1718 **Ordenes**. Commissary General: (1682) D. Salvador de Monforte, Salgado y Araujo (1689) D. Joseph de Salazar, (1693) D. Francisco Pingarron del Perral (1703) Frey D. Francisco Manuel Gutiérrez de Medinilla.
57 It became in 1707 regiment of **Rossellon viejo**, and in 1718 **Borbon**. Commissary General: (1633) D. Carlo Tasso (1675) D. Juan de la Capella (1680) D. Manuel del Pueyo (1686) D. Fernando de Toledo y Portugal; (1694) D. Joseph de Salazar (1695) D. Juan de Sentmenat y Toralla, I marquis of Sentmenat, (1697) D. Nicolas de la Rochela y Agramunt (1704) D. Luis Fernandez de Cordoba y Ponce de Leon.
58 It became later regiment of **Milan**. Commissary General: (1677) D. Julian de Lazcano, (1689) D. Francisco de Santa Cruz, (1690-1699) D. Alonso de Escobar (1699) D. Pedro Joseph de Aguirre, count of Ayanz (1704) D. Fabrizio Ruffo.
59 It became later regiment of **Estremadura**. Commissary General: (1689) D. Nicolas Rodriguez de Sotomayor, (1692) D. Miguel Gonzalez de Otaza y Tovar; (1694) D. Bonifacio Manrique de Lara y Luyando (1703) D. Melchor de Mendieta.
60 Commissary General: (1687) D. Gabriel Corada (1688) D. Juan Jeronimo Abarca y Villalon, II Count de la Rosa, Baron de Garcipollera; (1693) D. Joseph de Caro. Disbanded at some time between 1694 and 1695.
61 Commissary General: (1685) D. Juan Colon de Larreategui; (1694) D. Francisco de Santa Cruz (1696) D. Antonio Melgarejo. Disbanded in 1703.
62 Commissary General: (1678) D. Gaspar de Herrera Peñaranda (1686) D. Dionisio de Obregon (1689) Conte Marco Antonio di Valperga; (1697) D. Felix de Ballarò. Disbanded in 1698.
63 Commissary general: (1695) D. Manuel de Silveira y Becerra, (1696) D. Ángel de Mendoza.
64 Commissary general: (1695) D. Luis de Saa Rangel.
65 Commissary general: (1695) D. Albert count of Tilly, (1702) D. Iñigo de la Cruz Manrique de Lara Ramirez de Arellano, count of Aguilar, señor de los Cameros.
66 Maestro de campo: (168?) D. Juan Vazquez de Acuña, (1690) D. Diego Lasso de la Vega (1693) Count Maximilian Albert de Bossu, (1694) D. Francisco Domingo de Belbalet.
67 Maestro de campo of the *tercio* nuevo since 1695 D. Joseph de Armendariz y Perurena.

Spanish garrison, and were taken prisoner by the Austrians in 1707 when they conquered the kingdom. The dragoon *tercios*, by then already transformed into regiments, thus disappeared. In the early years of the War of the Spanish Succession, new dragoon regiments were created on the Iberian Peninsula.

Spanish Flanders

Governor General and Captain General

03/01/1686-December 1691 D. Francisco Antonio de Agurto, Marqués de Gastañaga.

December 1691-March 1701 Maximilian-Emanuel of Wittelsbach, Duke of Bavaria and Elector of the Holy Roman Empire.

Just after the outbreak of the Nine Years' War, in 1690, the army of the Spanish Low Countries included 9 *tercios* of Spanish infantry with 161 companies, 519 commissioned officers, 846 *reformed* officers and 4,795 private soldiers, in total 6,160 men; 3 *tercios* of Italian infantry with 45 companies, 147 in commission and 255 "reformed" officers and 1,049 soldiers for a total of 1,451 men; 3 *tercios* of Irish, Scottish and English infantry for a total of 153 men (which were to be reformed shortly due to the lack of recruits); a company of Burgundian infantry of 109 men; 9 *tercios* of Walloon infantry with 111 companies, 369 officers, 232 reformed officers, 4,045 soldiers for a total of 4,646 men; 6 regiments of German infantry with 64 companies, 466 officers, 89 reformed, 1,172 soldiers for a total of 1,727 men; 9 free companies, among which the 5 of Charlequint for a total of 677 men. Cavalry had 7 *tercios* of Spanish horse in 68 companies with 2,042 men, 2 *trozos* of Italian and Burgundian Horse with 15 companies and 494 men, 3 *tercios* of Walloon horse in 23 companies with 862 men, 9 regiments of German horse in 82 companies and 2,410 men, 6 companies of Guards of the Governor and of the generals with 845 men, 8 *tercios* of dragoons with 90 companies and 3,104 men[68].

---

68 A.G.S. Estado Flandes Leg. 3883.

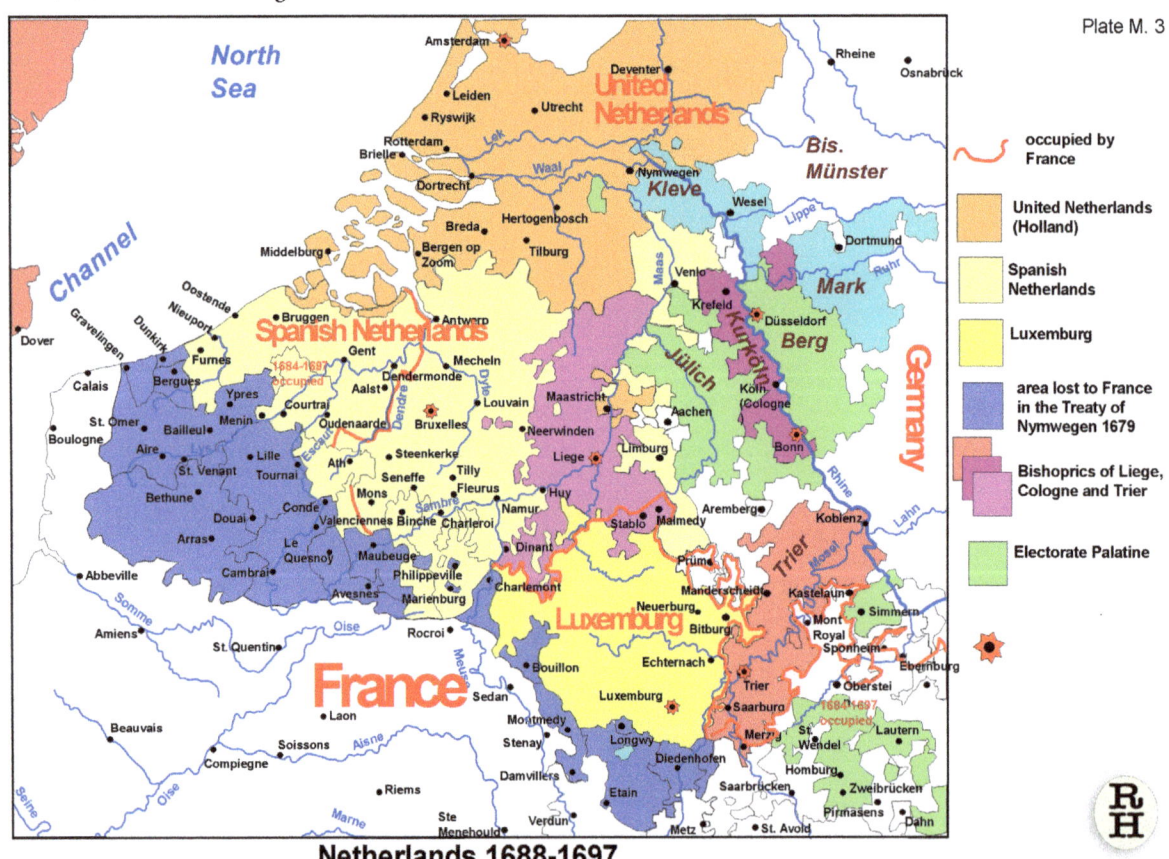

▲ *Area of the Netherlands. Spanish possessions and areas disputed by France. (Graphic design by R. Hall)*

In September 1698, at the end of the war, the army, reduced on the peace establishment, counted 14 *tercios* of infantry, with an average force of 576 men in 12 companies each, i.e. 6 Spanish of 12 companies each, 3 of Italian infantry of 8 companies each, 6 *tercios* of walloon infantry of 12 companies each, 3 regiments of German infantry, each regiment with 10 companies, besides 3 free companies. Line cavalry was composed of 3 *tercios* of Spanish horse, one *tercio* of Italian and one of Burgundian horse, each *tercio* being formed with six companies, three *tercios* of Walloon horse, each with 4 companies and three regiments of German cavalry, each one of them of 5 companies, besides the two companies of guards of the governor and that of the guards of the governor of the arms, 3 companies of guards of the general and of lieutenants-generals of the cavalry and the company of guards of the provost general of the army. There were also 3 *tercios* of dragoons, each of 9 companies. A certain number of these units remained in the service of Spain throughout the War of the Spanish Succession and passed from 1709-1713 to Spain to be incorporated for a long time into the Spanish army.

INFANTRY

Spanish Infantry

▲ *Maximilian II Emanuel of Bavaria by Constantij Netscher.*

The «old» or veteran Spanish *tercios* were the basis of the Spanish army in Flanders. They represented the most trusted body of men upon which the Governors based the defence of the Country from the continuous attacks of the French. Together with the veteran units, the seniority of which could go back to the previous century, a variable number (depending on the years) of other Spanish infantry units were present, sometimes just for a short while [being considered a *marching* unit] or for the ongoing campaign:

- **IRSP31** *Spanish Tercio of Zuñiga*[69]
- **IRSP32** *Spanish Tercio of Mariño → Hurtado de Amezaga*[70]
- **IRSP33** *Spanish Tercio of Grajal → Rocafull y Rocaberti → Diaz Pimienta → del Valle*[71]
- **IRSP34** *Spanish Tercio of Agüiar → Chacon → Borja*[72]
- **IRSP35** *Spanish Tercio of Manrique de Arana*[73]
- **IRSP36** *Spanish Tercio of Moncada y Aragon → Claros Perez de Guzman → Ibañez*[74]
- **IRSP37** *Spanish Tercio of the Marquis of Casasola*[75]
- **IRSP38** *Spanish Tercio of Fernando del Castillo*[76]

---

[69] According to Clonard the *tercio* was originally known as **Tercio departamental de Bravante**; in 1717 it became the regiment of **Soria.** Maestro de campo: (1682) D. Manuel Joaquín Lopez de Zúñiga y Sotomayor y Mendoza, X duca di Bejar, (1687) D. Gaspar Antonio de Zuñiga y Henriquez y de Salinas, (1693) D. Carlos Antonio de Zuñiga y Henriquez (1702) D. Pedro Antonio de Zúñiga Guzman Sotomayor y Castro.

[70] According to Clonard the *tercio* was originally known as **Tercio departamental de Flandes**; in 1717 it became the regiment of **Galicia.** Maestro de campo: (1685) D. Antonio Mariño de Andrade y Sotomayor, (1697) D. Juan Antonio Hurtado de Amezaga y Unzaga (1704) D. Francisco de Los Rios y de la Torre.

[71] According to Clonard the *tercio* was originally known as **Tercio auxiliar de Flandes**. Maestro de campo: (1683) D. Pedro Alvarez de Vega, conte di Grajal, marquis of Monraos, (1690) D. Gaspar de Roccaful y Roberti, (1692) D. Juan Diaz Pimienta, (1698) D. Luis Joseph Antonio de Valle, marquis del Valle.

[72] The *tercio* in 1717 became the regiment of **Toro** and in 1717 regiment of **Portugal.** Maestro de campo: (1683) D. Francisco del Castillo Fajardo, marquis of Villadarias, (1686) D. Luis de Agüiar y Toledo, (1691) D. Gonzalo Chacon y Orellana, (1695-1700) D. Luis de Borja, marquis of Taracena (1700) D. Juan de Idiaquez.

[73] The *tercio* was also called **Tercio de la Marina**. Maestro de campo:(1682) D. Martin de los Rios (1686) D. Juan Francisco Manrique de Arana (he was still in command at the beginning of 1700) (1700) D. Francisco Perez Mancheño.

[74] According to Clonard the *tercio* was originally known as **Tercio departamental de Holanda**; in 1717 it became the regiment of **Zamora.** Maestro de campo: (1682) D. Joseph de Moncada y Aragon, (1691) D. Juan Claros *Ignacio* de Guzman, (1701) D. Francisco Ibañez Rubalcava.

[75] Maestro de campo: (1687) D. Gonzalo Davila Pacheco, marquis of Casasola. The *tercio* was disbanded in May 1693.

[76] Maestro de campo: (1684) D. Fernando del Castillo Cabeza de Vaca y Carrasco. The *tercio* was disbanded in 1694.

▲ Plate 1 - Army of the Principality of Catalonia 1689-1694 1) Soldier of the Viceroy's horse guard company. 2) Pikeman of the Generalitat (Deputation) regiment; 3) Drummer of the City of Barcelona regiment; 4) Soldiers of the Vilafranca Company. (Plate by Francesc Riart, taken from "Soldats, Guerrers i Combatents dels Paisos Catalans" Rafael Dalmau Editor, Barcelona 2014)

▲ Plate 2 - 1694-1697) 1) Standard bearer of the tercio de la Generalitat; 2) Musketeer of the Tercio of the City (of Barcelona); 3) Flag of the tercio de la generalitat; 4) Flag of the tercio de la ciutat (of Barcelona); 5) Drum of the tercio della Città di Barcellona; 6) Captain of the tercio de la ciutat de Barcelona. (Plate by Francesc Riart, taken from 'Soldats, Guerrers i Combatents dels Paisos Catalans")

▲ Plate 3 - 1694-1697 Provincial tercios (Catalan) and miquelets. 1) Musketeer from the Talarn veguera company (Catalan militia); 2) Musketeer from the provincial tercio (Catalan) of the Count of Darnius; 3) Sergeant major from the provincial tercio (Catalan) of the Count of Darnius; Pikeman from the provincial tercio (Catalan) of Joan de Copons; 5) Miquelet. (Plate by Francesc Riart, taken from "Soldats, Guerrers i Combatents dels Paisos Catalans")

▲ *Plate 4 - 1674-1698 Tercios of the Kingdom of Valencia. 1) Arquebusier of the tercio of the Kingdom of Valencia 1674-1675; 2) Musketeer of the tercio of the City of Valencia 1684; 3) Pikeman of the tercio of the city (of Valencia) 1684-1695; 4) Pikeman of the tercio of the Kingdom of Valencia 1695-1698; 4) Drummer of the tercio of the Kingdom of Valencia 1684-1695 (Plate by Francesc Riart, taken from "Soldats, Guerrers i Combatents dels Paisos Catalans")*

▲ *Plate 5 - Army of Flanders 1692-1694 Zuñiga Tercio (Plate by Francesc Riart, taken from 'El vestuario: de los tercios a los regimientos (1550-1748)' BOERI GIANCARLO In 'Caminos Legendarios. Los Tercios y el Regimiento Soria en la Historia y la Cultura.' Las Palmas, December 2009)*

- **IRSP39** *Spanish Tercio of Pedro de Aldao*[77]
- **IRSP40** *Spanish Tercio of Sarmiento*[78]

There were two to three «veteran» Italian infantry *tercios* (that were considered the second most reliable nationality after the Spaniards); the Walloon infantry was constituted by eight to ten *tercios*. In order to compensate for the small number of soldiers that could be drawn from the subjects of the king of Spain, whose territories had been notably eroded by France, it was usual to form or capitulate the service of German regiments. During the war of the League of Augsburg there were serving about 7 German infantry regiments (reduced to three by the end of the war, because they were being replaced by the Bavarian regiments and financial assets did not allow the employment of all of them). The last formations of the infantry were three weak *tercios* (that soon after the beginning of the war were reduced to the force of a single company each) of English, Scottish and Irish Infantry:

Italian Infantry

- **IRIT06** *Italian tercio of* (1683) D. **Restaino Cantelmo, duke of Popoli, prince of Pettorano** (1695) D. **Carlo Giovanni Campi** (1698) D. **Paolo Piano Magni**.[79]
- **IRIT07** *Italian tercio of* (1675) D. **Fabio Bonamico** (1689) D. **Domenico di Francia** (1697) D. **Marcello, marquis Ceva-Grimaldi**.[80]

  IRIT08 *Italian tercio of* (1680) D. **Carlo Andrea Caracciolo, marquis of Torrecuso** (1691) D. **Domenico Acquaviva d'Aragona, marquis of Acquaviva**[81] (1701) D. **Antonio Ceva-Grimaldi**.

Walloon Infantry

- **IRWL04** *Walloon tercio of* (1685) **Count de Moucron**[82] → (1689) *Jean-Philippe Eugene de Merode, Marquis of Westerloo*[83]
- **IRWL05** *Walloon tercio of* (1688) *Marquis de Deynse*[84]
- **IRWL06** *Walloon tercio of* (1689) D. **Carlos Theodoro, barón de Winterfeldt** (1695) D. **Michel Xavier de Bournonville, baron de Capres**
- **IRWL07** *Walloon tercio of* (1688) *Count of Hornes*[85]
- **IRWL08** *Walloon tercio of* (1689) *Hugues de Noyelles, count of Falais (Fallay)*
- **IRWL09** *Walloon tercio of* (1684) *Baudouin Vanderpiet* → (1690-1701) *count of Grobendonq*[86]
- **IRWL10** *Walloon tercio of* (1688) *Francisco González de Albelda*[87]
- **IRWL11** *Walloon tercio of* (1682) D. *Jeronimo Alberto de Merode Varoux, Count de Thian, baron de Archies,* (1694) D. *Phelipe de Bete, marquis of Lede*
- **IRWL12** *Walloon tercio of Ferdinand Jacques Lindeman de Nevelstein,* (1689) *Sieur de Lannoy*[88]

English, Scottish and Irish Infantry

- **IREn01** *English tercio of Diego Porter*[89]
- **IRSc01** *Scottish tercio of* (1677) *Henry Gage*[90]
- **IRIr01** *Irish tercio of* (1673) *Dennis [Dionisio] O'Berny,* (1689) *Eugene O'Neil*.

---

77   Maestro de campo: (1689) D. Pedro de Aldao. The *tercio* was disbanded in April 1693.
78   Maestro de campo: (1689) D. Jacinto Sarmiento y Zamudia. The *tercio* was disbanded in May 1693.
79   According to Samaniego the *tercio* became the regiment of Italian infantry of **Basilicata**, and later (1718) **Corcega**; probably he exchanged it for another tercio formed in 1701.
80   Disbanded before 1715.
81   The *tercio* in 1718 became the regiment of Italian infantry of **Parma.**
82   *Jean François Hippolyte, marquis d'Ennetières Baron de la Berlière* **Comte de Moucron**.
83   The *tercio* in 1711 became the regiment of **Venloo** and in 1718 the regiment of **Namur**
84   *Maximiliano Alberto de Merode,* **marquis de Deynse**. The *tercio* became in 1711 the regiment of **Charleroi** and in 1718 the regiment of **Utrecht.**
85   *Felipe Manuel,* **Conde de Hornes**. The tercio in 1711 became the regiment of **Limburg.**
86   Called **Hainaut** in 1711 and in 1737 passed to the new army of the kingdom of the Two Sicilies. Finally disbanded in 1788.
87   The *tercio* was disbanded in 1693.
88   The *tercio* in 1711 became the regiment of **Gante** and in 1718 the regiment of **Flandes.**
89   Reduced to 2 companies.
90   In 1691 reduced to a single company.

German Infantry

- **IRAL06** *German regiment of (1681) Honoré Henry Arnoulde de Chastelet, Marquis of Trichateau*[91]
- **IRAL07** *German regiment of* (1681) *count Frederick Charles Wildt und Rheingraf,* (1689) *Antoine Lenoir Du Meny,* (1695) *Count Guillaume de Lannoy d'Hautpont*[92]
- **IRAL08** *German regiment of* (1671) *Hermann of Baden,* (1691-1701) *Philipp d'Ursel, count of Milan*
- **IRAL09** *German regiment of* (1681) *Charles Thomas of Lorraine,* (1693-1694) *D. Francisco Enrique Davalos Tapia*[93]
- **IRAL10** *German regiment of* (1676) *Godefrido Vanderstraten,* (1693-1701) *marquis Giovan Battista Spinola*[94]
- **IRAL11** *German regiment of* (1679) *Viscount of Ahere*[95].
- **IRAL12** *German regiment of* (1686) *Hans Hendrick Theyst van Braunsfelt,* (1692) *Juan Pedro Emering* (1693-1700) D. *Miguel Pérez de Mendoza.*
- **IRAL13** *German regiment of marquis* (1690) *Giovan Battista Spinola* (June 1693) D. *Geronimo Barceló*[96]
- **IRAL14** *German regiment of* (1688-1701) *Fabian, baron of Wrangel*[97].

The main places and forts were generally garrisoned by free companies (generally formed by inhabitants of the town or the surroundings), depending from the Governor of the place.

When in 1692 the Elector of Bavaria became Governor of the Spanish Low Lands he brought with him a number of Bavarian regiments, that were paid by the Spanish crown and were considered auxiliary troops[98]:

- **IRAL15** *Regiment of the guards of his Electoral Highness.*[99]
- **IRAL16** *Regiment of the Electoral Prince.*
- **IRAL05** *Regiment of Tattenbach.*[100]

CAVALRY

The line cavalry of the army of Flanders was composed of companies of Guards and tercios of horse (called cuirassiers= *Cavallos Corazas*) and of *tercios* of dragoons (called also Horse Arquebusiers= *Dragones Arcabuzeros a Cavallo*). The German units were ranged in regiments and were all cuirassiers.

The composition of the cavalry followed a similar pattern as regards the nationalities of the units. Each *tercio* was commanded by a mestre de camp, who also held a company, a sergeant major (= major) similarly at the head of another company, and some captains (normally a *tercio* had six companies). Each company had a captain, an ensign, a sergeant, a few corporals, a trumpeter and about 30 to 40 troopers. Each regiment of German horse was commanded by a colonel, a lieutenant colonel, a sergeant major and a variable number of captains. The formation of the companies was similar to those of the *tercios*, but there was also a lieutenant.

There were further companies with duties of Guards to the Governor General (a company of horse arquebusiers and one of cuirassiers), one company of horse guards for the Governor General of the Arms, one company of Guards to the General of the Cavalry and one each to his two Lieutenant-Generals. These companies had a number of troopers two or three times greater than the ordinary companies.

The Provost General of the army was also entitled to a small (around ten men) company of horse (sometimes called Archers).

---

91 Disbanded in 1686.
92 Disbanded in 1697-1698.
93 Disbanded in 1694.
94 Colonel of a previous regiment of low German infantry (1689-1693), disbanded in 1693
95 D. *Alexandro de Colins* [*Colens*]*, Seigneur et* **Vicomte de Ahere**. Disbanded probably in 1682.
96 The regiment was disbanded in November1693.
97 Swedish of nationality. Died in 1737 after passing to Imperial service.
98 The agreement for these troops was definitively made in 1694. The infantry regiments were to be 1,400 men strong each. These regiments replaced two infantry regiments from Brandenburg, which had previously been at Spanish service.
99 In 1691 and 1692 the regiment of Guards, together with that of De Pretz's, was employed in Piedmont as auxiliary forces to the duke of Savoy.
100 The regiment in 1695 passed to the army of Catalonia.

▲ Plate 6 - 1692-1694 Tercio de Aragon (plate by A. Manzano taken from SORANDO MUZÁS, Luis 'El Tercio de Aragon: Notes on its evolution, clothing and emblems (1678-1698)' Emblemata no. 1 Provincial Council of Zaragoza 1995

Companies of the Guards

- **CRSP16** *Company of Lances Guards of the Governor-General* (*Black Horses*).
- **CRSP17** *Company of Arquebusiers Guards of the Governor-General* (*White Horses*).
- **CRSP18** *Company of Spanish Cuirasses Guards of the Governor of the Arms* (*Bay Horses*).
- **CRSP19** *Company of Spanish Cuirasses Guards of the General of the Cavalry.*[101]
- **CRSP20-21**[102] two *Companies of Guards of the Lieutenant-Generals of the Cavary.*
- **CRSP22** *Company of Arquebusiers of the Provost-General of the Army.*[103]

Tercios and regiments

Spanish Cavalry

- **CRSP23** *Spanish tercio of Horse* of (1676) the **Count of Mastaing**[104] (1692) D. **Luis de Borja** (1695) D. **Leonel Gallo de Salamanca, baron of Noirmont** (1703) D. **Gabriel Cano de Aponte, Sr de Boulines**.[105]
- **CRSP24** *Spanish tercio of Horse* of (1688) D. **Juan Augustin Hurtado de Mendoza y Salvatierra, marquis of Gauna** (1694) D. **Diego de Veintemilla y Rodríguez de Santisteban** (later **Marquis of Cropany**) (1697) D. **Francisco Antonio Pascal.**[106]
- **CRSP25** *Spanish tercio of Horse* of (1685) D. **Gabriel de Buendia** (1690) D. **Joseph de Jimenez** (1695) D. **Francisco de la Puente Reisenberg** (1697) D. **Luis de Zuñiga y la Cerda.**[107]
- **CRSP26** *Spanish tercio of Horse* of (1687) D. **Joseph de Encio San Vicente** (1693-1701) D. **Joseph de Peñalosa.**
- **CRSP27** *Spanish (Burgundian) tercio of Horse* of (1679) D. **Felipe Carlos de Aremberg, duke of Arschot** (1691) D. **Alexandro de Bay, señor de Laëre** (1696-1701) D. **Joseph (conde) de Toulongeon.**[108]
- **CRSP28** *Spanish tercio of Horse* of (1688) D. **Alexandro de Bay, señor de Laëre** (1691) D. **Sebastián de Quincoces Hurtado de Mendoza**[109]
- **CRSP29** *Spanish tercio of Horse* of (1688-1701) D. **Gaspar Gomez de Espinosa** (dal 1693 **Count of Ribancourt**)[110]
- **CRSP30** *Spanish tercio of Horse* of (1688) D. **Antonio Jacinto de Landáburu y Zumarraga**[111]

Italian Calvary

- **CRIT01** *Italian tercio of Horse* of (1684) D. **Scipione Brancaccio** (1694) D. **Giovanni Giorgio Campi** (1695-1706) D. **Emanuel Fraula**

Walloon Cavalry

- **CRWL03** *Wallon tercio of Horse* of (1684) D. **Severin, Sr de Betencourt, señor de Audregny** (1693-1703) D. **Ignace, Chev. of Fourneau**[112]
- **CRWL04** *Wallon tercio of Horse* of (1675) D. **Nicolas Richard Du Puis** (1692) D. **Philippe Gourdin, Sr de Dessein et de Haubos** (1697-1701) D. **Alexandre Cecile de Scaillemont**[113]
- **CRWL05** *Wallon tercio of Horse* of (1667) D. **Philippe de Gulpen, Sr d'Audemont** (1695-1701) D. **Philippe, Chev. of Berghes**

---

101 In 1701 the company of the *General of the Cavalry* became a regiment, disbanded in 1715.
102 Later regiment **Conde del Real** and since 1718 regiment **Algarve**.
103 (1672-1694) D. *Benito de Castañeda* (1694) *Juan Francisco de Castañeda.*
104 *Carlos de Jauche, Comte de Mastaing et Sr de Bruxellet.*
105 In 1718 it became the horse regiment of **Barcellona**.
106 Disbanded in 1698-1699.
107 Disbanded in 1698-1699.
108 Disbanded in 1706.
109 Disbanded between 1693 and 1698.
110 Later it became the cavalry regiment **La Farina** and in 1718 the cavalry regiment of **Malta**.
111 Disbanded in 1691.
112 In 1701 it became the horse regiment of **Corral** and in 1718 horse regiment of **Farnesio**.
113 In 1701 it became the horse regiment of **Cecile**, that in 1718 took the name of **Alcantara**.

▲ *Plate 7 - Milan Standard Bearer of the State Cavalry. The ground colour of Cavalry guidons was usually crimson red. (Plate by Davide Grassi)*

▲ Plate 8 - Milan 1690 Spanish infantry soldier (red uniforms) and Neapolitan infantry soldiers (blue uniforms) (Plate by Davide Grassi)

German Cavalry

- **CRAL01** *German regiment of Horse* of (1689-1691) *François Dumont, Sr de Dielsem*[114]
- **CRAL02** *German regiment of Horse* of (1674) *Joseph de Noyelles, Baron of Torsy* (1690) D. *Nicolò Pignatelli, of the House of the Dukes of Bisaccia* (1693-1698) D. *Domenico Gaetano d'Aragona di Laurenzana.*[115]
- **CRAL03** *German regiment of Horse* of (1680-1701) *Nicolas Hartman,* (1701) *Charles Christien de Landas, vizconde de Fleurival, barón de Graincourt.*[116]
- **CRAL04** *German regiment of Horse* of (1682) *Charles Thomas of Lorraine*[117] (1693-1698) *Jean Joseph de Permillacq de Belcastel, Marquis d'Avesse;*
- **CRAL05** *German regiment of Horse* of (1684) *Louis-Ernest, Prince of Gavré, Count of Egmont* (1692) *François Joseph Pierre d'Ognies, Barone di Courrieres and of Ourges* (1700) D. *Domenico Gaetano d'Aragona di Laurenzana;*[118]
- **CRAL06** *German regiment of Horse* of (1689) *Martin Fernandez de Cordova* (1691) *Joaquim de Fuenmayor y Davila*[119]*;*
- **CRAL07** *German regiment of Horse* of (1688) *Charles-Louis-Antoine d'Hennin Liétard d'Alsace, Count of Bossu, Prince of Chimay,* (1704) *Philip Emmanuel de Lacatoire*[120]*;*
- **CRAL08** *German regiment of Horse* of (1688) *Charles de Croy, duke of Havré;*
- **CRAL09** *German regiment of Horse* of (1689-1690) *Anthon Ulrich d'Aremberg, Count of Fresin*[121]*;*
- **CRAL10** *German regiment of Horse* of (1689-1691) *François Hugues Ferdinand, Prince of Nassau*[122]*.*

DRAGOONS

The *tercios* of Dragoons were all composed of Walloon subjects (officers excluded) and had a force of 9 companies with 40-50 private soldiers each. Occasionally there were also some free companies of dragoons, that operated much as guerrillas (in the contemporary gazettes called also partizans) against the lines of communication and transport of the French, or raided French held territories, often imposing contribution in nature or money:

- **DRWL01** *Tercio of Dragoons* of (1676) D. *Gomar de Ville, Sr de Maugremont* (1691) *Ignace Chev. de Fourneau* (1693-1699) D. *Guillermo de Melun, Marquis of Risbourg*[123] (1699-1701) D. *Nicolas Ferrare*
- **DRWL02** *Tercio of Dragoons* of (1684) D. *François d'Ognies, Baron de Courrieres d'Ourges* (1692-1699) *Jean d'Arville* (1699-1701) D. *Guillermo de Melun, Marquis of Risbourg*[124]
- **DRWL03** *Tercio of Dragoons* of (1684-1705) D. *Theodore Valansart*[125]
- **DRWL04** *Tercio of Dragoons* of (1676-1691) D. *Mathias Gaspar Perez*[126]
- **DRWL05** *Tercio of Dragoons* of (1688-1691) D. *Fadrique de Castro*[127]
- **DRWL06** *Tercio of Dragoons* of (1689-1701) *Claude Richardot, Prince of Steenhuyse*[128]
- **DRWL07** *Tercio of Dragoons* of (1689) D. *Nicolas Agüero y Zarate* (1693) D. *Francisco Antonio de Pascal*[129]
- **DRWL08** *Tercio of Dragoons* of (1688) D. *Charles Ernst de Bossu, Chev. D'Alsace*[130]
- **DRWL09** *Tercio of Dragoons* of (1696-1697) D. *Jacques Pastur*[131]

---

114 Merged in 1691 withn the regiment of *Pignatelli*.
115 Disbanded in 1698-1699.
116 Disbanded in 1706.
117 Son of the prince of Vaudemont.
118 The regiment was disbanded in 1710, following the great reform of the army of the Spanish Low Countries.
119 Disbanded in 1693.
120 The regiment was disbanded in 1710, following the great reform of the army of the Spanish Low Countries.
121 Disbanded in 1690.
122 Disbanded in 1691.
123 In 1699 the marquis of Risbourg takes the command of another regiment of dragoons [**DRWL02**].
124 The *tercio* becomes the regiment of *Itre* and in 1718 *Belgica*.
125 It becomes the regiment *Boselli*, since 1718 *Batavia*.
126 Disbanded in 1691.
127 Disbanded in 1691.
128 It becomes the regiment *Ferrare* in 1701, then *Vendôme*, and in 1718 *Frisia*.
129 Disbanded in 1693.
130 Disbanded in 1690.
131 Disbanded in 1697.

- **DRWL10** *Tercio of Dragoons* of (1688-1693) D. *Guillermo de Melun, Marquis of Risbourg*[132]

German auxiliary Cavalry

The Auxiliary Bavarian cavalry was constituted by the squadrons and regiments of:

- **CRAL11** *Squadron of Horse Carabiniers*[133].
- **CRAL12** *Squadron of Horse Grenadiers*[134].
- **CRAL13** *Regiment of Cuirassiers of Arco*.
- **CRAL14** *Regiment of Cuirassiers of Weickel*.
- **DRAL01** *Regiment of Dragoons of Arco*.
- **DRAL02** *Regiment of Dragoons of Monastirol*.

The Cuirassiers regiments were to be 800 men strong each; the dragoons 480 each.

Italian possessions

The Italian territories that belonged to the crown of Spain were those of the Duchy of Milan (that included parts of present-day Lombardy and Piedmont as well as the small marquisate of Finale with its harbour on the Ligurian coast) and the kingdoms of Naples (i.e. southern Italy and the fortresses on the Tuscan coast known as the *Stato dei Presidi*), Sicily and Sardinia (at the time an integral part of the kingdom of Aragon and therefore Spanish territory). Each of these territories was governed by a Viceroy or Governor General (Milan) and had an autonomous army and administration.

---

132 Disbanded in 1693, when the marquis of Risbourg takes the command of the more ancient *tercio* of D'Arville.
133 Created in 1696 in Flanders.
134 Created in 1696 in Flanders,

▲ *States of Northern Italy; areas of war campaigns. (Graphic design by R. Hall).*

During the period of the war of the League of Augsburg (in Italy 1690-1696) the only territory that was directly involved and therefore mobilised a field army was the State of Milan. The other Italian kingdoms supplied reinforcements of men and resources in terms of money, food and ammunition.

While the armies were separate entities, the the squadrons of galleys often operated in concert. There was a squadron in Naples, one in Sicily and one of private Genoese galleys that served as mercenaries (*Escuadra de Particulares de Génova* [private, i.e. capitulated by *Asiento*], not to be confused with the state-owned one of the Republic); Sardinia had only 2-3 galleys. The main mission of these galleys (which were joined almost every year by the Spanish ones based in Cartagena) was to control the activity of the French fleets and to repress the activity of the Barbary pirates who infested the Mediterranean also carrying out raids on land to capture people to reduce to slavery, but they also served to transport troops from one territory to another[135].

Duchy of Milan

Governor General and Captain General

1687 D. Antonio Lopez de Ayala, Velasco y Cardenas, Count of Fuensalida y Colmenar.

1691 D. Diego Felipe de Guzman, Duque de S. Lucar la mayor, Marques de Leganes.

1696-1706 D. Charles Henry de Lorraine, Prince de Vaudemont.

Infantry

▲ Charles Henri de Lorraine, Prince of Vaudémont, Sovereign of Commercy, 1708.

The infantry of the field army of the State of Milan was composed of 5-6 *tercios* of Spanish infantry, 2 to 7 *tercios* of Milanese infantry, 2 *tercios* of Neapolitan infantry, 2 German infantry regiments and 1 Grison and 2 Swiss regiments (after 1691):

Spanish Infantry

- **IRSP41** *Spanish tercio of Lombardia*[136]
- **IRSP42** *Spanish tercio of Saboya*[137]
- **IRSP43** *Spanish tercio de la Mar de Napoles*[138]
- **IRSP44** *Spanish tercio of* (1685-1700) the **duke of San Pietro D. Francesco Maria Spinola**[139]
- **IRSP45** *Spanish tercio of Lisboa* (since 1691)[140]

There were for some shorter periods other Spanish *tercios*, such as that of **Francisco de Villalonga** from 1688 to July 1690, when it was disbanded (and the men merged into the existing *tercios*).

135 Spanish sailing warships also occasionally appeared in the Mediterranean, operating from Cadiz, Alicante and Barcelona against the French and North African fleets.

136 In 1707 it became the regiment of **Lombardia**. Maestro de campo: D. Diego de Benavides y Aragón, 3rd marquis of Solera (son of the Viceroy of Naples, killed at the battle of Orbassano in October 1693), 1694 D. Francisco Fernandez de Cordova, count of Aguilar.

137 In 1707 it became the regiment of **Saboya** [Savoia]. Maestro de campo: (1681-1691) D. Carlos Brizeño de la Cueva, marquis of Villanueva de las Torres, (1691) D. Manuel Fernandez de Velasco (1693) D. Pedro Pimentell.

138 Since 1718 regiment **Corona**. Maestro de campo: D. Francisco Fernandez de Cordova, Aguilar y Pimentell, (1691) D. Francisco Colmenero, D. Juan Zignuda, D. Lucas Spinola.

139 In 1700 this *tercio* was merged with that of Mar de Napoles, when Spinola became maestro de campo of the older unit.

140 Transferred from Sicily, where it was serving since the War of Messina (1674). Maestro de campo: (1691) D. Manuel de Orozco, D. Sebastian Pimentell y Zuñiga (December 1693) D. Juan Simon Henriquez de Cabrera (January 1695) D. Carlos Coloma, D. Diego de la Concha.

Italian Infantry
- **IRIT09** *Milanese tercio of* (1689-1707) *count Francesco Bonesana*[141]
- **IRIT10** *Milanese tercio of* (1685-1697) *Marquis Benedetto Ali*[142]
- **IRIT11** *Milanese tercio of* (1689-1692) *Marquis of Porlezza*[143]
- **IRIT12** *Milanese tercio of* (1690-1691) *Marquis Litta*[144]
- **IRIT13** *Milanese tercio of* (1690-1697) *Arese→Porlezza*[145]
- **IRIT14** *Milanese tercio of* (1690-1692) *Prince of Gonzaga*[146]
- **IRIT15** *Milanese tercio of* (1695-1697) *Fulvio Barile*[147]
- **IRIT16** *Neapolitan tercio of Colonna,* (1691) *Francia,* then *Caracciolo*[148]
- **IRIT17** *Neapolitan tercio of Dentice,* (1691) *Ciarletta Caracciolo*[149]

German Infantry
- **IRAL16** *German regiment of* (1682) *Miguel Ulbin,* (1693) *Cabrera,* (1693-1702) *Count of Leiningen*[150]
- **IRAL17** *German regiment of* (1686) *Cabrera,* (1693) *Melzi,* (1695) *Arteaga*[151]

From 1689 to 1693 there had been in existence a third German infantry regiment, given by Count of Fuensalida, then the Governor, to be commanded to his own son **count of Colmenar**, which in May 1693 was disbanded distribuiting the men into the two older regiments.

Swiss Infantry
- **IRSw01** *Grison regiment of* (1690) *Sprecher-Capuol,* later *Albertino*[152]
- **IRSw02** *German regiment of* (1692) *Besler*[153]
- **IRSw03** *German regiment of* (1692) *Mayer*[154]

In addition to these troops in 1690 the Governor General of Milan capitulated the service, for the duration of the war, of an infantry regiment from the Duke Regent of Württemberg[155].

- **IRAL18** *German regiment of Württemberg* 1690-1698[156]

Each Spanish *tercio* had a nominal composition of about 1,000 men, distributed in 12-16 companies. A similar composition should have applied to each Italian (Lombard or Neapolitan) *tercio*, even if it was expected that Lombard (=Milanese) infantry was at all times at full strength, being able to recruit from the country.

---

141 After the war the *tercio* of Bonesana was the only Milanese infantry *tercio* that was left standing.
142 In 1697 the *tercio* was sent to Catalonia, where it took part into the defense of Barcelona and was disbanded in 1698.
143 Maestro de campo D. Carlo Filiberto d'Este, marquis of Porlezza and Borgomanero; it was disbanded in 1692.
144 Maestro de campo: marquis Pompeo Litta; disbanded in 1691.
145 Maestro de campo: count Carlo Borromeo Arese (1692) Carlo Filiberto d'Este marquis of Porlezza; disbanded at the end of the war in 1697.
146 Disbanded in February 1692.
147 Maestro de campo: Fulvio Barile, June (1697) Giovanni Guglielmo Carré. In July 1697 the tercio was sent to Catalonia, where it was still serving in 1700.
148 Maestro de campo: D. Marco Antonio Colonna, (1691) D. Antonio di Francia, D. Tommaso Caracciolo.
149 Maestro de campo: (1689) Domenico Dentice, (June 1691) Ciarletta Caracciolo della Torella.
150 Colonel: (1682) Miguel Ulbin, May (1693) D. Fadrique Enriquez de Cabrera, November (1693-1702) Count of Leiningen [*Leiningen-Westerburg-Schaumburg, Heinrich Christian Friedrich Ernst zu*. The count of Leiningen early in 1701 with many officers of his regiment quits Spanish service and entered Imperial one. He dies in 1702 during the encounter at Cremona.]. In 1702 it became *Louvigny* and was transformed into a Wallon unit.
151 Colonel: (1686) Fadrique Enriquez de Cabrera, (May-October 1693) marquis Egidio Melzi, (1695-1702) D. Joseph de Arteaga.
152 Colonel: (1690) Ercole Capuol and Salomon Sprecher, (1697) Giacomo Albertino. In 1704 it became Buol and in 1706 passed over to the service of the Austrian pretender (later Emperor Karl VI).
153 Colonel: 1692-1697 Johann Karl Besler de Wattinguen. In 1697 the two Swiss regiments were merged together into one.
154 Colonel: 1692-1697 Hans Gaspar Mayer de Baldegg.
155 **Friedrich Carl of Württemberg-Winnental** (12th September 1652 –20th December 1697) from 1677 he was Duke Regent of the newly founded line of Württemberg-Winnental and Regent of the little Duke Eberhard Ludwig (1677-1733 (from 1677 to 1693). From the end of 1693 Duke Eberhard Ludwig came of age and governed in his own right and in his name the capitulation was renewed.
156 Colonel (nominal) Prince Karl Alexander of Würtemberg. the regiment was dismissed from Spanish service in 1698.

▲ Plate 8 - 1690 Grenadier from a German infantry regiment and musketeer from a Neapolitan tercio (Catalonia) (Coloured illustrations taken from a handwritten infantry exercise manual, National Library of Naples)

▲ Plate 9 - 1688-1696 Italian infantry tercios in Flanders, Campi-Magni, Acquaviva, Bonamico (Coloured illustrations taken from a handwritten manual of exercises for infantry, National Library of Naples)

The German infantry regiments should have had a force of 12 companies of about 100-150 privates each. A similar composition was foreseen for the two Swiss and the Grison regiments.

In addition to these troops, all the major places and fortresses of the State had garrisons, that could be of about ten to one hundred men, grouped in free companies, of one of which the Governor of the place was captain. During the war 3 companies of Spanish Invalids were also created to employ old and disabled Spanish soldiers in garrison duties.

Finale on the Ligurian coast, the possession of which was essential to guarantee a safe harbour for the galleys and vessels directed from Spain to Southern Italy or the other way round, and for convoying reinforcements from Spain, Naples and Sicily to Milan, had a garrison of 4-6 Grison free companies, 4 to 6 Italian free companies and 6 to 12 infantry companies detached from the Spanish or Italian *tercios* of the Milanese army.

Cavalry and Dragoons

The composition of the Cavalry of the army of Milan was similar to that of the other Spanish armies. The Governor General, the General and Lieutenants-Generals of the cavalry all had a company of Guards (two for the Governor General, one of Lances and one of Carbines). During the last part of the century there were no more Spanish companies of horse in Milan (even though many captains, officers and troopers could be Spaniards).

Companies of the Guards

Both companies of the Guards had the strength of about 100 soldiers. The captain of the Lancers company also had command over the Arquebusiers (Carbines) company.

- **CRIT02** *Company of Lances Guards of the Governor-General.*
- **CRIT03** *Company of Carbines Guards of the Governor-General.*
- **CRIT04** *Company of Cuirasses Guards of the General of the Cavalry.*
- **CRIT05-06** Two *Companies of Guards of the Lieutenant-Generals of the Cavary.*

The Milanese cavalry (called **cavalry of the State CRIT07**) was composed of about 30 companies of Horse (some of Gendarmes=*uomini d'armi*=men at arms and the others of light-horse).

These companies served normally as free companies and were not grouped into formations comparable to regiments, *tercios* or *trozos* and were subject to the command of a General of the Cavalry of the State[157] and some Lieutenant-Generals[158]. During the campaign they were grouped into operational squadrons. The strength of each company averaged between 30 and 50 men each.

Furthermore there were two units of **Foreign**[159] (=German; 8-9 companies **CRAL15**) and **Neapolitan**[160] (6-8 companies of horse **CRIT08**), that were commanded by a General of the foreign cavalry and a Commissary General of the Neapolitan Cavalry. All were subject to the General of the Cavalry of the State.

Among the mounted troops there was also the regiment **Dragoni dello Stato DRIT01** [called also the "**Yellow Dragoons**" from the colour of the dress][161] consisting in 8-12 companies (at different moments).

Since the time of the Thirty Years' War, the army of Lombardy had made use of units (companies) of Dragoons, mostly recruited from the hereditary territories of the House of Austria in Germany, but their use had always been judged by many to be unsuitable and in fact, from 1649 onwards, these units were gradually dismissed. Starting from the governorship of the Prince of Ligne, a few units of dragoons were created [which had been reintroduced into the Spanish army of the Netherlands by the Count of Monterey and shortly afterwards into that of Catalonia], but these were then sent to Sicily for the war of Messina. Of particular concern was the extensive use of these regiments in the French and Piedmontese armies, for which reason it was decided in the early 1680s to reintroduce this speciality into the Milanese army as well, especially after the French had since 1681 included some regiments of dragoons among the troops of the garrison of Casale, which had just been acquired by the Duke of Mantua.

---

157 1688 - **November 1693**. D. *Joseph Daza y Guzman*; **1696** D. *Filippo Spinola, duca del Sesto.*
158 **November 1678-1691** D. *Antonio de Olea;* **1691-1692** Marquis D. *Tommaso Casnedi;* **1693** Count *Bartolomeo Maria Visconti;* **December 1693-1695** Prince D. *Antonio Gaetano Trivulzio;* **November 1696** D. *Gaetano Coppola.*
159 Comissary general: Prince Antonio Gaetano Trivulzio, D. Gaetano Coppola, D. Francisco Ramirez de Valdes.
160 Comissary general: 1686-1692 D. Giuseppe Giudice, (1692-1694) D. Ambrogio Fiorenza, D. Tommaso Caracciolo.
161 Colonel: (1689) Count Prospero Crivelli, (December 1690) D. Antonio de Rojas, (1692) Count Albert d'Ursel, (1698) D. Diego Monroy. In 1702 it became the dragoons regiment of **Caylus;** passed in Spain after 1707, in 1718 it became the dragoons regiment of **Pavia**.

Auxiliary German Cavalry

In 1690 to meet the obligations with the duke of Savoy and to field and army of sufficient strength to oppose the French, in addition to with the infantry regiment from the duke of Württemberg, was capitulated the service of a cuirassiers and one dragoon regiment (that in 1692 were merged into just one regiment of horse) and one regiment of Bavarian cuirassiers (*Arco*), and one more of Imperial cuirassiers. These were paid for and under the general command of the heads of the army of Milan. (During the war in Piedmont along with the Allies there were also an infantry and a cavalry regiment belonging to the duke of Württemberg, but which were part of the Imperial contingent).

- **CRAL16** *Bavarian Cuirassiers Regiment* of (1690-1693) ***Arco***[162]
- **CRAL17** *Imperial Cuirassiers Regiment* of (1693-1696) ***Carafa***[163]
- **CRAL18** *Württemberg Cuirassiers Regiment*[164] (1690-1698)
- **DRAL03** *Württemberg Dragoons Regiment*[165] (1690-1694)

Kingdom of Naples

The main elements of the military structure of the kingdom of Naples during the Spanish rule were a regular force of professional soldiers and a territorial militia, called into service only when necessary.

There was in fact a regular force, made up of regularly paid soldiers (which included a Spanish infantry *tercio*, the **tercio fixo [de infanteria española del Reyno] de Napoles**, paid by the royal treasury (of the kingdom of Naples) i.e. the Camera della Sommaria, with the task of guaranteeing defence against external aggression and also against possible internal uprisings, and the cavalry endowed by the kingdom, the garrison soldiers of the castles, fortresses, places and coastal defence towers, to which were added a few bombers, Italian infantry and cavalry companies and the Viceroy's guard de corps), whose task was to garrison the main strongholds of the state and to constitute an initial nucleus of an army of the country in the event of an external aggression (or war). In the event of threats of aggression or open warfare, the regular forces were reinforced by troops from the other possessions of the Spanish Empire (primarily from the state of Milan and by sea from Catalonia) or by troops 'capitulated' almost always from the Habsburg Empire of Austria (German infantry). The fixed *tercio* of Spanish infantry also had the task of garnishing the Spanish galleys of the kingdom's squadron as marine infantry.

During the period we are dealing with, there were no permanently resident units of Italian infantry in the Kingdom of Naples at the level of *tercio*. However, some regular companies of Italian infantry were maintained for the garrisons of the Presidii di Toscana (each fortress governor was captain of a company of the garrison; the community of Longone from 1662 paid for the maintenance of two companies of Neapolitan infantry) and to provide the embarkation garrison for the auxiliary squadron of the Genoese galleys of the duke Doria of Tursi, which flanked the squadrons of Naples, Sicily, Sardinia and Spain.

For the defence of the land, the cities and the villages from internal (bandits and rebels) and external (French in the 16th century above all and raids and landings by Barbary corsairs) enemies, a national militia had been set up since the 16th century, chosen and paid for by the Universities (i.e. the communities) of the kingdom, known as the *Battaglione* the infantry and the *Sacchetta* the companies of the mounted militia.

As it is well known, the coasts of the kingdom were garrisoned by a network of towers, castles and fortresses[166], in which a highly variable number of soldiers and bombardiers were stationed to prevent and repel raids by Barbary corsairs

---

162 Colonel: (1690) Vasquez Coronado, Lieutenant Colonel count d'Arco, (1691) Col. Prince Trivulzio, Lt C. Arco; dismissed in 1693 and moved to Flanders once again in Imperial service.

163 Colonel: Carafa; (December 1693) Schrotembach, (1694) Prince of Hanover; dismissed in 1696 from Milanese service and once again in Imperial service.

164 Entered at Spanish service in May 1690 and dismissed in 1698.

165 Entered at Spanish service in May 1690. In June 1694 it was incorporated into the Cuirassiers regiment of the same Prince. Nominal Colonel was Prince Karl Alexander of Württemberg.

166 The Garrison Cities of the Kingdom of Naples are (excluding the State of the Presidi in Tuscany: Orbetello, Port'Ercole, and Piombino):
 In Terra di Lavoro: *Capua, Aversa, Nola, Surriento, Pozzoli, Gaeta*
 In Capitanata: *Viesti*
 In Terra di Bari: *Barletta, Bisceglie, Bari, Monopoli, Trani*
 In Terra di Otranto: *Brindisi, Galipoli, Otranto, Taranto*
 In Calabria Ultra: *Cotrone, Reggio, Tropea*
 In Abruzzo: In *Pescara* there is a large garrison [**BSNP Ms XXII.B.10** *Notice of the things pertaining to the position of Captain General of the Kingdom of Naples* (Post 1690)]

or other enemies; in the event of an enemy attack, these garrisons (many of the towers were guarded by a chief and one or two soldiers) were reinforced by the local militia. The major strongholds were entrusted to a governor, who had the support of his own 'staff' and a cadre of soldiers, often Spanish veterans of the *tercio fixo*, no longer suitable for active service in the corps. After the French attempt on the State of the Presidi in Tuscany in 1650, in the second half of the 17th century, the kingdom of Naples no longer had to suffer direct attacks by foreign armies, but was often put on alert, as already mentioned, by the presence of French and Barbary corsairs and the fear of more substantial incursions by enemy fleets. Moreover, during the Messina War, from 1674 to 1678, the whole of southern Calabria became a base of military operations against the insurgents and their French allies.

Viceroy's German Guard (Halberdiers)

To guard his person and the Royal Palace, the Viceroy also kept a foot guard, the *German Halberdiers*, i.e. a company of about seventy (initially around one hundred) German-speaking Swiss soldiers armed with halberds, as was the custom in most European royal and viceroyal courts at the time. The company was commanded by a nobleman, either Italian or Spanish, often a relative of the viceroy, as captain and a lieutenant of the same extraction; the staff was composed of a provost, three corporals, a drummer and the fifer, as well as the chaplain. The company of the Swiss halberdiers remained in existence until the accession to the throne of Charles of Bourbon in 1734, when it was replaced by a similar formation, composed, however, only of subjects of the Kingdom.

Spanish Infantry

Until the extinction of the Spanish branch of the Habsburg dynasty (at the death of Charles II in December 1700), the backbone of the Spanish military presence in Naples, as already mentioned, was represented by the *terzo fisso* of Naples, also known as the *terzo antico degli spagnoli* (to distinguish it from the *terzo nuovo* that existed for only a few years in the mid-1680s). From this *tercio*, during the wars in Piedmont, significant contingents were repeatedly detached to reinforce the Spanish infantry of the army of the Duchy of Milan. In 1705, during the reorganization taking place in all Spanish armies, three regiments were formed from the *terzo fisso* of Naples, which were then captured by the Austrians in 1707.

- **IRSP46 Fixed Tercio of Spanich infantry of Naples** of the Maestro di campo (1688) D. **Luis de Espluga** (1697) D. **Martin de Castejon y Medrano** (1700) D. **Joseph Caro**.

    The *tercio* of Naples originated in the army of Grand Captain Consalvo de Cordoba, who seized the Kingdom in 1503. Around 1600, the *tercio* was made up of 20 companies of 200 men each; towards the end of the century, the *tercio* had a strength ranging between 3,000 and 4,500 men, depending on the events of the moment, divided into around 30-40 companies. For example, in 1690, the *tercio* had 25 companies (of which 22 were stationed in the capital) with just under 3,300 men in Naples and 1,463 men in the garrisons of Tuscany. In 1693, the *tercio* had 481 officers and 5,000 soldiers. During the War of Messina (1674-1678), the *tercio* of Naples sent numerous infantry companies to reinforce the royal army on the island. From the *tercio* of Naples, throughout the War in Piedmont, from 1690 to 1696, replacements for the Spanish *tercios* of the army of Lombardy were also drawn heavily. During the War of the Spanish Succession, in early 1705, the *tercio* was reduced to a regiment, and in 1707, with the arrival of the Austrians in Naples, two Spanish infantry regiments were formed from the men left in the kingdom to serve the Austrian pretender, Archduke Charles (future Emperor Charles VI), who were then sent to Hungary in 1713.

Cavalry

The ordinance cavalry of the kingdom, in addition to the mounted units of the territorial Militia, as in the other armies of the Spanish monarchy, was divided into cuirassiers (the line cavalry), light horses (a few companies, including the *stradioti*, i.e. Greek-Albanian light cavalrymen, a few companies of lances, almost exclusively with guard duties and in every way assimilated to the cuirassiers, and in arquebusiers, which over time became the dragoons (in Naples there were never any units of dragoons on a permanent basis until the beginning of the 18th century. In the 1680s a few companies of dragoons were sent from Milan to instruct the Neapolitan cavalry in that service, but this was not followed up for the time being.

The heavy cavalry was composed, as in France or in the duchy of Savoy (and in the Milanese), of the companies of *uomini d'arme* (= *Gente d'arme* = *Gendarmes*), formed by the principal lords of the kingdom as a remnant of their feudal obligations to the king. This cavalry was used as an operational force until the mid-17th century but was then, in practice, assigned only to services within the state.

By the end of the 17th century, the regular cavalry (*uomini d'arme*) of the kingdom numbered 17-19 companies of armored cavalry (formed and maintained at the expense of the leading nobility of the Kingdom), including two personal guard companies for the viceroy, four companies of light cavalry (a term which soon began to indicate the new regular line cavalry), and one of *stradioti*. The strength of each company was generally around 60 men, plus the officers, on paper.

Companies of the Guards

The two companies of the Viceroy of Naples' horse guard had a strength that was on the average twice as large as the other cavalry companies, i.e. around 100 soldiers, in addition to the captain (nominally the Viceroy), the lieutenant, two trumpeters (only one in the ordinary companies), an ironmonger and an armourer.

- **RCNap01** *Company of the Lances of the Viceroy's Guard* Captain (1693-1698) D. Nicola Coppola (November 1698-1701) *Commendator Fra' Ventura Saracini.*
- **RCNap02** *Company of Cuirassiers of the Viceroy's Guard* Captain (1693-1695) D. Andres de la Rimpe y Muñoz (1696) D. Pedro de Niela (1696) D. Pedro Lopez April (1696-1698) *Commendator Fray Ventura Saracini (*November 1698-170)1 D. Domenico di Sangro
- **RCNap03** *Cavalry of the Men-at-Arms* (ordinance). With the men of these companies during the war the reinforcements (newly recruited cavalry) were formed and sent several times to Milan (and at the beginning of the War of the Spanish Succession two new regiments were formed).

Kingdom of Sicily

The military organization of the Kingdom of Sicily was, in general, similar to that of the Kingdom of Naples. Indeed, there was a strong fixed third of Spanish infantry, dating back to the time of the conquest of the island, divided between garrison duties in the fortresses (Palermo, Messina, Augusta, Saragozza [=Siracusa], Trapani, and Termini) and service as infantry for the royal fleet's galley. Additionally, there was a company of cavalry for the viceroy's guard, a company of Swiss halberdiers, and a territorial militia consisting of both infantry and cavalry.

The military hierarchy was the same as in other Spanish armies (in particular, the Captain General was the serving Viceroy, the Maestro de Campo General, the Artillery General, and the Cavalry General), though not all positions were always filled due to the island's distance from operational theaters.

The defense of the coasts, exposed to the threat of Barbary pirates and French privateers, was entrusted to the towers, the few artillerymen in service, the militia (the only service that locals could be called to), and, although it was limited during the reign of Charles II, the activity of the Sicilian Galley Squadron. Although some members of the Sicilian nobility served in high ranks in the armies of the monarchy, military service was not particularly attractive to the Sicilians. In fact, aside from brief periods (particularly during the Messina revolt of 1674-1678), no Sicilian infantry *tercios* were in service, nor were any cavalry units sent from the island for employment in other theaters of operation.

Spanish Infantry

IRSP47 *Tercio fisso di fanteria spagnola del Regno di Sicilia* [since 1718 Regiment **Africa**] Maestro de campo (1677-1695) D. *Duarte Correa de Castilblanco* (1695) D. *Lorenzo Brito* (1696-1704) D. *Pedro Lopez Pardo de Ribadeneira*.

Formed with a royal decree of 23rd October 1535 on the basis of 12 companies. During the War of the League of Augsburg (1689-1696), it sent several companies to reinforce the Spanish *tercios* of the army of the Duchy of Milan on several occasions. In 1699, the tercio was made up of 43 companies (with over 3,000 men).

During the War of the Spanish Succession, the fixed tercio was divided into three regiments, which later became Spanish infantry units. They remained on the island until 1713, when, on the cession of the kingdom to the duke of Savoy, they passed to serve in Spain.

Artillery (Spain, Flanders, Italy)

In the Spanish armies, a regular artillery corps was only established during the War of the Spanish Succession at the instigation and proposal of the French. The service of artillery was under command of a General of the Artillery and it was a body (or rather a group) of military engineers and architects (which were for the greatest part Italian or Flemish), a train of artillery, that was managed by a private contractor. The service of the pieces was entrusted to artillery gentlemen, a few military bombardiers (in Catalonia most of them came from Majorca) and in the major strongholds and fortresses there were

▲ *Plate 10 - 1697 Maestro de Campo of a Neapolitan infantry tercio (Illustration by Roberto Vela)*

▲ Plate 11 - 1692 Provincial Tercios of Burgos and Valladolid, and of Madrid (Plate by Roberto Vela)

▲ 1692 Provincial Tercio of Cordoba and drum of the regiment of the Costa de Granada (Plate by Roberto Vela)

▲ *Plate 13 - 1695 Grenadiers of the Tercio de las Ciudades (yellow uniforms) and Segovia (red uniforms) (Plate by Roberto Vela)*

▲ *Plate 14 - 1693 Dragoons of the State of Milan (Plate by Roberto Vela)*

sometimes some militia artillery-men and bombardiers. Furthermore in the major garrisons there was a major-domo of the artillery, a watch of the Arsenal and a few surveyors for the ammunitions and equipment.

As in the rest of the European armies, artillery was divided in two parts, the train of the artillery, or the field artillery, and the artillery of the different places, that was part of their defense.

This second class was served by the men coming from the artillery trains and usually was manned by residents of the same places directed by veteran artillery-men, normally too old to be able to serve on campaign.

The principal towns maintained schools of artillery, where future artillery-men and bombardiers were taught the handling and care of the pieces and other fireworks. From these schools, directed by teachers as well known as Fernández Medrano (in Flanders; a renowned writer about artillery and the Military Arts), would emerge the artillery-men who would in the following years serve in the campaign trains, the real backbone of the artillery.

In Catalonia the main garrisons that could count on standing artillery-men were those of Barcelona, with a well-known school of artillery, Gerona, Tortosa, Cardona and Rosas with other minor ones.

The places in Northern Africa, being exposed to a constant siege by the Moors, were all equipped with artillery and their garrisons included the necessary number of gunners.

In Flanders there were fifteen companies of artillery kept in the major garrisons, formed by a captain and a variable number of constables and artillery-men, depending on the importance of the place. Of the fifteen places the most important was the castle of Amberes with 5 constables and 49 artillery-men and the smallest Stevensweert with 2 and 9 respectively. The remaining of the places were those of Malines, Terramunde, the castle of Ghent, Ghent, Audenarde, Dama, Ostende, Nieuport, Mons, Ath, Namur, Charleroi and Gueldres.

Even in Milan, the artillery was under the command of a General of the Arm. The service included military engineers, who held a military rank, usually that of maestro di campo for the chief engineer, who during the war in Piedmont was Count Gaspare Berretta. For the service of the artillery in fortresses, bombardiers were employed; they belonged to the militia, though with special privileges. For field service, however, the artillery train was contracted out to a private entrepreneur, who provided mules, oxen, and drivers for transporting wagons, pieces, ammunition, and supplies, as well as the pontoon bridge for crossing rivers Italian and Spanish noble artillerymen ensured targeting and fire direction, while bombardiers and soldiers handled the artillery pieces. Ordinary infantry provided security and artillery defense in the field, while dragoons or cavalry escorted them on marches.

▲ *Bombardier, by Fernández de Medrano, Sebastian 'The Perfect Artificer, Bomber and Gunner (1699)'*

For engineering works, local peasants were generally employed and paid for the task, or alternatively, infantry soldiers were used, receiving a special reward for their labor.

In the duchy of Milan artillery-men were distributed in 16 places, the castle of Milan being the most important. Besides these they also served in Pavia, Lodi, Tortona, Serravalle, Pizzighettone, Trezzo, Lecco, Domodossola, Como, fort of Fuentes, Rocca of Arona, Cremona, Novara, Alessandria and Valenza.

In 1686[167] the artillery was made up of its general, two lieutenant generals, 8 gentlemen, a butler, the army's chief engineer, 3 military engineers, 4 of their assistants, the munitions officer of Pavia, the munitions officer of Alexandria, a chief of fireworks and his aide, a chief of miners, 2 chiefs of the ironworkers, a chief ironmaster, a smelter, his aide and an armourer a chief of artillerymen, 14 ordinary and 36 extraordinary artillerymen, a captain of boatmen, his lieutenant and 5 boatmen; there were also 60 artillery students at the Milan School and 40 at the Pavia School. During the war campaigns, some of these numbers varied considerably: for example, in 1691, there were 9 gentlemen, 5 ordinary military engineers, 7 engineers' assistants, there was also a military architect, the butler of the artillery had 4 assistants, the fire chief had 3 assistants, there were 2 master craftsmen, there were 6 ironworkers' assistants, 8 carpenters' assistants, 2 foundrymen's assistants, 90 boatmen, 19 miners, 33 porters and 104 artillerymen[168].

The artillery train that in 1689 followed the army on boats along the course of the Po in the expedition against the Mantuan area, the first war rehearsal in a long time and before the start of the campaigns in Piedmont, consisted of 10 medium guns and another 17 guns, including sages and quarters, 4,000 bombs and other military equipment, as well as numerous munitions of war and mouthpieces.

The artillery train that left Pavia in 1690 for the war in Piedmont consisted of 300 trucks of ammunition and military equipment, with boats and planks to make bridges, followed by 350 mules with powder, balls and fuse, twelve artillery pieces, 4 small, 6 large and 2 culverins pulled by several suits of horses.

In the Kingdom of Naples, the supreme military hierarchy included, as in other Spanish armies, the General of Artillery. Under his command were the cadets and the gentlemen artillerymen (equivalent to artillery officers) and the bombardiers, who were stationed in various fortresses across the kingdom. Among his duties was the supervision of the maintenance of all artillery pieces, the casting of cannons (at the Naples arsenal), the management of the arsenal itself, the production and maintenance of gunpowder, the supply of munitions for both the artillery and the troops (until the 18th century, munitions included both "war and subsistence" supplies, including clothing), and fortifications. The General of Artillery was sometimes assisted by Lieutenant Generals and a Chief Engineer (for fortification matters).

Naples did not have a permanent artillery train, meaning an organization responsible for transporting artillery pieces and baggage in the event of a military campaign. When necessary, a contract was signed with a private "assentista" (contractor), who was always overseen by the General of Artillery.

Officers Deputies for the Royal Artillery

General of Artillery *(General de la Artillería)*: D. Marzio Origlia, Duke of Arigliano, Neapolitan nobleman, *Caballero de Alcántara, Comendador de Valencia del Ventoso*, assisted by a Lieutenant General and two aides; his Lieutenant; Captain of the Artillery School; Assistant of the Foundry; Captain of Artillery in Cotrone; Artilleryman of Manfredonia; Other Artillerymen; Master Craftsman of the Artillery Chests and Wheels; Clerk of the Artillery Officer; Captain of Artillery of the Tuscan Presidios; Artilleryman in the same Presidio; Munitions Officer of said Artillery.

In each garrison, there were some bombardiers. *(regarding matters of the Captain General after 1690).*

(List of Fortresses): Tuscan Presidios, Naples, Gaeta, Civitella del Tronto, Pescara, Bari, Otranto, Taranto, Reggio.

In Sicily, with an organisation very similar to that of Naples, the main strong places into which the artillerymen were distributed, consisted in Messina, Augusta, Zaragoza, Trapani, Termini e Castellamare di Palermo. Followed in order of importance the places and forts of Cefalu; Milazzo; isle of Lipari; Iaci; Catania and Brucoli among others.

The North African strongholds, being exposed to a continuous siege by the Moors, were all supplied with numerous artillery and their garrisons included the necessary number of gunners.

The composition of trains of artillery was similar in most of the armies and within those of the same state varied in their importance on the base of the money disposable at any moment. It should be remembered that even if officers and those manning the pieces were military people, the great majority of personnel was composed of civilians who served for pay for a determined period.

---

167 **A.G.S. Estado Leg. 3407.**
168 **A.G.S. Estado Leg. 1405.**

Let us present two examples of trains of artillery:

Milan Army 1697	Flanders Army 1690
General	General
Three Lieutenants-generals	Four Lieutenants-generals
Chaplain	Chaplain
	Counsellor of the artillery
Steward	Steward
Five assistants of the steward	Four assistants of the steward
Eight labourers	Three labourers with an assistant
Five Spanish gentlemen	Four Spanish gentlemen
Three Italian gentlemen	Five gentlemen of the Country
	A master of school
	Quarter-master and his assistant
	Provost and his assistant
	Five drivers
Chief of blunderbusses and mortars	A master of fireworks
Captain of blunderbusses and mortars	
Nine assistants of blunderbusses and mortars	Six artificers and three bombardiers
A master of foundry with two aids	A master of foundry with an officer
Two gunsmiths	
Chief of ironsmiths with six assistants	A master caulker
	A master charlier with an officer
Seven assistants-carpenters	A master carpenter with two officers
	A master of horses
	A chief of storekeepers with six keepers
A surgeon	A surgeon
	An apothecary
	A cooper
Engineer major	
Seven ordinary engineers	
Nine assistant engineers	
Two ammunitioners	
Chief of miners	Two chiefs of miners
28 miners	18 miners
Two chiefs of artillery	
114 ordinary, extraordinary and above-number gunmen	
Two chiefs of the matrosses	
Captain of the pontoon-bridge	Two captains of the companies of sailors of the train
Lieutenant of the pontoon-bridge	Two lieutenants of the said companies
Chief of the making of boats	
63 boatmen	2 pilots, 2 grooms and 22 sailors

To these there should also be added the personnel necessary for the administration of the train and caring and victualling of the animals belonging to it.

Only in 1701 in Flanders, in 1702 in Milan and in 1704 in Spain was there organised in each of these territories a regiment for the service of the Artillery in the Spanish armies, modelled upon the French regiment of *Fusiliers de l'Artillerie*.

MILITIA

In all the territories subject to the Spanish Crown, as elsewhere in Europe, there existed (often essentially on paper only) the organisation of a territorial Militia based on the enlistment of the local population in companies of foot that could be grouped into "sargentias mayores" under the command of a sergeant-major [=major in modern terms] for a given province or district (as was the case in Castille or in Sicily) or in *tercios* (as was the case in Estremadura or in Milan). In many of the kingdoms and provinces there was also a mounted militia (of a particular significance in the Kingdom of Naples). As a last vestige of the feudal obligations of the nobles there were also the mounted companies of Men at arms or of Ordinance, that during this period were mostly converted into regular forces. A special case was represented by the **Guardias Viejas de Castilla**. These horse units were generally to be commanded by old soldiers and/or by local nobles, the care of which was entrusted to the Councils and municipalities.

Except at the frontiers (Extremadura, Catalonia, Flanders and Milan) or in cases of threats of war, the militia seldom assembled or was exercised. Militia units were rarely employed in the field or in offensive actions with the sole exception of Catalonia It nevertheless represented the first resource when reinforcements for the standing army were urgently demanded. The performance of the militia when employed on the field was generally very poor, excluding Catalonia, where the resistance of many villages and small towns to French attacks was often sustained by the militiamen [the Miquelets], where more than often squads of Miquelets and "*veguerros*" in platoons and companies also took an active role in harassing French lines of communication and embarrassing convoys. Militia was normally employed for garrisoning walls and gates of cities and for guarding small towns and villages in order to free line troops from these duties and to make them available for field operations.

In Flanders militia units were often involved in defending towns and villages, and in the State of Milan in guarding the frontier positions on the Monferrat border (where a large French garrison was positioned in Casale threatening Alessandria and Novara) and small fortresses and towns, thus relieving regular forces. The Milanese militia helped successfully in preventing the French from crossing the border of the Milanese state during the whole war.

In 1690, the island of Sicily was militarily divided into Sergeanties, with militias grouped into *tercios* governed by their respective *Sergeant Majors*. These included those of Taormina, Girgento, Lentin, Jaca, Termines, Pati, San Phelipe, San Fratelo, Castagirón, and Xicle. Each of the three valleys of the kingdom (*Valdemone, Val di Mazara, and Val di Noto*) had an *Ordinary Captain of Arms* with a small retinue of about a dozen soldiers. Additionally, there was a *Royal Campaign Captain* and a *General Provost*, each with their own entourage of men[169].

As a final consideration it should be noted that the major losses in total caused to the French, who had won most of the field battles, was caused by the resistance of the peasants supported by the militia, especially in Italy (Piedmont) and Catalonia.

---

169 **AHN. Estado, libro 497**

▲ *Grenadier Company by Fernández de Medrano, Sebastian 'El Perfecto Artificial, Bombardero Y Artillero (1699)'.*

▲ *Plate 15 - 1650 Pikemen and arquebusiers of the Spanish infantry tercios stationed in Naples (Plate by Massimo Mannocchi, based on a painting exhibited at the Certosa di San Martino Museum in Naples).*

UNIFORMS

General notes on military clothing

In order to be able to better follow how the adoption of a 'uniform' dress in military units came about, we consider it useful to mention general elements of military clothing in Europe, and in particular among the armies of the Spanish monarchy. Up until the end of the 16th century, the captains of the ordinary companies were obliged to provide clothing for their soldiers, bearing the cost by means of a direct deduction from the men's pay; this system lent itself to many abuses and deficits, to remedy which many states and kingdoms began to grant private contractors contracts for the supply of clothing to the troops according to imposed models at pre-established prices and conditions. Officers were excluded from these supplies of very unrefined clothes and therefore provided for their own clothing, although they then generally received a special allowance from their prince. Of course, at the beginning there must have been a certain hostility and resistance to wearing uniform clothes, because soldiers were traditionally accustomed to dress as they liked and sometimes, if the spoils of war permitted it, with luxury or extravagance; those of some divisions, being royal guards or nobles of the 'first sphere', i.e. the major titled, had been accustomed to wear rich and ostentatious liveries and they too must not have welcomed the change to uniform and too sober clothing with enthusiasm.

Naturally, the supply of "ammunition" clothing, i.e. on royal or public account, greatly favoured the expansion of a cloth manufacturing industry, which until then had been predominantly artisanal, with the birth of embryonic industrial enterprises, which then developed and transformed and, in some cases, remained in existence for centuries. As far as the territories and kingdoms of the Spanish crown were concerned, the national productions made available cloths, twills, canvases and laces, even of a good quality, but, when something better or large quantities were needed in a short time, for example to dress recruits hastily raised in moments of international tension, many products had to be imported and this fact was very common, especially in terms of cloth from England and cloths from France or Flanders; these fabrics often arrived at their destination even when there was war with the producing countries.

From 1580 onwards, a number of items of clothing began to be supplied 'of ammunition' to third parties serving on board the fleet and those in the Spanish army in the Netherlands, starting with the tunic alone, then adding breeches, shoes, hats, stockings and so on. The earliest known examples of a 'party' ('asiento' in Spanish), i.e. a contract, by which whole garments were supplied in two sizes, relate to the supply of 2,000 garments for the infantry of the ***Armada***[170] in February 1594[171]; the supply included tunic, bodice, breeches, shirts and stockings and these were clothes for which no uniform colour or style was prescribed, a red band or scarf often being sufficient to distinguish soldiers of the Catholic King or the House of Austria. Shoes, hats, shoulder straps and other leathers were also supplied, while the supply of linens had to wait until the 18th century; a separate consideration should be given to coats for sentries, which were supplied long before the above-mentioned dates. According to Clonard, the coats were usually dark brown in colour and often some garments, such as breeches and stockings were red; according to the above-mentioned contracts, those supplied to the tercio of marine infantry in 1598, however, had to be bleu and green.

Paintings illustrating the Battle of White Mountain, fought in 1620 near Prague[172], show us, however, that the thirds of the army that the King of Spain had sent to reinforce the Emperor, including one of Neapolitans and one of Florentines, were distinguished by a sort of tunic or cape-like surcoat, called 'all'ungara' or 'ungarina' [=*Hungarian style*], in uniform colours (red with greenish lining for the Neapolitan *tercio*) and on their backs they mostly wore the Burgundian cross. Breeches, stockings and hats, on the other hand, were not always uniform in colour.

---

170 D. Diego de Bargas Manrique mi Corregidor de la Villa de Medina del Campo aze visto una carta de los 17 del presente y el contracto *firmado de Sevastian Pascual que con ella ymbiasteis y las condiciones con que se obligara de hazer los 2500 vestidos que se os a mandado para la Infanteria de mi Armada Real del paño lienço y façiones en el contenidas 6666 ducados y 7 reales y 11 mrs que son las 2/3 partes de los 10.000 ducados que se avian proveido para los que se avian de hazer en essa Villa y la de Valladolid ... del que se hazan en la Ciudad de Burgos otros mill ... por lo que importa a mi Servicio que los dhos vestidos se hagan ya con mucha brevedad por la necessitad que tiene de ellos la dha gente de guerra .... De Madrid Noviembre 1588 el Rey*
Ropilla de paño catorceño de mezclae y açule y verde de la mesma ley que lleve bara y media de paño cada una de a seis palmos de ancho. El dicho paño /o en proporcion siendo mas angosto/ aforrada en negrillo /o en bayeta de Burgod/: un collare y bebedeos? Forrados en fustan con botones o ojales de seda y grequescos del proprio paño en que entra otra bara y media del paño en la forma dicha aforrados en malohin?
Archivo Provincial Valladolid Seccion Protocolos 6145 Notario Francisco de Victoria de Medina.
171 **Geoffrey Parker**, "*The Army of Flanders and the Spanish Road. 1567 - 1659*", Cambridge 1972.
172 Church of S. Maria della Vittoria in Rome.

Again, a fresco in the Pinacoteca dell'Ospedale Maggiore in Milan shows the Plaza Mayor in Madrid in the mid 17th century with two groups of soldiers, clearly all in uniform, the first group wearing red robes with yellow facings and white stockings and the second with green robes, yellow facings and stockings.

Of course, even in the case of clothing, as in other branches of the military intendancy of the time, the timeliness and efficiency of supplies were often not exemplary: for example, the Italian *tercios* who crossed Mont Cenis in 1620 had neither hats nor shoes and were so badly dressed that about a third of the soldiers died on the journey; the Spanish troops sent to Flanders often arrived in such poor condition that they looked like frozen scarecrows[173]. In 1640, an asiento [=contract] was made with Pedro de Miranda for the provision of 4,000 clothes for the infantry of the army in Spain, to be paid for with goods confiscated from the French[174].

Around 1650, soldiers were dressed in coarse wool cloths, almost always a grey colour tending to the brown (in Spanish *pardo*) of untreated natural wool. Officers, with clothes made of a better quality fabrics, were distinguished by a large red scarf almost always wrapped around the waist, or even over the shoulder, and often wore a morion helmet and breastplate. As already mentioned, soldiers often wore red socks and breeches[175]. There was not yet a uniform in the modern sense with defined colours per outfit and uniform, i.e. facings, to distinguish the different corps and specialities, however, there was uniformity in the appearance of the soldiers as the clothes were all made from pieces of the same cloth for the same unit. However, the surplus clothes were kept in ammunition and, in the case of soldiers added later to a company, they could be given clothes that were different in make-up, and also in colour. It could also happen on the occasion of a sudden increase in the number of troops due to wartime contingencies that the cloth available from the usual suppliers was not sufficient, and so different suppliers could be used with different qualities and colours of cloth, just as different tailors could make clothes for the troops at the same time. It is evident that on such occasions some soldiers or companies might appear dressed differently from the others. In the case of troops in the countryside, then, they were supplied with clothing wherever they happened to be, often taken from the enemy or from the unfortunate civilians living in the districts over which the enemy armies fought, when the soldiers were left covered in nothing but rags.

The French justaucorps (*casaca*) was introduced into the Spanish army in the years 1668-69[176]. It reached almost to the knee and had very wide sleeves that rolled up to the elbow. On both sides, towards the bottom, there were pockets closed by buttons; at the neck, to fix the shirt, a tie was worn (from the term *croata* or *crovata* because it was introduced into use by the Croatian troops) generally white or black, made of linen or cotton, while Spanish-style trousers and stockings remained in use. Drummers and fifes wore the dress trimmed with lace and with the design of the livery of the royal house, of the viceroy, or of the house of the colonel of the regiment (especially for the German infantry regiments) or of the maestro de campo of the *tercio*.

The following year the low and wide hat called at the French style or Schomberg's, also came into use. It may be interesting in this regard to report what Giovanni Battista Pallavicino, envoy of the Most Serene Republic of Genoa to the Spanish court from June 1668 to August 1676, noted relative to the year 1669; he reported as follows: "... ***It was considered and proposed by the Marquis of Aytona, chief Master of the House of the Queen and of the Council of Government, that in order to make Her Majesty esteemed and obeyed his orders more promptly, it was necessary to form a regiment of three thousand men of the best people and officials of Spain, with the title of Royal Guard, which later took the nickname of Chiamberga because all the soldiers and chiefs who had fought against Portugal were dressed in the same manner as the Portuguese army, which was commanded by Monsieur of Sciomberg***[177]. There were many great contradictions in forming such a body, [because it was said that the king had no need of such a guard since the whole Spanish nation was the guard of its king] ***Aytona, however, always remained firm in his plan, alleging that princes should not live at the mercy of the people, and so finally he instituted the said regiment in which the best of the soldiers of Spain were enrolled and the captains of it were the majority Great [=Grandes] of Spain and also the lieutenants, and the Marquis of Aytona was created colonel of ot. From this body then the said captains were very quickly elected who for general and other singular posts, and the said Chiamberga then continued for eight years without any news.***"[178]

---

173 **G. Parker**. op.cit.
174 **A.G.S. Contaduria Mayor de Cuentas III leg. 47.**
175 See the painting "*Il Cardinale Filomarino visita il Vicerè*" Museo S. Martino, Napoli.
176 **Conte de Clonard** "*Historia orgànica de las armas de infanteria y caballeria española* etc." Madrid 1854.
177 **Frederic-Armand, count of Schomberg**, French (huguenot) general who was in charge of the command of Portuguese troops fighting against Spain.
178 **Raffaele Ciasca**, "*Istruzioni e relazioni degli ambasciatori genovesi - 1494-1780*", Roma 1951 Vol. IV.

The entire military clothing was modernized over the years, especially during the War of the Grand Alliance, when it was established that for an infantry soldier, the clothing should consist of a *justeaucorps* of woolen cloth lined with serge, an undergarment (vest or *chupa*) also of cloth, cloth trousers, canvas shirt (usually two were provided), neck tie, woolen socks, hat, a hanging "*batticulo*", that is, a sword holder slung over the shoulder, and a pair of shoes. Each nation of those that made up the armies of the crown of Spain maintained the make of the clothing in accordance with its own national style; but all the different styles became increasingly Frenchified in the second half of the seventeenth century and up until the accession to the throne of Philip V, who even imposed on all his armies the colour (white) of the uniform of the French infantry.

The widespread adoption of the new French military style throughout almost all of Europe consequently brought with it the need to distinguish the various corps and armies by means of distinctions more conspicuous than the simple coloured band; therefore, uniform colours began to be adopted for clothing, and they soon stabilised in two basic colours, that is, the colour of the dress, which could also be common to all the infantry or to several cavalry regiments of the same state or kingdom (the typical colour being red for the vast majority of military corps in Great Britain), and the colour of the "facings", which instead distinguished the individual corps and concerned, in whole or in part, the sleeve cuffs, the vest, the trousers and, later, also the turnbacks of the dress itself.

From the mid-1660s, indications on the colours of clothing began to appear for the Spanish armies corps, meaning that the adoption of fixed colours for the regular army corps was earlier than what is normally placed in 1670, or even 1680. Ample evidence of this can be found in various receipts for types of clothing made in Spain or Flanders or even in Naples and in the receipts of soldiers hospitalised at the Hospital of Barcelona. It should be noted, however, that for the Spanish corps there was not a single, unique or main base colour, such as yellow with red facings, as was instead written in various texts of the past; yellow, however, until almost the end of the century, was a colour often used for corps with guard functions. The dress worn by the soldiers (normally called **casaca** or even **ungarina** in Spain, **justacorps** in the Low Countries, **marsina** in Milan and **giamberga** in Naples) often resulted of a uniform appearance and of matching colors simply because it was cheaper to bulk-order cloth when available. Wealthy commanders and guards units outfitted their troops uniformly as a status symbol or dynastic tie.

Catalonia

Infantry

The foot soldier of the Spanish army in the 1690s was dressed in a woolen cloth suit (in Spanish called **casaca** as mentioned before; generally produced in the country where the soldier came from or where he was serving, although it was not uncommon for the cloth to come from as far away as France!!), lined with baize; cuffs turned up; the suit was closed in front by a row of buttons (usually 2 to 3 dozen buttons could be used for a suit) or covered in cloth (with a heart of wood or metal) or metal (usually tin, but also brass). It reached the knee and was normally worn open in the front, it had two pockets, generally arranged horizontally, closed by two flaps and held in place with a few buttons. Other buttons closed the cuff on the sleeve. Underneath, from a certain period onwards, the soldiers began to wear a sleeved robe (**chupa** or **almilla**) made of a lighter cloth (**kersi**), which was often worn instead of the dress in the hot season.

The breeches were of the same cloth (and often the same colour) as the dress. They reached the knee, the Spanish style ones were rather tight, and were fastened with ribbons or buttons. In order to cover the lower part of the leg, wool or cotton stockings were distributed, usually in the colour of the exhibitions, unless for reasons of economy at a certain time large quantities of them were supplied all of the same colour (often white) for several units or quantities in storage were used for other bodies for which they were not initially intended. The equipment or "ammunition", as the Spanish army called clothing and equipment, was completed by a pair of cowhide shoes (the leather often came from Flanders) with wooden heels, closed with fabric straps or fastened with metal buckles, two linen or hemp shirts, two hemp or Indian cotton ties (one of which was usually white, but could also be red or black) wrapped around the neck to secure the shirt, and a felt hat that could be white, grey or black (traditionally the Spanish infantry had worn light-coloured hats, while Italians and Walloons wore black ones; over time, after 1695, French fashion led most units of the Spanish armies to wear black hats); the hat was often decorated with coloured plumage (predominantly red) and with a red band at the base. Each soldier was provided with a shoulder bandolier, usually made of leather, to hold the sword (**tahali** or **bridicu**).

The common soldiers were armed for two-thirds of their strength with a firearm, a sword and a bayonet or with a pike (one third) and a sword; those armed with muskets carried a baldric for charges and towards the end of the century a pouch to store powder and balls. All the leather accoutrements were of natural colour. The pouches were generally darkened, sometimes blackened. The scabbards of the swords and bayonets were generally of darkened leather.

In the 1690s the pikemen, at least on the battlefield, no longer wore the helmet and breastplate (which were still used on the ramparts of a fortress and sometimes on board ships), but only the coat (*casaca*) and hat like the musketeers. Curiously, at least the *maestro de campo*, used in battle a round iron shield [*rodella*], a relic of the past, which was normally carried by an attendant until it was used. In a French account of the Battle of Orbassano (October 1693) it is noted that the Marquis of Solera, field master of the tercio of Lombardy, fought like a lion with his sword and shield surrounded by enemies (and lost his life on the field).

The grenadiers, created in 1685, wore a woollen cap with a ridge on the forehead initially made of cardboard covered with cloth; probably towards the mid-1690s for some units the cap was surrounded at the base by fur; the grenadiers were armed with a sabre, a bayonet, an axe, a pistol in addition to the musket.

Drummers and fifers either wore the same dress as the soldiers with the addition of braid and, probably, ribbons on the shoulders, in the livery of the *maestro de campo*, or of the kingdom or even of the province whose name the unit bore, or they could also have a particular livery.

In the illustrations accompanying the monumental (and oft-cited) work by count Clonard *"Historia Organica de la Infanteria e Caballeria Española"* the chevrons of the drummers are depicted in red and white checks, the colours of the royal livery, but from some contracts for the supply of clothing to the Neapolitan and Walloon troops it appears instead that still in 1702 the colours varied from one regiment to another (often the livery of the field master) and only the units of the Guard used the chevrons of the royal livery.

The colour of the dress and the sleeve facings distinguished the unit (it is well known that the provincial *tercios* were also named according to the colour of their dress (as was also the custom in other countries): **colorados** (reds), **amarillos** (yellows), **verdes** (greens), **azules** (blues), **morados** (dark blues), **plateados** (silveries), **blancos** (whites); the Spanish *tercios* stationed in Italy were traditionally dressed in red and those in Flanders in grey-white); the dress was mostly the same colour as the facings; the breeches were either the colour of the facings or that of the coat. From 1694 to 1696, in order to quickly dress the troops in Catalonia, almost all the infantry corps of the various nationalities were provided with a white vest (***chupa*** or ***almilla***) and natural wool breeches of a dark grey-brown colour.

Sergeants were generally dressed similarly to soldiers, but employing cloth of a better quality. German regiments and some Walloon units were exceptions; with regard to their tradition the sergeants and **forieri** could be dressed in a different colour, often that of the facings.

In the Spanish armies, excluding German units, officers usually were clothed in the same colours as their soldiers, even if their dress was made of finer fabrics, at the neck and wrists they wore lace more or less rich depending on the finances of the person. Sometimes the coat was enriched with golden or silver laces and embroideries (officially forbidden). Similarly the buttons, instead of tin or brass or copper, or even cloth, were of silver or golden. The quality of an officer was designated by a cane, and the quality of the wood and the metal of the pommel distinguished the rank.

Generally the officers wore either at the waist or across the breast a red sash (the colour of the Imperial house of the Habsburgs, worn as well by German and Austrian imperial troops until the early years of the Spanish Succession War). Often N.C.O.'s and the private soldiers, especially in the mounted troops, also wore a red band at the waist or across the breast. Sometimes red plumes were also worn on the hat.

Anyhow in the field officers and n.c.o.s very often dressed in dark coloured coats or tan brown ones (the equivalent of a off-duty dress in the XIX century) probably in order to save the more costly parade one.

In the following we list available information on the dress of units of the armies of the Spanish Monarchy during the last quarter of the 17th century (for the 15 *tercios* of provinces the documents present a somewhat different picture to that which you can see in the work of Clonard.).

It should also be noted that the artist who created the illustrations for the Clonard volumes misinterpreted a contemporary image (exhibited at the Spanish Army Museum) in which a soldier was shown with his suit slightly opened and he deduced that there was a strip of cloth on both sides of the suit down to the bottom of it, as if they were breast plates ante litteram, which is why for a long time all subsequent designers represented the uniforms of the time of Charles II in this (incorrect) way. Furthermore, since the colours of the linings were not known (they only reference was to the name of the *tercio* – colorados, azules, amarillos ...) the artist (or whoever gave him the instructions) left them blank, and this was then interpreted by everyone as the colour actually employed.

Old provincial Tercios

The *tercio* of *Toledo* or *de los azules viejos* (**IRSP01**), was dressed in blue with red facings and stockings.
The *tercio* of *Valladolid* and *Burgos*, or *de los amarillos viejos* (**IRSP02**), was dressed in yellow with blue facings and stockings.
The *tercio* of *Cordova* or *de los verdes viejos* (**IRSP03**), was dressed in green with red facings; red stockings[179]. In 1693 it received green breeches.
The *tercio* of *Sevilla* or *de los morados viejos* (**IRSP04**), was dressed in deep blue with red facings and stockings[180].
The *tercio* of *Madrid* or *de los colorados viejo* (**IRSP05**), was dressed in red with blue facings and stockings.

These data, which remain valid until the early eighteenth century, come from numerous confirmations from contracts for the purchase and distribution of effects (established as early as the 1660s during the Portuguese War), as well as from the records of the effects worn by soldiers hospitalized in the Hospital of the Holy Cross in Barcelona. It should also be noted that this source shows that after a certain time from the distribution of the new clothing, the soldiers of the provincial *tercios* found themselves not always dressed in the pre-established colours, this because there were frequent changes of soldiers from one *tercio* to another or because the men also dressed with effects that they took from the dead, even enemies, (perhaps because they were in better condition than those worn at that time) or because for hospitalization they preferred to wear old clothes so as not to risk losing the good ones. For the other *tercios*, especially the non-Spanish ones, the variability of the goods worn is much less marked.
See for example (four of the five tercios were present at the time, the data is replicated over the years without substantial variations in the colours):

December 9th, 1679 Barcelona. The General Inspector reports the 2,000 doubloons sent to clothe the provincial tercios and the settlement with a resident of Barcelona, P. Juan Graelles, for the provision of 901 dresses at 122 reales in Catalonian currency[181].
*** I, Domingo Marlet, a master tailor living in Barcelona, hereby oblige myself to make 901 ammunition dresses for the four provincial tercios serving in the army of this principality of Catalonia, consisting of a 22nd cloth ungarina lined with baize, breeches of the same cloth lined with canvas, a cordellate vest, a canvas shirt, wool stockings, 3-soled leather shoes, a ranis tie, and a hat for each tercio, the number of dresses and colours that will be stated below in this manner:
For the *tercio* of the Maestre de campo D. **Diego de Mirafuentes** 211 dresses composed of a coat of a blue 22nd cloth[182], 7 palms wide, each one to be 5 palms long and 10 wide, lined with red Solsona baize with two dozen tin buttons, breeches of the same amusco [*dark*]-colored cloth that must be 3 and a half palms long and as wide and hollow in the good proportion that the cloth allows, lined with Piedmont canvas, a white cordellate almilla, a Ghent cloth shirt, 5 palms long and 7 palms wide, wool stockings, 3-soled hook-knot shoes, a ranis tie and a brown hat 211.
Tercio of Don **Antonio Serrano** 261 dresses composed of a jacket of the same twenty-second straw-colored cloth lined with blue baize, breeches of amusco-colored cloth of the same quality and with the same pieces that the tercio of D. *Diego de Mirafuentes*.
Tercio of Don **Pedro de Villacis**: 268 green jackets lined with red baize with two dozen tin buttons, breeches of the same raisin-colored cloth the length and width...
Tercio of Don **Tomas Arias Pacheco**: 161 ungarinas of said twenty-second purple cloth lined with red baize, breeches of the same amusco-colored cloth of larco...
In total, 901 garments, which he undertakes to deliver by mid-February 1680.
Each garment is paid for at 12 silver reales. Barcelona, December 6th, 1679

February 24th, 1690. Memory of the Cities with whose name the Provincial Tercios of Catalonia serve and the Colours they wear[183]
Toledo: The Tercio of Mr. de Campo D. *Manrique de Noroña* serves under the name of *Toledo* and its colour is blue lined in red;

---

179 In December 1691 the clothing of the *tercio* was composed of: *casaca de paño 22° de color verde aforado en bayeta colorada de Solsona, calzón del mismo paño de color amusco aforado en lienzo crudo, almilla de cordellate blanco, zapatos de vaqueta, corbata de ranis, sombrero pardo* (green wool jacket lined in a red bay of Solsona, breeches of the same dark brown colour lined in raw linen, white cordellate hat, vaqueta shoes, ranis corbata, leopard sombrero.) **A.G.S. Guerra y Marina, leg. 2881**.
180 In November 1694 the dress of the tercio was composed of: *justacor y calzón de paño morado, chupa de sempiterna, dos camisas, dos corbatas, zapatos, medias de lana, sombrero con su colonia, espada, bridicu, mochila y bandola. El justacor forrado de bayeta de Córdoba y calzones y chupa en lienzo crudo.* **A.G.S. Guerra y Marina, leg. 2949**
181 **A.G.S. Guerra y Marina. leg. 2475.**
182 The quality of the cloth was designated by the number of wool threads that made up the fabric.
183 **A.G.S. Guerra y Marina. Leg. 2829.**

Madrid: The Tercio of Mr. de Campo D. *Joseph Creel* serves under the name of *Madrid* and its colour is red, lined in blue;
Valladolid and Burgos: The Tercio of Mr. de Campo Pedro Tolesano serves under the name of *Valladolid and Burgos* and its color is yellow lined in blue;
Seville: The Tercio of Mr. de Campo D. *Thomas de los Cobos* serves under the name of *Seville* and its colour is morado [=*very dark blue*] lined in red;
Cordoba: The Tercio of Mr. de Campo D. Carlos de Eguia, which is in Pamplona, serves under the name of *Cordova* and its colour is green lined red.

These five Tercios were constituted as Provincials in Extremadura the year of 1664 and they were been paid by the said Cities whose names they maintain nowadays.

Tercios of the Kingdom (Iberic Peninsula)

The *tercio del Casco de la Ciudad de Granada* (**IRSP07**) was dressed in green (1690), probably with green facings. In 1691 it received a new clothing grey with blue facings with bottons of cloth of the two colours[184];
The *tercio de la Costa del Reyno de Granada* (**IRSP08**) was dressed (1691) in grey with blue facings; in the years 1694-1695 the coat was yellow; in 1695 drummers with a blue livery; 1696-1697 drummers with red coats, sergeants with white coats, private soldiers with a white cloth dress[185].
The *tercio* of *Aragon* (**IRSP09**) was dressed in blue with yellow facings and tin buttons. Officers had a dress of the same colours as soldiers, but of a finer quality and with lace. Drummers were dressed as the soldiers, with the addition of silk lace (possibly blue and yellow, that is the kingdom's livery, or yellow and red as its armories or even red and silver as the livery of the Count of Guara). [186]
The tercio of the Marquis de Torres (Aragon **IRSP09bis**) in December 1693 was dressed with: *22nd blue cloth coat lined with Solsona baize with two dozen tin buttons, breeches of the same cloth lined with raw canvas, canvas shirt, cordellate vest, woolen stockings, leather shoes, hats.*[187]
The *tercio del Reino de Valencia* (**IRSP10**) was dressed in blue with red facings and vest.

New provincial Tercios in 1694

The new *tercio* of *Burgos* (**IRSP16**), was dressed in blue with red facings and stockings.
The second *tercio* of *Valladolid* (**IRSP17**), was dressed in blue with red facings and stockings.
The *tercio* of *Cuenca* (**IRSP18**), was dressed in green with [*probably*] green facings and stockings.
The *tercio* of *Leon* or *de los amarillos nuevos* (**IRSP19**), was dressed in yellow with blue facings and stockings.
The *tercio* of *Murcia* or *de los azules nuevo* (**IRSP20**), was dressed in blue with red facings and stockings.
The second (new) *tercio* of *Sevilla* (**IRSP21**) was dressed in blue with red facings, red breeches and stockings; white hats.
The *tercio* of *Gibraltar* or *de los colorados nuevos* (**IRSP22**), was dressed in red with blue facings; blue breeches and stockings.
The tercio of *Jaen* (**IRSP23**) [*plateado*=silvery] was dressed with coat and breeches of a grey colour (*mouse-grey*) and white facings and stockings.
The second (new) *tercio* of *Toledo* or *de los blancos nuevos* (**IRSP24**), was dressed in white with red facings and stockings.
The *tercio* of *Segovia* or *de los plateados* (**IRSP25**), was dressed in silvery white with red facings and stockings.
The *tercio de las ciudades* [*de Avellaneda*, (**IRSP06**) that later was merged into that of *Gasco*] was dressed in a blue coat lined yellow, blue breeches and stockings, straw-yellow waist-coat, white hat [actually each town clothed their levies with slight differences]. Hat, breeches and shoes had blue ribbons[188]. Some companies were clothed in red and others in white.
The *tercio de Gasco (Gremios de Madrid)* was clothed (1694-96) in white-grey with yellow facings and linings. Between 1694 and 1695 it received many recruits dressed in blue with yellow facings.

February 8th, 1697 <u>War Council</u>. *Regarding the officers who are to go to the cities of Castile to lead the people of the neighborhood... the corregidores will be informed of the names, as well as the colors of the dresses and linings they will have to make...* [189]

<u>Relacion of the cities of Castile where the officers of the Spanish infantry tercios of this army will be recruited, with information on the uniforms each one is wearing</u> (Catalonia)

---

184 **A.G.S. Guerra y Marina. Leg. 2881.**
185 **A.G.S. Guerra y Marina. Leg. 3068.**
186 An article by Luis Sorando with illustrations by Antonio Manzano supplies many additional details on the subject. **Sorando Muzás, Luis** "*El Tercio de Aragon: Notas sobre su evolucion, indumentaria y emblematica (1678-1698)*" Emblemata 1 Diputacion de Zaragoza 1995
187 **A.G.S. Contaduría Mayor de Cuentas IIIª, legajo 3106.**
188 Personal comunication **Antonio José Rodriguez Hernandez**
189 **A.G.S. Guerra y Marina Leg. 3043**

▲ *Plate 16 - 1683-1688 Naples. Officer of the Viceroy's guard (on horseback) and soldier of a Neapolitan infantry company (Plate by Massimo Mannocchi)*

▲ Plate 17 - 1689 Naples. Pikemen and arquebusiers from a company of the tercio fixo garrisoned in the Presidi di Toscana (on the ramparts of the fortifications, pikemen could sometimes wear armour). In the background, an arquebusier from a company of the tercio de Lisboa (plate by Massimo Mannocchi).

▲ Plate 18 - 1694 Naples. Grenadier of a Neapolitan tercio, sergeant and drummer of a company of the tercio fixo (Plate by Massimo Mannocchi)

▲ *Plate 19 - 1694 Naples. Officer and arquebusier of a Neapolitan infantry tercio (Plate by Massimo Mannocchi)*

▲ *Plate 20 - 1694 Naples. Standard bearer of a Neapolitan infantry tercio (Plate by Massimo Mannocchi taken from a contemporary painting)*

▲ Plate 21 - 1690 Swiss halberdier guarding the Viceroy of Naples (Plate by Massimo Mannocchi, taken from a contemporary painting at Schloss Rorau, Austria)

▲ Plate 22 - 1689 Naples. Soldier from a newly recruited company of cavalry sent to Milan (Plate by Massimo Mannocchi)

▲ *Plate 23 - 1687 Naples. Soldier from a company of cavalry belonging to the Viceroy's guard (Plate by Massimo Mannocchi)*

Burgos, 6 captains of the third of D. *Esteban de Olalla* with their officers, insignia, green with red lining and cuffs (***Old Cordova***)

Toledo, 6 captains of the third of D. *Miguel Gasco*, insignia, white with yellow lining and cuffs (***New Madrid***)

Valladolid, 6 captains of the third of D. *Manuel de Toledo*, yellow lining and blue cuffs (***New Leon***)

Cuenca, 6 captains of the third of D. *Fernando Davila*, yellow with lining and cuffs blue (***Old Burgos***)

Leon, 3 captains with their officers from the Tercio of Don *Francisco Domingo*, blue, lining, and red cuffs (***New Valladolid***)

Oviedo, 3 captains from the Tercio of the *Marquis of Torres*, blue with lining and red cuffs

It could be the one from Murcia or the one that had Jaen, 6 captains from the Tercio Don *Antonio de Lima*, green lining and red cuffs (***New Burgos***)

Murcia, 6 captains with officers from the Tercio Don *Francisco Ibañez*, red lining and blue cuffs (***Old Madrid***)

Segovia, 6 captains from the Tercio Don *Diego Alarcon*, blue lining and red cuffs (***Old Toledo***)

Those from *Gibraltar* and *Seville* do not come with the detail of the colours of other years…

Catalan Tercios

The *tercio de la Ciudad de Barcelona* (**IRSP11**) was clothed with a red coat with yellow facings, waistcoat and breeches.

The *tercio de la Generalitat* (**IRSP12**) was dressed in grey with red facings (1694).

March 15th, 1692, <u>Barcelona</u>. Duke of Medina-Sidonia, regarding the attire of the Miqueletes, which number 800, that coats or gambetos be made for them from 22nd cloth, which they call Portuguese, and that each jacket must be 5.5 palms long and 12 palms wide, lined with red baize with two dozen tin buttons and with tabs of the same red baize; that each jacket be paid for at 80 reales de ardites.[190]

Tercios de la Armada

The *Tercio viejo de la Armada de la Mar Oceano* (**IRSP26**) of D. *Geronimo Marim* was clothed in dark cloth 1689[191]; in blue with red facings (1703)

The *Tercio nuevo de la Armada de la Mar Oceano* (**IRSP27**) of D. *Juan Flores de Septiem* was clothed in red in 1694[192], later in yellow with blue facings (1703)

The tercio of *Villalonga* (**IRSP28**) in 1691 and 1694 was dressed in red [**Hospital Barcelona**]; in 1702 (when sent to Naples) was clothed in green with red facings.

Italian Infantry

The tercio *de Napolitanos viejo de l'Armada* (**IRIT05**) was probably clothed in blue with white facings and at a later stage in grey with yellow facings [data of 1701], while the companies and tercios of Neapolitan infantry (even when serving aboard the galleys) were traditionally dressed in blue with red or white facings.

The tercio of *Ferdinando Pignatelli* (**IRIT01**) was clothed in blue with white facings[193].

The *Tercio* of the *Prince of Macchia* (**IRIT02**) was clothed with a blue coat with red lining and facings; red stockings, tin buttons (1692-1694). In 1692 it wore white hats, that later became black.

The Milanese infantry was generally clothed in grey-white (*Sechi* **IRIT04bis**)[194]; in one case with yellow facings (Bonesana), while the tercios levied in the early XVIII century had blue or red facings. The tercio of *Carè* (**IRIT15**), that reached Catalonia in 1696, was dressed in green as were the Italian tercios formed in Lombardy in 1692-1693.

Walloon Infantry

Walloon infantry was generally clothed in grey-white as in Flanders; one of the *tercios* (*Noyelles* later *Maulde* **IRWL03**) in 1702 had blue facings. When formed in Flanders for employment in Catalonia the two tercios, *Noyelles* (**IRWL02**) and *Lede* (**IRWL03**), were dressed in grey-white with red facings; drummers with a red or green coat. Probably in the following years one of the two *tercios* had the facings changed from red to blue as a distinction from the other one.

German Infantry

The two regiments of German infantry long in the service of Spain, those of *Baron de Beck* (**IRAL01**) and of *Simon*

---

190 **A.G.S. Guerra y Marina Leg. 2906**
191 **Hospital Barcelona BC AH**
192 **Hospital Barcelona BC AH**
193 **Hospital Barcelona BC AH**
194 **Hospital Barcelona BC AH**

Henriquez de Cabrera (**IRAL02**) were dressed in grey with blue lining and facings, white metal buttons, dark-grey felt hats (the data refer to the regiment of Simon Enriquez de Cabrera[195], later *Gorcey*.) But in 1697 the regiment of *Baron of Gorcey* was clothed in red[196], while the regiment of *Baron de Beck* was still clothed in grey[197].

The Bavarian regiment of *Tattenbach* (**IRAL05**) was clothed in a mid-blue dress with yellow facings, that is it kept its own uniforms and flags. In 1701 it had yellow camisoles and may already have had this colour at their introduction in 1696. The cartridge pouches had brass plates with the Bavarian arms. The flags of Tattenbach in 1694 were white with blue flames each with 5 tongues in the 4 corners. In the middle the golden cypher **EME** mirrored beneath the Electoral cap. The colonel's or Leibfahne was recorded in 1694, when the regiment was *Rivera*, as being white with the Patrona Bavariae on both sides and with the Electoral cipher in all 4 corners (***Anton Hoffmann***).

The Imperial regiments (*Zweibrücken/Deux-Ponts* and *Saxe-Coburg* **IRAL03-04**) were dressed with a grey-white coat.

Deux-Ponts [**IRAL03**] had a grey-white dress with red facings.

Saxe-Coburg [**IRAL04**] had facings, vest, breeches grey-white, brass buttons and black stockings [according to Knötel black facings]. White border on the hat. N.C.O.'s were dressed as the soldiers with a border of yellow lace on the cuffs. Officers wore a red coat and the remaining as the soldiers. Drummers wore a black coat laced with yellow, white stockings.

Cavalry and Dragoons

The dress of the cavalry of the army of Catalonia consisted in a coat (***casaca***) of woollen cloth with facings, generally made of light bay and lining, metal buttons, sometimes made of cloth, breeches and vest (***chupa***), felt hat, a neck tie, gloves, high riding boots and ordinary shoes, woollen stockings. The colour of the coats was generally grey or sometimes blue. All mounted units were equipped with cloaks, normally of the same colour as the dress or natural wool, generally lined in the facing colour. Until the mid 1680's cuirassiers and lancers wore breast and back plates, or at least the breast plate; regiments of German cavalry and the companies of horse of the State of Milan wore a leather ***Kollet*** and a lobster helmet, like Austrian cuirassiers. Mounted troops were armed with a carbine, a broad sword and pistols, dragoons with a musket, sword or sabre, bayonet and a pistol, beside a hatchet and a spade. Saddle-cloth and pistol-holsters were in the colour of the dress or of the facings, usually bordered with a plain lace or of the livery, often carrying at the corners the arms of the captain, or of the maestro de campo, the general commissary or the person to whom they were the Guards.

Cavalry (Caballos Corazas)

Information on the cavalry's clothing is somewhat less frequent than that for the infantry in the archival documentation, but it still allows us to form an overall picture. Two notes taken from the correspondence of the Marquis of Villahermosa inform us about the composition of his clothing and equipment and also provide indications on the colours adopted for some of the corps.

March 1690 [For the Cavalry] [198] 1,608 22nd cloth coats, half five and a half palms long and the other half six palms long as well, and all 16 palms wide, without seams, lined with serges of bright colors, as it will be indicated, with 28 round tin buttons, and two canvas small pockets in the front, with cloth, and sleeves three and a half palms long, one palm wide each without seams, and full at the turn-up, which has to be like a boot [rolled up], also two palms long each, and this has to be covered with the aforementioned serge, with a declaration that the 550 jackets, more or less, have to be of a very bright red color, and permanent ... and the remaining 1,058 jackets of a lead colour or by another name, whitish with a mixture of black.

1,608 overcoats of 22nd cloth, half six and a half palms long each and the other half six palms long, with a flare in proportion to the said length and the cloth... with a round collar six fingers wide, with linen interlining, and a large metal clasp, 550 of them more or less reddish in color and very deep... and the remaining 1,058 of a lead color...

1,608 brown hats of Aragon wool, each two and a half fourths high at the crown, and with a skirt barely three-quarters high... 175 reales de ardite, the principality's currency, for each garment consisting of a jacket, cape, and hat.

---

195 In March 1691 it received an "ammunition" clothing composed with "*a iustacor of 22º cloth of whitish color of 5 palms long and 10 of flare, lined in blue Solsona bayeta with two dozen tin buttons, breeches of 22º cloth of three and a half palms long lined in raw canvas, with two pouches of the same canvas, white cordellate vest, Ghent cloth shirt of five palms long and seven of flare or width, wool stockings, shoes of Muscovy leather with 3 soles, ranis tie and brown hat.*" **AGS. Guerra y Marina, legajo 2881. AGS. Contaduría Mayor de Cuentas IIIª, leg. 3106.**

196 **Hospital Barcelona BC AH**

197 **Archivo Historico Ciudad de Barcelona Deliberacions del Consell de Cent**

198 **B.N.M. MS 2404. Correspondencia de Villahermosa.** fol. 336-336vº

A first reference for a part of the units is this presentation relating to the troops who in the year 1691 had received the complete clothing:

Clothings that were made for the Cavalry in the year 1691[199]

By contract of April 5th, 1691, Juan Graells, master tailor, manufactured one thousand 22nd cloth jackets of whitish or blue colour at a price of 86 1/4 reales for each coat and 10.5 rs for each hat, and 96 3/4 reales for both pieces.

To the Trozo de *Osuna*, 326 white-colored suits.
To the Trozo de Estremadura, 226 blue suits.
To the Trozo de las Hordenes, 216 white-colored suits.
To the Trozo de Milan, 232 white-colored suits.
For the three Guard Companies, 264 suits were manufactured.
For the company of Don Juan del Campo of the Tercio of Dragoons, 50 suits.

The companies of the Horse Guards of the *Capitan General* (=Viceroy, **CRSP01 to 03**) wore (1690-1697) a blue coat and red facings, with silk galloon, gilt buttons, black hats with a silk border, red cloak; saddle-cloth and pistol holsters red with initials and border of galloon.

In the years 1687-1689 the Guards wore red coats with buff breeches, yellow or white waist-coats and, probably yellow facings[200]; in 1699 these companies were dressed in yellow with red facings[201]

The company of the Guard of the Governor General of the Arms [**CRSP04**] was clothed in red[202].
The company of Horse of the Provost general of the army was clothed in red (blue facings?)[203]
The *Trozo* of *Ordenes* (**CRSP08**) was dressed grey-white (red facings in 1703)
The *Trozo* of *the Rosellon* (**CRSP09**) was dressed in blue (red facings in 1703)
The *Trozo* of *Milan* (**CRSP10**) was dressed in grey-white
The *Trozo viejo* of *Extremadura* (**CRSP11**) was dressed in blue with yellow facings
The *Trozo* of *Osuna* (**CRSP12**) was dressed in grey-white; for some years it went dressed in yellow with red facings.
The *Trozo nuevo* of *Extremadura* (**CRSP15**) was dressed in blue with yellow facings, black hats
The *Trozo* of *Flandes* (**CRWL01**) was dressed in grey-white [blue facings in 1702]
The *Trozo* of *Brabante* (**CRWL02**) was dressed in grey-white [1702 dressed in blue with red facings];
The *Tercio viejo* of *Dragones* (**DRSP01**) was dressed in red, yellow facings; yellow vests. Red saddle-cloth.
The *Tercio nuevo* of *Dragones* (**DRSP02**) was dressed in yellow with red facings[204]

Note Facings in the cavalry were yellow, white and red with blue coats; yellow, red and blue with grey-white ones. The saddle-cloth was generally the colour of the dress.

Spanish Flanders

Infantry

The traditional colour of the dress of most of infantry corps in the Spanish army of Flanders, of all nationalities, was grey-white. In facts Spanish, Italian and Walloon *tercios* and near all German regiments were dressed in that colour (that varied from definite grey to whitish), different units being distinguished by the colours of the facings (blue, white, red and yellow being the most often employed)[205]. We can to a certain extent reconstruct the dress of many corps, both on the basis of the receipts of the payments made in Flanders[206] and on some inspection returns dating from 1701 to 1702, because until 1704 traditional colours of existing units should not have been reasonably altered.

Spanish Infantry

In 1677 a contract was made for clothing 1,000 men of the Spanish infantry in coats of dark natural wool with facings of the

199 **A.G.S. Guerra y Marina Leg. 2881**
200 **Hospital Barcelona BC AH**
201 **Hospital Barcelona BC AH**
202 **Hospital Barcelona BC AH**
203 **Hospital Barcelona BC AH**
204 At least this was the clothing supplied to some of the free companies which constituted the new *tercio*.
205 **A.G. Simancas G.A. - A.G.R. Bruxelles Contaduria y Pagaduria**...
206 In the **Archives Generaux du Royaume** of Brussels there are quite a few records about the clothing of the army.

three colours: green, blue and red and with white metal buttons. In the following coats for most of the Spanish *tercios* were grey-white or white, with facings mostly red or blue.

The *tercio del Conde de Grajal* (**IRSP33**) was dressed (1680-1684) in grey-white, yellow facings.

The *tercio* of *D. Joseph de Moncada y Aragon* (**IRSP36**) was dressed (1684-1685) in grey-white with red facings and lining. In 1687 it received 7 blue coats with red facings, red breeches and stockings and tin buttons; we think these were drummers' liveries.

The *tercio* of the *duke of Vexar (Bejar)* (**IRSP31**) was dressed (1685) in iron grey, coats lined with a blue bay, grey stockings and a black felt hat. Drummers wore a red coat lined in blue

The *Tercio* of *Mariño*, later *Amezaga* (**IRSP32**), was dressed in grey-white with (1701) red facings, vest, breeches and stockings. White metal buttons. Sergeants had a silver lace on the cuffs. Officers were dressed as the soldiers, but captains had gilt buttons and lieutenants of a grey cloth. Drummers wore the livery of the maestro di campo.

The *Tercio* of *Mancheño* (**IRSp46**) was dressed in grey-white (1701) red cuffs and cloth buttons. Vest of red kersey with white metal buttons, grey breeches and red stockings. The hat was bordered with false silver. Sergeants had a silver lace on the cuffs and on the hat. Officers were dressed as the soldiers, but had gilt buttons on the red vest and the hat bordered with a golden lace.

The *Tercio* of *Zuñiga* (**IRSP31**) was dressed in grey-white with blue facings and white metal buttons; blue vest, breeches and stockings (1701). Sergeants had a silver lace on the cuffs and on the hat. Officers were similarly dressed, but had silver buttons and silver lace around button-holes on the coat and the vest and lieutenants silver lace at button-holes only on the vest. Drummers had the livery of the maestro di campo, that is red coats with blue facings and livery lace on the coat.

The *Tercio* of *Guzman* (1701 later *Ibañez*) was dressed in grey-white with red facings, vest and stockings. Cloth buttons. Drummers had an entirely blue livery.

The *Tercio* of *Benavides* (1701) was dressed coat and breeches grey-white with white lining; blue facings and vest. Drummers dressed as private soldiers, but with a yellow lining.

Walloon Infantry

Walloon infantry was similarly dressed in grey-white with facings white or of another colour.

Tercio of *Adrian de Aurech* (later *Hornes*) (**IRWL07**) in 1687 was dressed in grey-white lined blue.
Tercio of *Hornes*, when *Nassau*, (1701) was dressed with grey-white coat and breeches, white lining, blue facings. Drummers had a blue coat, yellow facings, vest and lining (*Nassau's livery*); breeches as private soldiers.

Tercio of count of *Falais* (**IRWL08**) was dressed in iron-grey (1690).

Tercio of *Deynse* (**IRWL05**) was dressed in grey-white with yellow facings and vest, breeches and stockings grey-white; cloth buttons (1701). Drummers wore a livery of buff colour. In 1695, probably due to a temporary shortage of white cloth, the *tercio* was dressed in red with yellow facings.

Tercio of *Grobendonc* (**IRWL09**) was dressed in grey-white with red facings and vest, breeches and stockings; tin buttons (1701). Drummers wore the livery of the maestro di campo, this being a red coat lined yellow.

Tercio of *Capres* (**IRWL06**) was dressed in grey-white with yellow facings, vest, breeches and stockings; tin buttons (1701). Drummers had the livery of the maestro de campo of yellow.

Tercio of *Moucron*, then *Westerloo* (**IRWL04**), was dressed (1701) in red with facings, vest, breeches and stockings blue. Drummers had the livery of the maestro de campo of a buff colour.

Italian Infantry

Italian infantry *tercios* that received their organisation in Flanders were dressed along the traditional lines of a grey-white coat as the majority of the other units of that country, but *tercios* formed in the Kingdom of Naples were generally dressed in blue.

Tercio of *Campi*, later *Magni* (**IRIT06**), was dressed (1701) in grey-white with blue facings, vest, breeches and stockings; pewter buttons. Drummers had a blue livery with buff facings (1701).

Tercio of *Bonamico, Francia, Acquaviva*, later *Grimaldi* (**IRIT07**), was dressed (1687) with grey-white coat and breeches, red facings and stockings. Drummers had a red livery, blue facings and the rest as the soldiers.
In 1701 dress white-grey with red facings, vest, breeches and stockings; white metal buttons. Drummers wore the livery of the maestro de campo.

Tercio of *the Marquis of Torrecuso*, later *Acquaviva* (**IRIT08**), was dressed (1684-1692) in blue with facings, vest, breeches and stockings red; pewter buttons.

German Infantry

Old German infantry regiments were usually dressed with stronger colours than grey, starting from the end of the century

▲ Plate 24 - 1690 Naples. Soldier from a company of cavalry belonging to the Viceroy's guard (Plate by Massimo Mannocchi)

▲ Plate 25 - 1688 Soldier from a company of avalry of the Foreign Cavalry (Milan) (Plate by Massimo Mannocchi)

▲ *Plate 26 - 1690 Naples. Standard bearer of a company of horsemen belonging to the Viceroy's guard (Plate by Massimo Mannocchi)*

they were gradually dressed in grey or grey-white.

Regiment of *Marquis of Trichateau* (**IRAL06**) (1684) coat grey-white with white lining and red facings.

Regiment of *Theys* (**IRAL13**) dress white lined blue (1687).

Regiment of *Baden* (**IRAL08**) (1687) dress white with red lining. When it became the *Regiment* of *Ursel conde de Milan* (1701) it was dressed entirely in grey-white with red facings and vest; tin buttons. Drummers had the red livery of their maestro de campo (facings probably yellow).

Regiment of *Prince Charles Thomas of Lorraine* (**IRAL09**) (1688) dress, lining, facings and stockings white; silver border on the hat. Drummers had the green livery of the House of Lorraine (probably with breeches and stockings as the soldiers)

Regiment of *Spinola* (**IRAL10**) was dressed (1701) in grey-white with green facings and red vest and breeches; tin buttons. Drummers were clothed in green with a black and white lace of the livery of the maestro di campo. Officers had a red dress with golden buttons and lace.

Regiment of *Wrangel* (**IRAL14**) was dressed:

(1685) blue coat with red facings, lining, breeches and stockings. Natural leather. NCO's wore a leather *kollet* and red breeches and stockings.

(1701) grey coat with blue facings, blue breeches and vest; tin buttons. Officers with a blue dress and white facings and breeches, gilt buttons. Drummers wore the livery of their maestro de campo, light buff.

English, Irish, Scottish Infantry

Tercio of Scottish infantry of *Henry Gage* (**IRSc01**) had (1681-1684) a yellow coat with red facings, breeches and stockings.
Tercio of English infantry of *Diego Porter* (**IREn01**) had a blue coat with red facings, breeches and stockings.
Tercio of Irish infantry of *Eugene O'Berny* (**IRIr01**) had a red coat with blue facings, breeches and stockings.

German auxiliary Infantry

The Bavarian regiment *Guards of his Electoral Highness* (**IRAL15**) was clothed in a mid-blue with white facings according to the ordonnance of 1694. Stockings were white. Breeches for all infantry regiments were of leather. The cartridge pouches were decorated with the complete arms of Bavaria surrounded with the Order of the Golden Fleece, probably on blue cloth or a brass shield. Lace on the buttonholes is not mentioned for any regiments at this time. All infantry were equipped with a large, loosely cut, blue mantle with wide sleeves "in the Danish manner". Waistcoats or camisoles were introduced only in 1696 following the French fashion and were probably all blue at first. Musicians and drummers were in the Bavarian livery with laces "in the style of the Guards of Piedmont". The officers wore blue with silver lace, sashes blue with silver fringes. In 1683 it had carried a colonel's flag of white with the "Patrona Bavariae" or Madonna in natural colours[207]. The battalion flag was white with a blue-white flamed edge, in the middle a gold lion holding a sword and a wreath, surrounded by a laurel wreath tied with a red ribbon. The same gold lion occurs in all four corners of the middle field[208].

The Bavarian regiment *Electoral Prince* (**IRAL16**) was clothed in mid-blue with blue facings, leather breeches. Officers were in blue with gold lace, sashes blue with gold fringes. (Therefore the men would have had yellow buttons.) At first the cartridge pouches were plain red leather but in 1696 they became similar in style to those of the Guards but with the Electoral cipher ("**EME**" under the Electoral cap). Its flags in 1683 were made up of 3 horizontal fields; the upper and lower white-red checked, that in the middle a blue band[209]. In 1694 they received blue/white striped flags for the 7 battalion companies and the Virgin on the white colonel's flag[210].

Cavalry

The dress of the cavalry was, almost independently of the nationality of the corps, white-grey often lined and faced in the same colour, sometimes in blue or red. The companies of the Guards of the Governor General and of the Governor of Arms represented an exception to this rule. Hats were generally black felt, with a silver narrow border, larger for the companies of the Guards. Breeches are never mentioned, we can infer that they were either buff or natural wool, or even of the colour of the coat. The vest is also not mentioned with the exception of the three companies of Guards. Troopers received further-

---

207 **Kühn**: Painting of Sobieski's relief of Vienna and **Anton Hoffmann**
208 "*Triomphes de Louis XIV*", **Belaubre**
209 Communication **August Kühn**.
210 **Staudinger**, Hoffmann.

more buff gloves, leather belt and a bandoleer, woollen stockings, probably white, riding boots, a broadsword, a cavalry musket and two pistols.

From 1688 to the end of the century, based on the contracts for the supply of the dress to these corps, the companies of **Guards of the Governor General** (**CRSP16-17**) were dressed in blue with facings in the same colour, silver buttons and lacings, buff vest and breeches.

The **Guards of the Governor of Arms** (**CRSP18**) were instead dressed in red laced silver; at the end of the century, in 1698, they also adopted a blue dress with red facings.

The company of the **General of the Cavalry** (**CRSP19**) was dressed in white with red facings, saddle-cloth, pistol-holsters and cloaks. Towards the end of the century it also received red vests.

The Companies of **Lieutenant Generals of Cavalry** (**CRSP20-21**) were dressed in white with red facings, but *Scipione Brancaccio*'s had blue facings (see his *tercio*). **Count of Valsasines's**, Lieutenant General of dragoons, was dressed entirely in red (1688), with overcloak, shabraque and pistol holsters red[211].

The tercio of horse of D. *Mastaing* (**CRSP23**) had a white dress with red facings[212].

The tercio of horse of D. *Juan Augustin Hurtado de Mendoza* (**CRSP24**) had a completely white dress[213].

The tercio of horse of D. *Gabriel Buendia* (**CRSP25**) had (1686) grey-white dress with blue facings.

The tercio of horse of D. *Alexandro de Bay* (**CRSP28**) had an entirely white dress.

The tercio of horse of D. *Espinosa* (**CRSP29**) had a white coat with red facings[214], white facings in 1696[215].

The tercio of Italian horse of D. *Scipione Brancaccio* (**CRIT01**) had (1688) grey-white dress with blue facings and lining, white facings in 1696[216].

The tercio of horse of *Betencourt* (**CRWL03**) had an entirely white dress (1689)[217].

The tercio of horse of *Dupuy* (=*Du Puis* **CRWL04**) was dressed (1687) completely in white[218], white breeches and stockings, silver border on the hat.

The tercio of horse of the *Count d'Audemont* (**CRWL05**) had a white dress with blue facings (1689).

The German Cavalry Regiment of *Dumont* (**CRAL01**) had an entirely white dress[219].

The German Cavalry Regiment of *Torsy* (**CRAL02**) had a white dress with green facings[220].

The German Cavalry Regiment of *Hartman* (**CRAL03**) had a white coat with red facings[221].

The German Cavalry Regiment of *Lorraine* (**CRAL04**) had a white dress with red facings[222].

The German Cavalry Regiment of the *Count of Egmont* (**CRAL05**) had (1687) grey-white coat, white lining, red cuffs.

The German Cavalry Regiment of *Martin Fernandez de Cordoba* (**CRAL06**) had an entirely white dress.

The German Cavalry Regiment of the *duke of Croy* (**CRAL08**) had white coat and lining.

The German Cavalry Regiment of *Fresin* (**CRAL09**) had a white dress with red facings[223].

The German Cavalry Regiment of the *Prince of Nassau* (**CRAL10**) had white coat and lining.

Dragoons

The following list presents some of the main data about clothing of Dragoons. The first units of Dragoons in the army of

211 08/10/1688 Orden tocante los vestidos y armas de la Compañia del Theniente General de la Cavalleria Estrangera Conde de Valsasines ... 645 baras de paño rojo, las 390 para 60 capas a seis baras y media para cada una y los 255 restantes para los Justcorps y calzones a quatro baras y una quarta y de bayeta del mismo color 489 baras para los aforros de las capas y de los justacors ... y usas, capas de las pistolas, armas y demas equipage ... **A.G.R. Secretariat d'Etat et de Guerre T100, legajo 73**.

Janvier 1691 Costi di cui chiede il rimborso il Conte di Valsasines per aver vestito la sua compagnia (1688-1689) 120 chapeaux, 120 paires de pistolets, 120 selles, 120 paires de bas, galon d'or et d'argent pur et large d'un grand pouce pour border les bandoliers, chapeaux, pattes de poches et manches, 120 baudries de bufle et autant de larges bandolieres; 120 paires de gands de bufle; 120 housses de drap verd avec leurs chappes et bordé de drap de couleur

120 cartouches de drap bordé avec leurs centures de bœuf; façon de 120 habits et autant de manteaux ayant fourny toille pour les culottes ... 120 cravattes noires faisants deux tours au col; 120 paires de bottes cuir de somelles avecq leurs esperons; 32 tentes; 120 espeées a garde de cuivre et large lame. **A.G.R. Brux. Contadorie et Pagadorie des Gens de Guerre T 005 L. 115.**

212 Gerpines list
213 White with red facings in Gerpines list
214 Gerpines list
215 Ath Camp List
216 Ath Camp List
217 White with red facings in Gerpines list
218 White with red facings in Gerpines list
219 Tilroy camp list
220 Gerpines list
221 Gerpines list, Ath Camp list
222 Gerpines list
223 Gerpines list

Flanders were dressed in red, a colour that in almost Europe was usually adopted for the speciality, even if there were some exception to the rule.

1676 *Tercio of Salzedo*[224] coat, cap and cloak red (probably facings were also red); drums were painted in red.

1676 *Verloo-Nicolas Hartman-Risbourg* (**DRWL01**) red coat with red facings, in the following it probably took a blue coat with red facings.

1676 *Vanderpit-Valanzart* (**DRWL03**) green dress

1683 *Mathias Perez* (**DRWL04**) coat red, facings, lapels, linings of blue bay, 72 tin buttons, chamois leather breeches, blue stockings and hat with a false silver edge and cord (also for 1687). A red cloak, lined with blue at the front. Sword belt, musketoon bandoleer and pouch of buffalo. A sword and a musketoon[225].

1687 (Free) company of Captain *Nicolas Ferrar* blue coats lined red, red breeches and stockings and black felt hat.

1689 *Bossu Chevalier d'Alsace* (**DRWL08**) red dress

1693 *d'Arville* (**DRWL02**) red dress

1696 *Jacques Pastur* (**DRWL09**) Clothing blue cloth; cloak, coat, vest and cap (edged with fur), linings and lapels of blue serge, breeches leather, boots, hat, sword, musketoon, two pistols[226].

Auxiliary (Bavarian) Cavalry

Squadron of Horse Carabiniers (Bavarians CRAL11)

These wore a tricorn with silver lace and a silver button and loop on the left. A leather **Kollet** was worn over the blue coat with crimson red cuffs and linings. Silver buttons with silver lace on the buttons, buttonholes and cuffs. Breeches were blue. Belts were buff edged with silver/blue lace, n.c.o.s having black cloth covering and silver lace on the belts. The cloak was plain blue. Saddle cloths and holster covers were blue with silver edging. We do not know what the standards looked like.

Squadron of Horse Grenadiers (Bavarians CRAL12)

These wore blue uniforms with white facings and white lace on the buttons, buttonholes and cuffs. Waistcoats and breeches were blue, the waistcoat having white lace as on the coat. Buttons white (tin). Dark brown bearskin caps with a red bag having silver lace. The cloak was blue without decoration. Belts were buff and edged with blue/silver lace[227]. The still existing guidon of this squadron is medium/light blue strewn with the Electoral cipher ("**EME**" mirrored beneath the Electoral cap) and grenades (black with red/yellow flames) alternating in four rows with only the last four in a row visible, the others being covered by the emblem at the staff. The emblem on the obverse was the Bavarian arms in a Baroque shield, surrounded by the order of the Golden Fleece and superimposed upon palm leaves. Below it the motto "**UNI DOMINE**" on a ribbon. Above the arms the eye of God in a triangle with light streaming out, clouds around the sides and above the motto "**UNI DEO**" on a ribbon. On the obverse lightning bolts issuing from the top corner at the staff crash upon a rock at the bottom. Below the rock a motto "**HIS OMNIA CEDUNT**" on a ribbon.

Regiment d'Arco Cuirassiers (Bavarians CRAL13)

Cuirassiers of the Bavarian army were dressed in light-grey, the regiment of Arco having blue facings. Of the same colour were saddle-cloth and holsters, bordered with white lace (silver for officers and n.c.o's). Troopers wore a cuirass (breast and back plate) and a pot helmet. Usually officers, n.c.o's and trumpeters were dressed with reversed colours with lining and facings of a light grey colour; trumpeters had fake sleeves of the regimental colour sewn at the shoulders and covered with lace. Cloaks were grey for all. Trompeters would have been dressed in reversed colours with false sleeves, all covered with lace in the button colour. In the Archives Nationales at Paris there is a description of the Arco livery for 1708. This may well have been the livery of the trumpeters too. It was blue lined with feuille-morte (orange-brown) with white/silver lace and white buttons.[228]

---

224 Disbanded in 1685.

225 [**AGR Bruxelles** *Justeaucorps rouge avec parements, revers, doublures de baie bleüe, garni de 72 boutons d'estain, des chausses de peau passé en chamois, bas bleus et un chapeau avec un galon d'argent faux et cordon (idem 1687). Un manteau rouge, au devant doublé de baie bleüe. Baudrier et porte-mousqueton de buffe et une tasse de buffe (gibeciere); une épée, un mousqueton.*]

226 [**AGR Bruxelles** *Tenue de drap bleu: manteau, habit, veste et bonnet (garni de fourrure), doublure et revers de serge bleue, culottes de peau, bottes; chapeau; épée, mousqueton, deux pistollets.*]

227 **Anton Hoffmann**

228 Estat des Draps et gallon quil faut pour la Livrée de son E Monseigneur Le Mareschal d'Arco pour l'an 1708. Quatre vingt trois aulnes de Drap bleu, Quatre vingt quinze aulnes de Drap feuille morte, Deux cent vingt sept aulnes de serge feuille morte, Trente six douzaines de bouton d'argent fillé, Quarante huit douzaines petit boutons fillé d'argent à veste, Soixante et neuf douzaines bouton d'estain à Justaucorps, Quatre vingt douzaines boutons d'estain à Vestes, Dix neuf marc quatre gros de gallon d'argent, Quatre cent quatre vingt trois aulnes du gallon de soye blanc, Deux cent soixante et onze aulnes de gallon soyé feuille morte. **A.N. Paris**

An illustration of the regiment in 1683 by Nemetz shows the standard as plain white with the Bavarian arms in the middle. Anton Hoffmann shows a white standard with the Bavarian arms on one side and the "*Patrona Bavariae*" on the other, with the Electoral cipher in the 4 corners, the field of the standard covered in gold decorations. The squadron standards were probably in the facing colour.

Regiment Weickel Cuirassiers (Bavarians CRAL14)

Weickel Cuirassiers, previously Salburg, was dressed as described for Arco but the facings were crimson red, as were linings and waistcoat. The above description of the standards would also be valid here.

Regiment d'Arco Dragoons (Bavarians DRAL01)

In the period concerned this regiment had blue coats with red facings and in 1694 yellow camisoles are recorded. Equipment was typical of the dragoons of other states at the time. The officers wore a red coat with silver lace (indicating that the buttons were white for the men). Note that the dragoons all had blue saddle cloths and holster covers and a red sack behind the saddle, all edged with white borders. The ordnnance of 1694 describes their guidons as being blue but gives no other details.

Regiment Monasterol Dragoons (Bavarians DRAL02)

Was created by dividing the regiment of Arco into 2 in 1694. It took a blue uniform with grey facings, the officers having grey coats with golden lace (indicating that the buttons were yellow for the men). The guidons were blue in 1694.

State of Milan

As it concerns the units of the army of the duchy of Milan information on uniforms is not abundant as for other territories of the Spanish Monarchy, due to the devastations during the wars of Milanese Archives, nevertheless we can have an overall picture of the situation.

Infantry

The following description is of the end October 1689 printed in a gazette from Milan: ***Thursday afternoon … … while the Cavalry of the State marched by land, being followed along the Po [river] by the infantry distributed, with a wonderful view, aboard 82 large barges, laden with 8,000 foot armed and clothed in dress of 3 colours, viz. red, blue and white for Spaniards, Germans and Italians, except 500 Grisons clothed in grey*** …

<u>Spanish Infantry</u>

Spanish *tercios* wore red coats, as that was the traditional colour reserved to Spanish foot troops in Italy[229]. In 1693, a report of the time, indicates that all the Spanish foot in the army of Milan was clothed with the same colour, that is red. The Spanish foot in the kingdom of Naples (***tercio fixo del reyo de Napoles***), consistent detachments of which were repeatedly sent as a reinforcement to Milan, had red coats with facings, lining, breeches and stockings of a yellow colour. Until the 1695 the hat of the Spanish infantry-man was probably of a whitish felt, even if on the Spanish mainland some *tercios* had black hats and Italian and German infantry were supplied with black felt hats and it is therefore probable that even the Spaniards found this merchandise more easily available on the market in Lombardy.

Following the battle of Staffarda in 1690 in order to organize anew the units of the army it was deemed necessary to supply coats of three different colours (500 of each): blue, red and silvery (that is grey-white). Furthermore we know from a contemporary French report on the battle of Marsaglia, that at least one of the Spanish *tercios* was clothed in red. In 1692 the Governor had 500 red coats made (for the Spanish infantry) and 3,000 green ones for the Lombard foot, but we do not know the colours of the facings.

<u>Milan Infantry</u>

At the beginning of the military operations in 1690 it is likely that all the milanese infantry (**IRSP41 to 45**) was dressed in grey-white with different facings. The tercios levied at the end of 1692 were instead dressed in green with different facings[230]. The *tercio* of **count Bonesana** (**IRIT09**) was probably dressed in grey-white with yellow facings (1709 at least as it regards the facings).

---

229 **A.G.S. Guerra y Marina Leg. 2790** and **Gazzetta di Milano year 1689**
230 ASMi Antichi Regimi - Cancellerie dello Stato

Neapolitan Infantry

Neapolitan infantry (**IRIT16-17**) serving in the army of Milan was traditionally dressed with a blue coat with white or red facings and tin buttons. Usually vest and stockings were the same colour as the facings; breeches could be of various colours, often natural wool. In 1694 the coats were dark bleu and the facings white[231].

German Infantry

German infantry (levied in Austrian territories or in some of the German principalities belonging to the Empire and among German-speaking Swiss cantons) was dressed with blue coats and red facings and vests (the stockings were very probably red as well), as it appears from the Capitulation for the regiment *Ulbin* in 1685 (*Melzi* at the end of 1692 **IRAL16**)[232].
The second regiment, that of *Fadrique Enriquez Cabrera*, later *Leiningen* (**IRAL17**), was very likely dressed in the same colours.

We do not have information about officers, n.c.o.'s, drummers and fifers. It is probable that, according to the fashion of German armies of the time, these could wear a dress of a colour different from the soldiers. Usually they had reversed colours, that is red coats with blue. Officers should have worn a red waist-sash, quite certainly their dress was adorned with golden or silver lace and on the hat they wore white or red plumes. Drummers and fifers could also have had the livery of the colonel or of different colours from those used by the soldiers.

The infantry regiment of the duke of **Württemberg** (**IRAL18**) was dressed in a grey-white coat with red facings and lining, white cloth buttons, buff vest and breeches and white stockings, red neck-tie, black felt hat with a white border; fouriers, sergeants and drummers had red coats with white facings and lining, and tin buttons, white cloth neck-ties[233].

Swiss and Grison Infantry

The **Grison** regiment (**IRSw01**) was dressed in grey with blue facings.

From a note of the Papal Nuncio in Turin we learn that in 1696 some officers of the **Swiss** regiments [probably from the Milanese army] which were withdrawing to their camp were dressed in blue with white plumes on the hat. May de Romainmotier in his "*History of the Swiss at Foreign service*" (1787) states that the Swiss regiments in Milanese pay were dressed in red.

Cavalry

The two companies of the *Guards of the Governor* (**CRIT02-03**) in June 1692[234], were dressed with blue coats and silver lace. The facings were probably red to imitate the French Guards du Corps. Since the arrival of the prince of Vaudemont as Governor General in 1696, his Guards was dressed wholly in red with golden buttons and lace.

Neapolitan cavalry companies (**CRIT08**) *newly levied* sent to Lombardy by the Viceroy of Neaples at the end of 1689 were dressed with a red coat and breeches with blue facings, lining and vest, tin buttons, black felt hat with a white lace. Saddle-cloths and pistol holsters were red with a white lace. At the corners of the saddle-cloths there were the family arms of the captains of each company[235].

We don't know how German or foreign cavalry (**CRAL15**) was dressed. It is likely that their dress was red with white or blue facings (as it was the German cavalry in Spain).

In the State Cavalry (**CRIT07**) *men-at-arms* and *cuirassiers* were still equipped with old full cuirasses.

---

231 ASNA Partito con Mº Biase Califano di mille vestiti Gennaro 1694 (Contract for clothing 1000 Neapolitan Soldiers)
Havendo S.E. con suo viglietto de 16 Novembre 1693 ordinato farsi Partito di 800 vestiti violetti per servitio de soldati Italiani in conformità della mostra venuta da Milano e dopo con altro biglietto de 4 Gennaro 1694 ordinato che fusse fatto il precedente Partito per infino alla summa di mille ...
27/8/1694 Si fa fede haver ricevuto dal Mag.co Biase Califano 1000 vestiti intieri de monitione de panno violeto di S. Severino, complite con sue spade per servizio dei soldati Italiani in conformità della mostra venuta da Milano .... cioè le ciamberghe foderate de cusano bianco e le smerze delle maniche e colaretto de panno bianco S. Severino della vecchia fabbrica, e li calzoni di panno di d.ª vecchia fabrica color bianco, e detti vestite sono 700 mezzani, e 300 grandi e per ogni centenaro sono 30 bandolere meno conforme il solito. [**Note** The term *violeto* indicates a dark blue colour]

232 **A.G.S. Estado Leg. 3428** *The Colonel is also obliged to dress the Regiment every two years, giving each soldier a coat of good blue cloth with good red lining, his red cloth breeches, stockings, shoes, hat, shirt, tie, bandolier and sword belt.*

233 Personal communication of the late **August Kühn**

234 **A.S.Vat. Segreteria di Stato Avvisi**

235 **A.S.Na. Notai Paolo Colacino Reg. 43**

▲ *Plate 27 - Officer of a German regiment in field uniform (Flanders) (Period portrait, private collection)*

Practically all the State and the German cavalry on campaign wore a heavy leather coat (***Kollet***) and a metal helmet, of the style used by Austrian cavalry[236].

July 1690 *The Company of 60 Horses levied by the Marquis [Guasco] of Alessandria all dressed with a leather kollet and well mounted ... is ready to march.*

During the campaigns in Piedmont in the years 1691-1692 a uniform dress was distributed to the Cavalry of the State (**CRIT07**). It is probable that the coat was white-grey (as the infantry) with facings blue or of another colour, since one of the regiments formed in 1702 with these companies (***Valdefuentes***) had this uniform.

As for the Cavalry of the State we have found an offer to the duke of Savoy for levying a regiment of Milanese cavalry by a subject of the king of Spain (dating early 1690's) [the proposal was not accepted, but it is interesting for the description of the dress the soldiers should have worn, that very likely was similar to that of the Milanese cavalry].
Proposal of prince of Carpegna for a regiment of 1,000 Italian horse for service of H.R.H. ... 1,000 horse in 10 companies of the State of Milan clothed with a coat, breeches and cloak of a light-grey cloth lined blue with tin buttons, a large sword-belt and a sling for the carbine of leather with large boots, a hat bordered with silver with its ribbons, saddle-cloths, cloth pistol-holsters with cyfres ... armed with a sword, pistols and carbines ....[237]
At the same time we must record that a reinforcement of 500 troopers sent from Spain in 1692 was dressed in red with blue waist-coat and facings[238]

The regiment of ***dragoons of the State*** (**DRIT01**), is often defined as the ***yellow dragoons***, from the colour of the dress. Since in the following years the regiment had, besides the yellow dress, red facings, it is probable that also in the years 1680's and 1690's the Milanese dragoons were thus dressed.

Auxiliary Cavalry

The regiment of ***Württemberg Cuirassiers*** (**CRAL18**) were dressed with coat, vest and breeches of a buff colour, black facings and brass buttons, white neck cloth, helmets, blackened breast-plate and carabine bandolier, yellow saddle-cloth and pistol holsters with a black lace[239].

The regiment of ***Württemberg dragoons*** (**DRAL03**) was dressed with a red coat[240] and black facings, grey-white vest and breeches, tin buttons, white neck-cloth, black felt hat and boots, yellow saddle-cloth and pistol holsters with a black lace[241].

After 1694 the horse (cuirassiers) regiment created merging the two previous ones (**CRAL18**) had a coat of a buff colour with red facings and tin buttons, black felt hat bordered in white (discarding the helmet), red saddle-cloth and pistol holsters with a white lace[242].

d'Arco Cuirassiers Regiment (Bavarians CRAL16)

Cuirassiers of the Bavarian army were dressed in light-grey; the regiment of Arco having blue facings. Of the same colour were saddle-cloth and holsters, bordered with white lace (silver for officers and n.c.o's). Troopers wore cuirasses (breast and back plate) and a pot helmet. Usually officers, nco's and trumpeters wore a dress with reversed colours of those of the troopers with lining and facings of light-grey; trumpeters had fake sleeves of the facings colour sewn at the shoulders and laced around. Cloaks were grey for everybody.

Cuirassiers Regiment of Carafa-Hanover (CRAL17)

All Imperial cuirassier regiments wore the *Kollett* of leather, mostly with red facings. In the field all men wore (trumpeters excluded) breast and back plates and the lobster helmet, usually blackened. As a rare exception to the rule Carafa wore light blue facings. The standards were also light blue with golden fringes, embroidery and an emblem showing pillars on a square base with a golden crown above. On a white ribbon the motto "**QUI LEGITIME CERTAVERIT**". The reverse showed the usual Imperial double eagle.

---

236 **ASMi Registri**
237 **ASTo Sez.I MatMil**
238 **AGS Guerra y Marina L. 2905**
239 Communication **August Kühn**.
30/06/1691 "*The villagers near Invrea yesterday led to Turin 14 Yellow Dragoons from Vittemburg, [actually the cuirassiers] of those who came recently, who were destined to support the Duke's forces there to drive the French out of the Aosta valley and went to throw themselves into their party.*" **A.A.Vat. Segreteria di Stato Savoia 1691**;
01/11/1690 Milano ... *Six companies of Yellow Dragoons of the Duke of Virtembergh (= Cuirassiers see above) of the Duke of Virtemberg sent by order of King William] have passed through Genoa to the camp at Turin and four other companies of Red Dragoons have already arrived in Damaso on behalf of His Catholic Majesty.* **Avvisi di Foligno**
240 In some gazettes of the time the dragoons were also called the *red dragoons of the King* (of Spain) to distinguish them from the Savoyard ones.
241 Communication **August Kühn**.
242 Communication **August Kühn**.

Naples and Sicily
Kingdom of Naples

For the Kingdom of Naples we have abundant information on the clothing of the troops raised or stationed in the kingdom; in fact many of the contracts that the Royal Court, through the Chamber of the Sommaria, stipulated with merchants and tailors to make the soldiers' clothes have been preserved. In 1683 a specific ordinance was issued which imposed uniform colours for the clothes of the troops of the kingdom. We have not found the text of the military ordinance which, between 1682 and 1683 and the first in the history of Naples, placed order on the colours of military clothing, but it was taken up in a civil pragmatic promulgated shortly afterwards by the viceroy on duty, Gaspar de Haro y Guzmàn, who thereby prohibited male civilians from wearing clothes of the style and colours used by the military. The aforementioned pragmatic is first read about in the Confuorto's newspapers: *"On the 6th of the said month (6th of November 1683), on the occasion of the 'compleaños' of our lord the king, the Viceroy put out a new livery, since he dressed the halberdiers in yellow otherwise citrine, the Spanish infantry in red, the Italian in blue and the cavalry in dark blue. And he had a regulation issued that no one else could dress in that colour.*[243]*"*

Spanish Infantry

The fixed tercio of Spanish infantry of the Kingdom of Naples was traditionally dressed, since at least 1683, in red with yellow facings; yellow breeches and stockings, yellow vest and lining, tin buttons.

Italian Infantry

The Neapolitan infantry levied in the kingdom, whether it served in the dependencies of the kingdom itself (that is, as free companies in the southern places or in those of the Tuscan Presidi, or even as garrison to the galleys), or sent to the various possessions of the Crown, from 1683 was always dressed in blue (according to the specific Pragmatic of the Viceroy) with usually red or white, or sometimes yellow, facings; with the exception of *the tercio viejo de infanteria napolitana de la Armada real de la Mar Oceano*, which was instead dressed (at the expense of the crown of Castile) in grey with yellow facings.

Cavalry

Companies of the Guards

The two companies of mounted cuirassiers of the guard of the viceroy of Naples [**RCNap01-02Nap**], which, born from the reform of the previous company of lances, appeared in public for the first time on January 17, 1691, were described by Bulifon as follows: *"On the said day, being the feast of St. Anthony the Abbot ... for the first time the two companies of cavalry newly raised to guard the lords Viceroys appeared. The first, led by captain Mr. D. Nicolò Coppola, marched: first four with swords in hand, then the trumpeters behind a kettledrum, the page of the valise, the captain, then the company, dressed in blue with yellow lining, the baldric of crimson velvet and in gold cloth the arms of the lord Viceroy, the flag or pennant with the arms of His Excellency. Of the other company without kettledrums was captain D. Andrea de la Rimpe, formerly a horseman of His Excellency, which came after the carriages of the cortege..."*[244].

From the description of the same cavalcade made by Confuorto we learn that the second company wore the same uniform as the first: *"... the two companies on horseback, again made up of good and beautiful people but of the same ... uniform ..."*[245]

This uniform soon changed because the Viceroys and their tastes alternated. In the report that Buliflon wrote about the cavalcade held in Naples on the 6th of January 1701 to celebrate the acclamation of Philip V as the new king of Spain, we read: *"One of the two mounted companies of the cuirasses of the guard of the Lord Viceroy preceded, so richly dressed, as you know, for the great quantity of yellow velvet, and large silver braid, commanded by the Commendator Saraceni ..."* and in May 1702 to the cavalcade for the entry of the Papal Legate Cardinal Barberini, he added *"... a company of the Viceroy's guards, nobly dressed of just-au-corp in fine yellow cloth with the sleeves-facings of blue velour, garnis de larges galons d'argent ..."*

Company of (Swiss) Halberdiers Guard of the Viceroy.

Finally, it remains to describe the uniform of the only Neapolitan corps that always maintained its own particular costume, that of the German halberdiers of the viceroy's guard, German-speaking Swiss mercenaries who inspired their own

---

243 **Confuorto**, op.cit., year 1683
244 **A. Bulifon**, "*Giornali* ecc.", year 1691.
245 **Confuorto**, op.cit., year 1691.

dress to their traditional costume and to that of the royal halberdiers in Madrid, but above all to the Swiss Guard of the Pope and other Italian princes, such as the Duke of Savoy, the Doge of Genoa, the Dukes of Parma and Modena and the Grand Duke of Tuscany, each of whom had a guard company made up of Swiss halberdiers (German-speaking and therefore called German).

A complete estimate of the military expenditure during the time of the Viceroy de Los Velez, that is, a few years before 1680, informs us that *"at the entrance of each new Viceroy"* the new clothing was given to the German guard, which, like all European palace guards, had always worn a specific livery[246]. The style was the one that the German mercenaries, since the time of Charles VIII, had made known throughout Italy. The Viceroys who succeeded each other in Naples left it substantially unchanged, limiting themselves - at least in the second half of the seventeenth century - to sometimes inverting the prevalence of one of the two fundamental colours, yellow and crimson, which characterised that livery. Yellow had long been a favourite colour for the liveries of the royal palace guards in Spain and of many Viceroys or Governors of other territories.

1696 Contract for the German Guard's Livery.
H.E. with a bill dated 4th October 1696 ordered that the Royal Chamber should apply itself to have the necessary Clothes made for the Soldiers of the German Guard's Company, in accordance with what had been done on other occasions, ... Contract was made with Pietro Vitale of ... 76 clothes:
Four suits of crimson velvet with yellow satin strips, with vest, and sleeves lined with taffeta, with four ferrayoli (cloajs) of Venetian saya, and four halberds trimmed with velvet with gilded nails and four points of Partisans with their knots, and silk ribbons for the three Corporals and Proposito [the Sereant] of the said Company. Six other suits of yellow damask for the six Trumpeters and four knots and usual laces for each Trumpeter and Banners printed with gold fringe around and silk with the Arms of H.M. and H.E. with their Hats. One suit, or Royal Jacket for the King of the Arms of crimson damask lined with yellow taffeta, with its embroidery on the breast and back with the Royal Arms, and with four Arms of H.E. in the four parts. One dress for the Chaplain of the said Company consisting of 10 canes of black Boratto, with shoes, socks and hat. And 64 others dressed as usual, with gilded swords, and Bradicù with Ferrajoli of crimson-colored Cimosone Cloth from Milan, with crimson silk socks, and yellow silk Hangers, with crimson velvet hats, and another white hat for each soldier, with their silk cord of various colors; all as shown by His Excellency. And a tambourine with all its adherents trimmed with crimson-colored cowhide, covered with velvet of the same color with fringes, and galloons.

Sicily

German Guard of the Viceroy

The Guard Company of Swiss halberdiers, in service at the Royal Palace of Palermo, was dressed in a yellow Swiss costume (as shown in the painting of the Royal Palace in the Pepoli Museum of Trapani), while in the past it had been distinguished by a sixteenth-century cut dress of entirely red colour.

The fixed tercio of the Spanish infantry of Sicily was dressed in red with blue facings.
*The company (of Spanish infantry) recruited by Antonio Pilo for [the **fixed tercio of**] **Sicily**] in 1690 was adorned with coloured [=red] coats, like the trousers, having blue facings*[247].

---

246 *"Stato del Regno di Napoli e spese occorrenti per il suo mantenimento"*, **S.N.S.P.** Ms. XXVII.A.17.
247 Letter of Conde de Altamira, Valencia 10th September 1690. *Relación del género y piezas que han de ser los vestidos que ha de dar el capitán don Antonio Pilo..., 28 de abril 1690.* **A.G.S. Guerra y Marina. Leg. 2.850**.

FLAGS AND STANDARDS

The flags of the armies of the Spanish monarchy (not only Spaniards, but also of the other vassals of the King of Spain such as Italians and Walloons) of the sixteenth and seventeenth centuries were characterised, for almost all the corps, by the presence of the Cross of Burgundy (in Spanish *Aspa*, two knotted sticks crossed in an X), very often red, placed in the centre of the flag, a characteristic symbol from the early years of the sixteenth century to the present day (one of the first uses of this symbol in the field was at the battle of Pavia in 1525).[248]

Spanish tercios during Carlos II's reign had a standard for each company, even if during field operations they carried the maestro de campo's one and a couple more, and the remaining were left with the baggage in the rear. The reason for a company standard was tied to the fact that originally companies recruited on their own, being the obligation of each captain to keep his company at level; this was done exposing the standard in a given site, indicated by authorities and receving there the recruits. In other instances the recruits were made for the whole tercio and some officers were delegated to operate also on behalf of their fellows in order to reach the desidered number of recruits.

a) Infantry Flags

As for the infantry flags, they were square in shape, very large (towards the end of the century, however, they had been reduced to around 2 m per side), the field of which was often divided by the four branches of the Cross of Burgundy into squares and geometric segments of various colours (obtained by sewing together pieces of cloth and canvas on a light canvas base), among which white, blue, green and yellow in various combinations predominated. Very often, the edge was also made up of squares or flames of alternating colours. The poles, until the last years of the 17th century, were very short and ended with a knob; the flag bearer held them with his fist and they could be supported on a special support added to the belt at the waist. There are various depictions of the flags of the *tercios* of infantry (especially those of Flanders) from the first half of the 17th century in various paintings[249]. These flags were very large and had very picturesque motifs. In the second half of the century, the dimensions were reduced and the geometric motifs became relatively simpler. In this regard, see the book "*Arte del Sastre*" [*Art of the Tailor*] published in 1580[250] (and then replicated in various editions for several decades), which provides instructions for the construction of an infantry flag made of taffeta with white and blue squares and a red Burgundy cross in the centre, very similar to some flags depicted in various illustrations.

In addition to what is indicated in the tailor's manuals mentioned above, we have not been able to find written sources on the Spanish flags of the time, even though there are numerous representations of them relating to different periods and moments in history.

A document dated in Madrid on 5th of April 1694 provides us with a report of the cost incurred for the recruitment of the provincial Tercios who served in Catalonia ...

> "*To Mr. Nicolás Laurel, Master Flag-maker, for the value of 10 Flags that have been bought from him to give them to the captains who have gone out to raise people at the price of 120 reales each... To Juan Méndez, master blacksmith, 98 reales have been paid for the value of 14 flagpoles with their spearheads that he made for the Flags at the price of 7 and a half reales each... 3 companies march to Madrid*".[251]

For the period we are dealing with, that is, the War of the League of Augsburg, the main source [which Jean Belaubre has very well documented in his study on "*Les Triomphes de Louis XIV*"] comes from the collection of the Bibliothèque Nationale in Paris[252], in which are represented (sometimes in a simplistic manner) the flags captured from the enemy during the long wars waged by Louis XIV.

---

248 The *aspa* [*Burgundian cross*] comes from the fact that Juana, the daughter of the Catholic Kings, married with Felipe *el Hermoso* and added it to his own shield, referring to the territorial origin of her husband, Burgundy, who was under the patronage of San Andrés, representing the *aspa* the instrument of his martyrdom. The *aspa* began to become the international insignia of Spanish armies, placing itself above the flags as well as above the clothing of footmen. It was first used in the Battle of Pavia in 1525 and allowed a clear distinction before the French, who used a white cross, precisely the same signal that they used the Spanish imperial troops in the war of the Communities, ended in 1521. **Antonio Manzano Lahoz** "*La evolucion de las banderas*". in Militaria, Revista de Cultura Militar n: 9, Madrid 1997

249 See for example the series of paintings by Denijs van Alsloot of 1615 set in the Grande Place in Brussels and the reproductions in "*Il Libro del Sarto*" **Fondazione Querini Stampalia,** Venezia 1987.

250 Indication by **Luis Sorando Muzas**.

251 **A.H.N. Est Lg 805**.

252 **Bibliothèque Nationale de France,** Paris «*Les Triomphes de Louis XIV et de Louis XV*», Id 42, Id 43, Id 44, Id 45, Id 46, Id 47

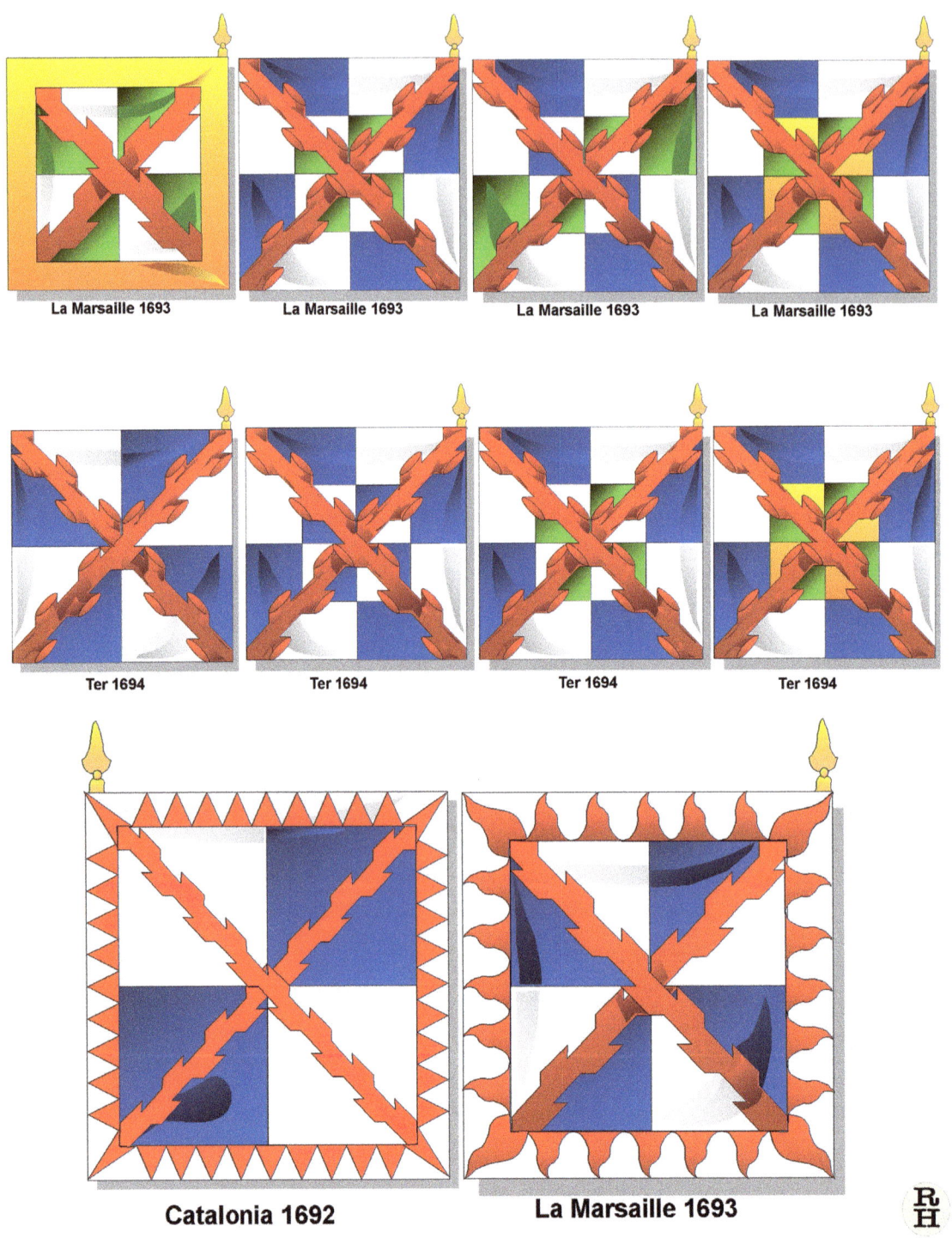

▲ *Plate 28 - Spanish infantry flags captured by the French in Catalonia (1692-1694) and at the Battle of Marsaglia in Piedmont (October 1693) [Drawings by Robert Hall from 'Les Triomphes de Louis XIV' Bibliotheque Nationale Paris]*

▲ *Plate 29 - Spanish infantry flags captured by the French in Catalonia (1692-1694) and at the Battle of Marsaglia in Piedmont (October 1693) [Drawings by Robert Hall from 'Les Triomphes de Louis XIV' Bibliotheque Nationale Paris]*

▲ *Plate 30 - Spanish infantry flags captured by the French in Catalonia (1692-1694), at the Battle of Fleurus (1690) and at the Battle of Marsaglia in Piedmont (October 1693). Note the two flags with the imperial eagle bearing a Burgundy cross superimposed on it: they are believed to belong to a regiment of German infantry in the service of the King of Spain. [Drawings by Robert Hall from 'Les Triomphes de Louis XIV' Bibliotheque Nationale Paris]*

▲ Plate 31 - Spanish infantry flags captured by the French in Catalonia, probably belonging to the tercios of the Kingdom of Granada (1690s) and Piedmont (1690–1693); others whose capture has not been recorded. [Drawings by Robert Hall from Les Triomphes de Louis XIV, Bibliothèque Nationale, Paris]

▲ *Plate 32 - Cavalry banners of the Spanish armies (1690s), Milan and Flanders. [Drawings by Robert Hall from 'Les Triomphes de Louis XIV' Bibliothèque Nationale Paris]*

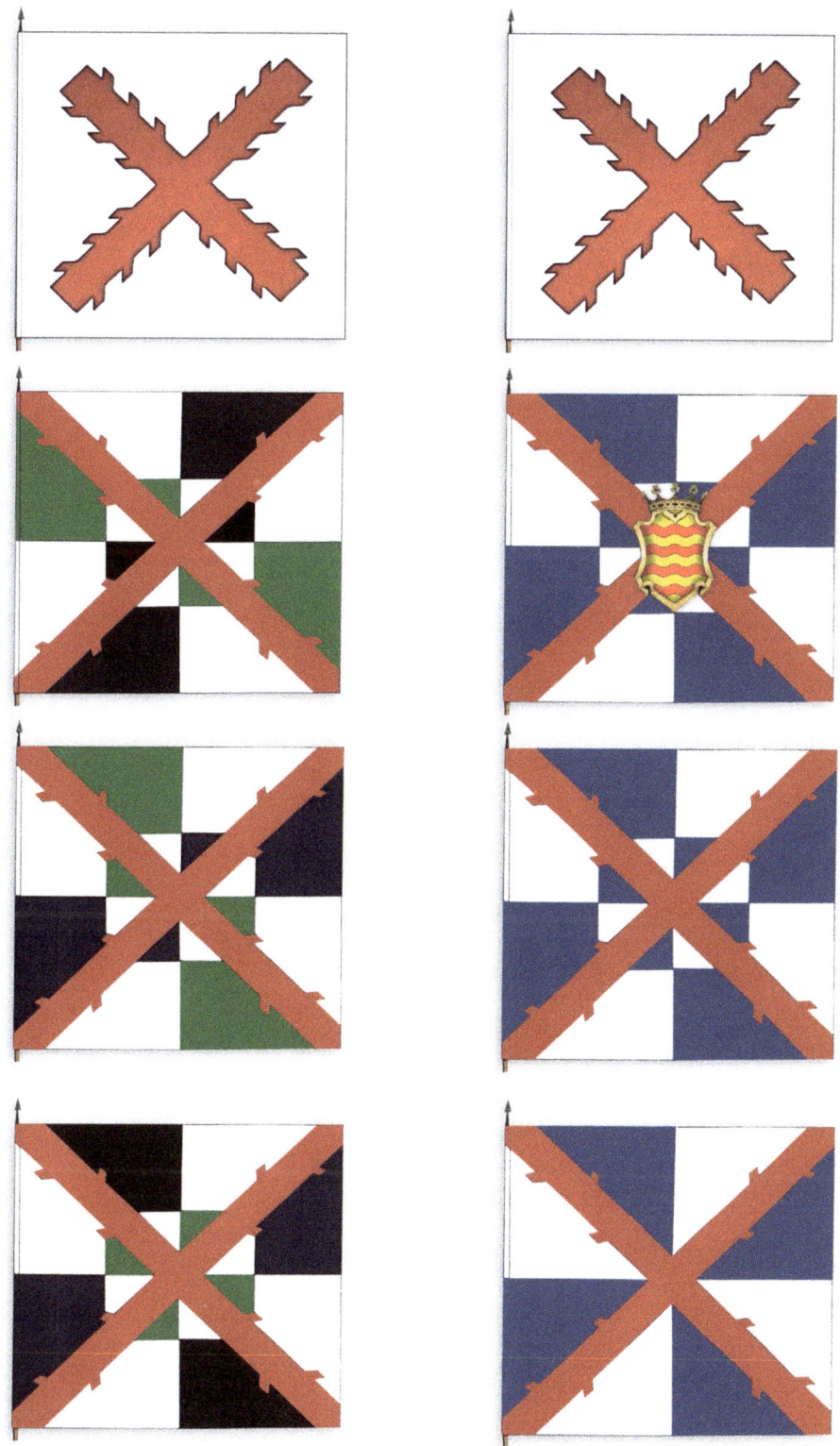

▲ *Plate 33 - From 1694 onwards, the tercios carried four flags onto the battlefield: the field master's flag was normally simpler, perhaps with a white background and a red cross, while the other three, belonging to the captains, were perhaps similar in design and colour. The table shows a hypothetical grouping of flags shown in the Triomphes of Louis XIV (hypothesis and reconstruction by A. Manzano).*

▲ Plate 34 - 1-2-3 Flags of Milanese militia tercios (from several contemporary paintings); 4 flags of the Tercio de la Diputacion de Cataluña and 5 of the Ciutat de Barcelona (From RIART, Francesc; HERNANDEZ F., Xavier. 'Soldats, Guerrers i Combatents de los Paisos Catalans' 2014) and finally the 6th an Asturian infantry company flag (from 'Dragona')

The problem is that it is very difficult to attribute the flags to a specific unit because there the name of the unit from which it was taken is not written next to the drawing and the flags are non characterized by particular elements that can lead to the identification of the specific unit. Jean Belaubre, in his study cited above, attempted to attribute them on the basis of the knowledge he had of the orders of battle, made more complicated because the *tercios* were often known only by the names of the officers commanding and there was a certain turn-over amongst the *mestres de camp* (passing from one tercio to another as a function of their seniority) and the Count of Clonard (the only available source for the period) doesn't always give enough information to reconstruct the changes which occurred.

During recent years, Luis Sorando Muzás and Antonio Manzano in Spain have made painstaking research into the ancient (and modern) Spanish flags adding many other new elements of knowledge and related images. In their publications as well as in others (see bibliography) there are various representations of flags, especially for the first half of the seventeenth century.

The current state of research allows us to conclude that in all the Spanish infantry *tercios* the flags (one for each company, at least unitl 1694) always had a (red) Burgundian cross in the middle and often reaching from one corner to the other. The field was, in most cases, divided into geometrical elements (squares, triangles, etc.) of various colours (with the dominance of green, white, blue and yellow), sometimes with a border also consisting of geometric elements (squares or triangles). The distribution of colours remains complicated throughout the century, but towards the end there is a reversal of the trend towards a combination of eight pieces of varied colours, with more or less variations: a border of triangles or small flames, etc., always with the presence of the (red) Burgundy cross.

An important variant is the one in which the Virgin Mary appears in one of her various apparitions, on a full-colour field (red, blue, yellow, etc.) without the cross of Burgundy. These flags were considered the "principal" of the tercio, until at the end of the century they became white with a red cross.

We can find a good example of the variety of these flags among the representations of the Triumphs of Louis XIV already mentioned, in which appear a group of flags of *tercios,* captured by the French in the unfortunate defeat that, at the river Ter, the Duke of Noailles imposed on the Marquis of Villena and his army of recruits on May 27th, 1694. In the plates that we present appear many of the captured flags with the only common motif of the cross of Burgundy in the form of knotted branches. Of all these only two have some symbol that can differentiate them and provide some clues as to their owner.

In the same collection there is another plate with another series of 8 flags taken by the French in their raid on Cartagena and of which three are presumably infantry. The difference with those taken in the battle of the Ter is that in two of the first the cross of Burgundy, always red, has been drawn with straight branches, while the others show knotted branches (probably a simplification by whoever made the drawings). Another group of Spanish flags captured by French troops, this time on the fields of Italy, in the battle of Marsaglia, or Orbassano on the 4th October 1693 show us a similar general situation.

According to Manzano[253], after 1694 the flags in the infantry tercios were reduced to only four (at least on the battlefield), that of the maestro de campo (white background with the cross of Burgundy in the center) and those of the first three captains, basing this statement on the examination of those captured in those years by the French in some battles in Spain, Flanders and Italy. Indeed, from the examination of the known representations, a resemblance between some of them can be seen, which suggests belonging to the same unit, even if to date no written provisions have been found in this regard which explain the criteria for the variants.

The flags of the two *tercios* raised in 1677 by the kingdom of Aragon were regulated by the chapters established by the king: **A.G.S. Guerra y Marina Libro** ... Conditions for forming 2 tercios of Aragon. "(The 4th is that) ... *the flags of the companies bear the branches of Burgundy in the best place and that to ensure that they are different from those of Catalonia there must be some other insignias from the arms of Aragon and I deem it well also that both tercios are clothed in blue as requested in the fifth condition.*"[254]

The flags of the Catalan tercios were made of white taffeta with a red cross (*Ciudad*) or of crimson taffeta (*Generalitat*).[255]

In the "*Historia de Vigo*" it is stated that the flags and drums of the *tercio* of the city (D. Fernando de Valladares y Sarmiento) bore the arms of the maestro de campo.

According to the Count of Clonard (Vol. 9 page 19) the flags of the *tercio provincial de Sevilla*, by decree of 3 April 1642, had a red background with crossed Burgundy batons of a bright red, distinguished from the background by a black profile and surmounted by a golden crown.

A painting dating back to the mid-17th century shows a Spanish company guarding the Royal Palace in Naples with a similar flag with a crimson red background.

---

253 **Manzano Lahoz, Antonio**. "*Las Banderas del Ejercito Español a lo largo de la Historia Siglos XVI a XXI*" Editorial Atenea, Madrid 2017
254 **A.G.S. Guerra y Marina Libro ....**
255 **A. Espino Lopez**. "*El Esfuerzo de la Corona de Aragon.*" ... **A.C.A. Generalitat G. 121/7** *Libro de cuentas del tercio* 1689-1692.

The Walloon and Flemish *tercios* in Flanders generally had white flags with the Burgundian cross, usually crimson-red, in the centre; from what can be deduced from the capitulation for the formation of one of them in 1689 (*Deinse*) each Walloon third had only three flags. However, in a tapestry on the conquests of Louis XIV relating to the capture of Dole in January 1668, a Walloon third is shown with a blue flag with a white Burgundian cross. A painting, now preserved in a Belgian castle of the Marquises of Westerloo, also shows the Marquis's regiment in 1702 with a similar flag, and the flag of the Walloon Guards was also similar; it is therefore probable that many Walloon infantry units had flags of this type. The same seems to have been the case with the cavalry standards of Walloon units (see below). Bandiere Fiandra 1

The Swiss corps almost certainly had flags with flames of several colours and a white cross in the centre (similar to those of the Swiss in the service of the House of France or of Savoy); and, in the absence of more precise information, which we have not been able to find, we are unable to attribute the flags, among those captured by the French, to the regiments to which they belonged.

From a collection of drawings of flags used by the allied armies (Spanish in aid of the Imperials) at the beginning of 1600 we note that even the German regiments of the army of Flanders had flags with the double-headed eagle superimposed on the cross of Burgundy. Still in the 1670s the foreign regiments that were raised for service of the King of Spain in Flanders bore on their flags the emblem of the cross of Burgundy[256].

The same was established in the case of the two Dutch regiments "bought" in 1677 by the Spanish court, which had to place the Cross of Burgundy in the center of their flags[257].

From some contemporary paintings (relating to the battle of Seneffe in August 1674, preserved in the Museum of Dijon) we can see some (old fashioned) flags with horizontal bands of various colors, probably belonging to German regiments in Spanish service. In fact, in more ancient times many regiments, probably those that had capitulated to private subjects, appeared with fields striped in various colours (various paintings of battles between opposing sides represent them in this way).

German regiments in the Milanese army had colours with a Burgundy cross that could be yellow or red upon which there was an Imperial eagle, so as to denote the origin of the unit; in the center there were the Royal arms of Spain with a royal crown at the top. It is very likely also, that the German regiments in the Catalan army had colours similar to those.

Foreign corps that were temporarily brought into service for the State of Milan (Württemberg and Bavaria) or for the army of Flanders, and later also in Catalonia, generally kept the flags of their princes, sometimes overimposing a Burgundian cross.

Milanese *tercios* originating from militia had particular colours; the colonel's had a red field with a central white cross (instead of being white with a red cross as we would have expected on the basis of today's arms of the City), some of the others with waving bands of yellow and black or blue, or white and blue (as can be derived from a painting of 1702 and from the representations of those taken by the French at Orbassano [Marsaille]). The colonel's flag of one Milanese *tercio* carried in the middle a Madonna framed with laurel branches[258] and has been till now attributed to a Bavarian unit, because it closely resembled a Bavarian colour. According to information from the Serbelloni family, the flags of the *tercio* of the Urban Militia of Milan had a white field and a red cross and on the other side the coat of arms of the maestro de campo of the *tercio*.

B) The banners of the cavalry and dragoons

"The Ensign on the day of combat must carry it himself - the standard -, and must defend it, and not abandon it while his life lasts, because by losing it, he dishonours himself, and dishonours his company, and the Nation[259]."

While there are few provisions for the infantry that allow us to get an idea of what their flags looked like, for the cavalry there are, to our knowledge, even fewer written sources to refer to.

According to the Regulations of 1638, each squadron was to fly a damask standard with the royal arms embroidered on the obverse above the cross of Burgundy, and the corps' own arms on the reverse, the first squadron's being normally white and the remainder blue or crimson red. Bandiere Fiandra 2

The cavalry standards were much more decorated and embroidered than the infantry colours, and unlike those with a greater profusion of designs, heraldic insignia or religious or mythological representations. They were very small in size (50 to 60 cms) and square in shape and it appears that they were almost always crimson red, with Burgundy batons also red, or silver or even gold. Probably those of the Guard units bore the arms of the owner of the body on one side. This hypothesis is based on the fact that there are few representations of cavalry standards, and these almost all red, and that even

---

256 **A.G.R. Brux. Secretairie d'Allemagne.**
257 **A.G.S. C.M.C. III.**
258 **Mercure Galant Oct. 1693** The Allies had three colours for each battalion. Among the flags taken on the field ... *& mesme d'un Regiment Milanois d'ont on voyoit le Drapeau Colonel avec une Nostre Dame & un Christ.*
259 **Don Joseph Antonio DE ZELARAY, natural de la Villa de Tambarria** "*Arte de la nueva guerra, segun el pie de Francia, sacada de los escritos del Señor de Gaya.*" 1707 Pag. 47.

in the Bourbon period this rule was maintained. From some contemporary paintings, however, it appears that blue, yellow, white and other colours were also in use. Perhaps some had one side red and the other in the colour of the owner, as was later used in the Spanish army, in the French army and in other European armies of the time.

The mounted arquebusiers and dragoons had, as in other European armies, double-tailed ensigns, called guidons, of small dimensions, similar to those of the cavalry and like them embroidered in gold and silver relief.

It is also likely that the standard or guidon of the maestro de campo or of the colonel were on a white (or other livery colour) ground.

Among the few identified is that of the *tercio* of Horse of **Toulongeon** [**CRSp27**]: A blue banner with a Burgundy Cross, and on the other side the Effigy of the Madonna [**1706**]. It is therefore probable that for the Walloon cavalry, at least for many units, there was the tradition of banners with a blue background with a white Burgundy Cross on one side. The guidons of the Dragoons of *Steenhuis* [**DRWL06**] had the coat of arms of the Count of Monterey.
The tercio of the Dragoons of *Berloo* [**DRWL01**]: had 4 pennants that did not conform to the ordinances, since the first was White with the Arms of the Count of Monterey with two knots intertwined at the edges on one side and on the other different designs in which two men with 2 swords, two horses and an emblem **EQUESQUE PEDESQUE FORTUNA FERET** are distinguished. This guidon as it is said is the same from its formation and for memory it was preserved without renewing it by virtue of an order of Cardinal Alberoni at the time of his Ministry which was lost with other papers stolen from the count of Ytre at the time colonel of the Corps.[260]

In the graphic representation of the uniforms and flags, in addition to the extraordinary work of Robert Hall, rearranged for this occasion, we also wanted to include several contributions from various authors and friends who over the last twenty years have been able to provide on the subject, and who probably not all have had the diffusion they would have deserved.

---

260 **Luis Sorando Muzas**. "*Estandartes de Dragones* (I)" in *Dragona*, pp 17-20

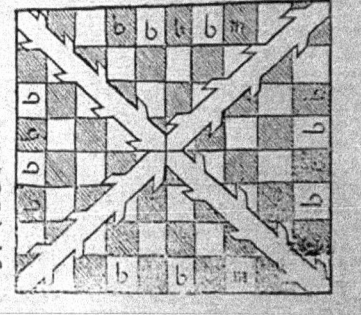

▲ *The first edition of the book (instructions for tailors) on how to make an infantry flag and some subsequent editions. (see also pag. 148)*

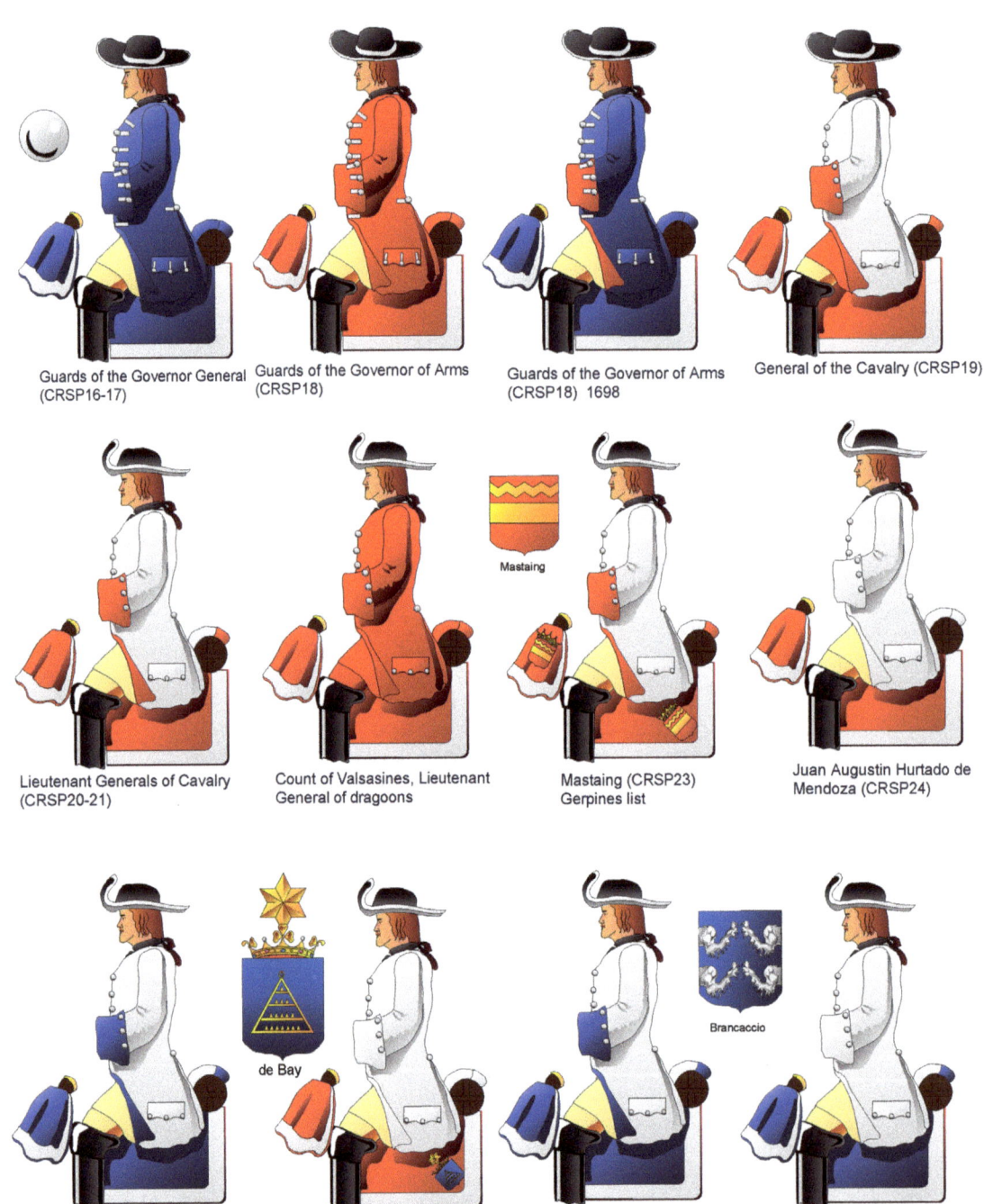

▲ *Plate 35 - 1688-1698 Companies of guards and tercios and regiments of cavalry (Cavallos Corazas) (Flanders) [Drawings by Robert Hall]*

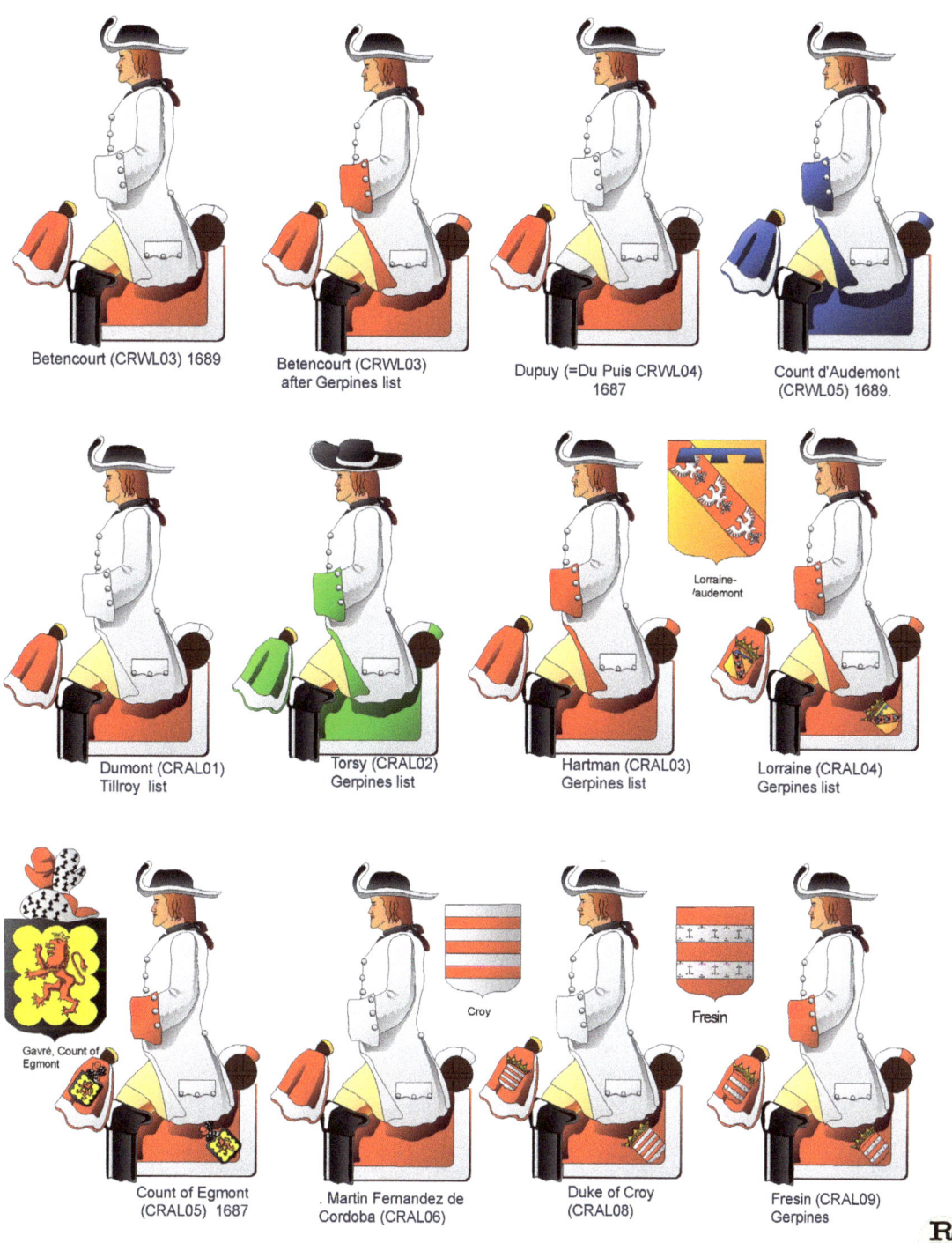

▲ *Plate 36 - 1688-1698 Tercios and regiments of horse cavalry (Cavallos Corazas) (Flanders) [Drawings by Robert Hall]*

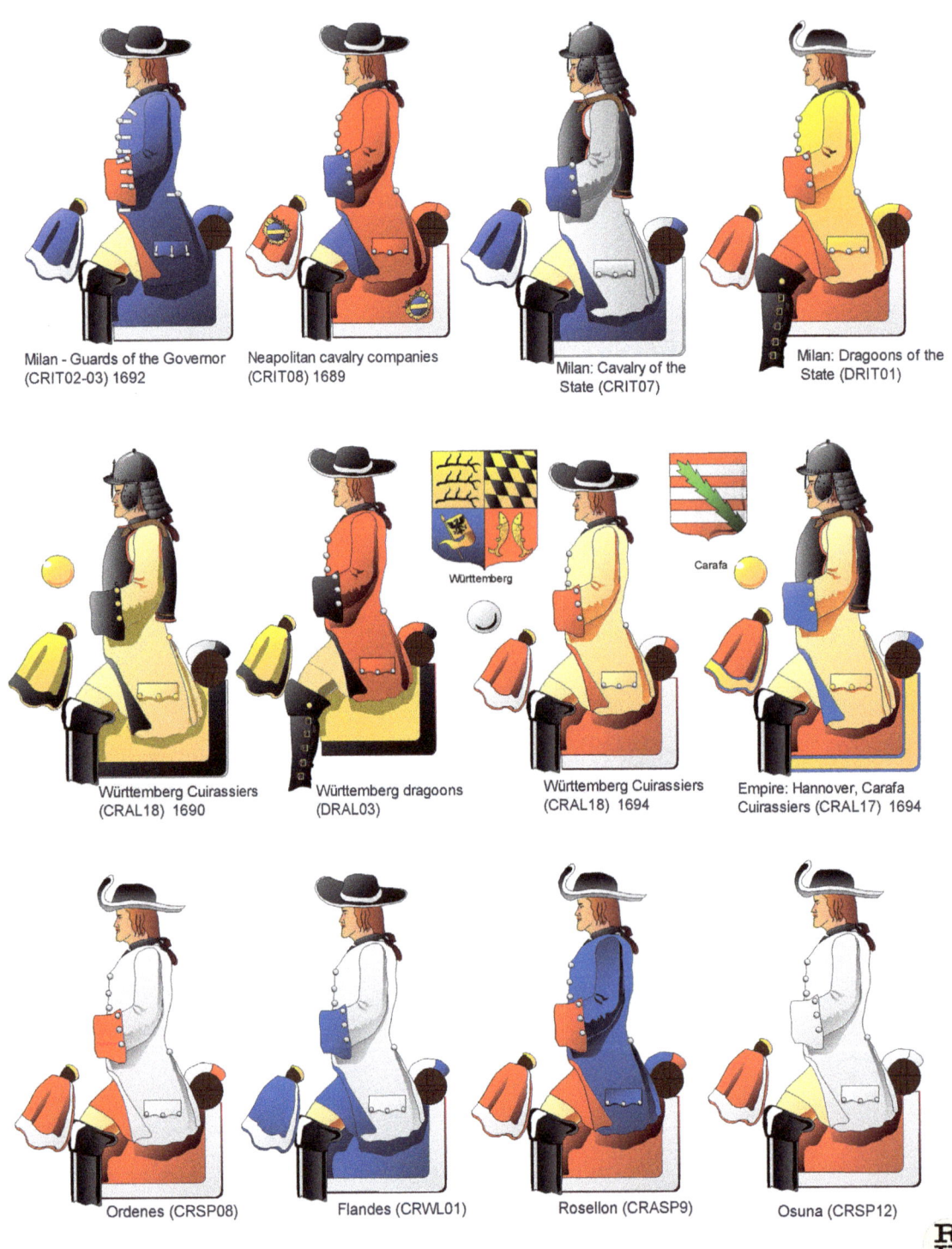

▲ Plate 37 - 1690-1697 Tercios and regiments of horses cavalry (Cavallos Corazas) (Milan and Catalonia) [Drawings by Robert Hall]

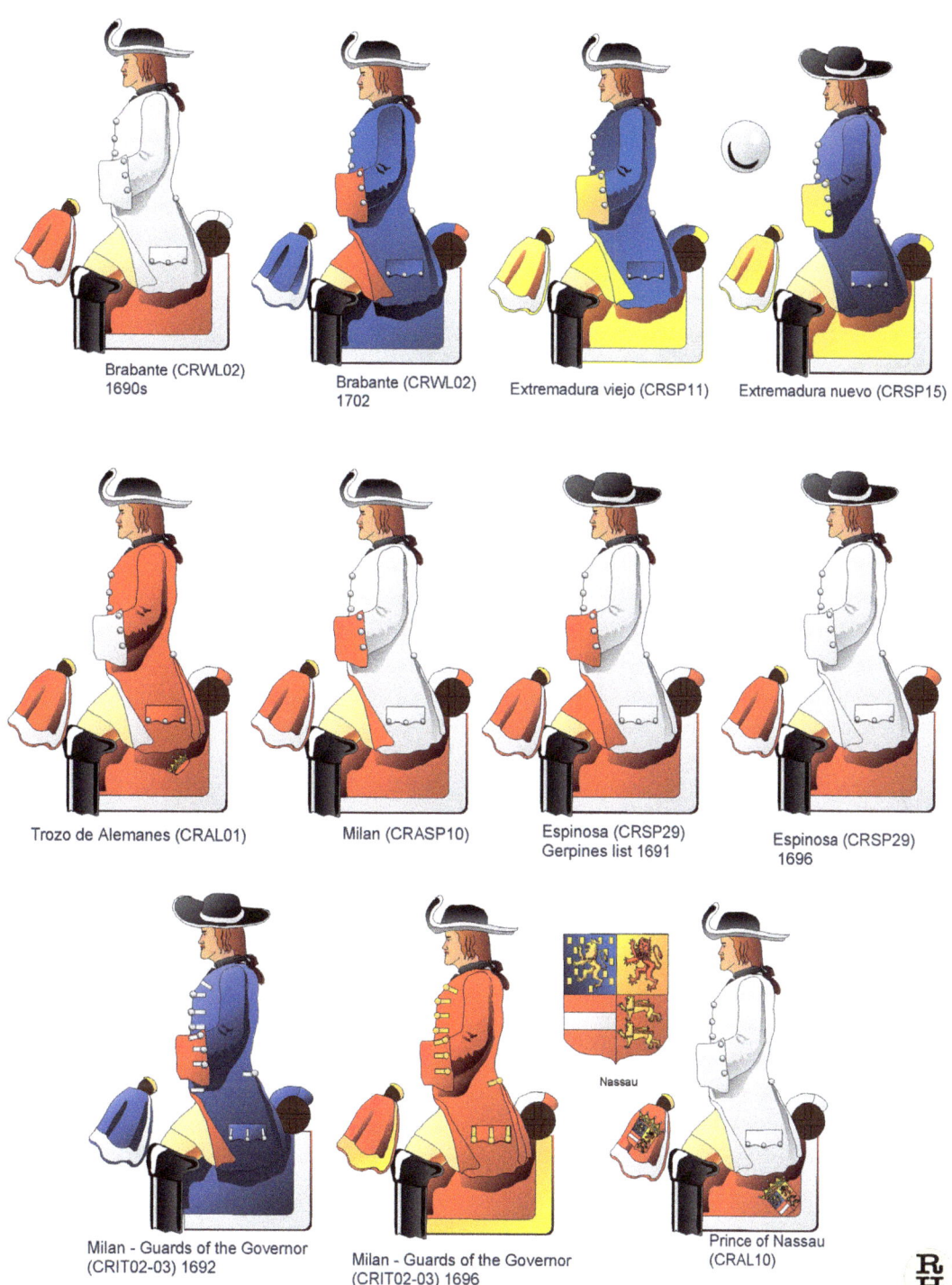

▲ *Plate 38 - 1688-1698 Companies of guards and tercios and regiments of cavalry (Catalonia and Milan) [Drawings by Robert Hall]*

▲ Plate 39 - 1698 Tercio de Cavallos Corazas by D. Joseph de Toulongeon and banner, typical of Walloon units. [Drawings by Robert Hall]

A BRIEF SUMMARY OF THE WAR CAMPAIGNS DURING THE PERIOD

In the following we will quickly review the main events that characterized the war operations on the various fronts upon which the armies of the King of Spain were engaged. While there are numerous "classic" works that describe the events that occurred from the French, English (Flanders front), German and Austrian points of view and therefore also providing data on the participation of the units of their nationalities (and exalting their courage and their enterprises), the same cannot be said for the troops of the Spanish Monarchy. The count of Clonard in the general part of his work deals with the main events, but mainly for the period preceding the reign of Charles II, and the period following the accession of the Bourbons to the throne of Spain. In the part dedicated to regimental histories there are more details referring to single units, but never an overall picture. History books deal with the subjects from a general point of view, but almost never go into detail on the events of the individual corps that made up the Spanish armies, and in any case almost never mention the non-Spanish military corps that made up these armies (also due to the difficulty until recently of being able to find the relevant information). A partial exception is represented by the facts and events that concern the principality of Catalonia, in which case works of considerable depth have appeared (see bibliography and notes in the following paragraphs). A source that has proved notable for the wealth of details that it has been able to provide and which has so far often been overlooked by studies in the sector, is represented by the reports provided by the news sheets and gazettes of the time, as well as by the reports of diplomats and figures of the time; particularly interesting is the series of information provided by the different papal Nuncios in the various Courts of Europe.

The war that upset Europe from 1688 to 1697, sometimes called the *War of the League of Augsburg* or of the *Grand Alliance*, since England was added, or *the Nine Years' War*, was essentially linked to the interests of Holland and Great Britain, with those of the Austrian Emperor (Leopold I of Habsburg) on the one hand and those of Louis XIV on the other. The interpenetration of the Dutch and the English, since William III of Orange assumed the government of both nations, immediately gave the conflict a vital commercial and colonial dimension and allowed England to rise to the role of a maritime and continental power. Spain at first apparently did not take part in this dispute and Louis XIV tried to keep her out of the conflict as long as he could. Spanish security was inevitably affected. In 1689, the Spanish ambassador to the Hague, Emanuele Colonna, invited Dutch troops to occupy the strongholds of the Spanish Netherlands to help defend them, since French designs on that domain had never ceased. At the same time, the governor of the Spanish Low Countries, the Marquis of Gastañaga, agreed with the Elector of Brandenburg to "buy" some regiments that were to act as auxiliaries to reinforce the Spanish infantry, while in Spain the diplomatic route was attempted in the hypothesis of exchanging the Netherlands for the Roussillon, which had long been occupied by France. However, neither military preparations nor diplomatic negotiations served to avoid the conflict: on 15th of April 1689, Louis XIV declared war on the Spanish Netherlands, on the pretext that the initiatives of Colonna and Gastañaga were of an offensive nature. A month later, on June the 6th, the Spanish king Carlos II denounced the unjustifiable aggression of the French. The consequence was that on June 7th, 1689, Spain joined the military coalition of the Allies against France, whose troops invaded the Netherlands without no one being able to oppose serious resistance; another French army had penetrated Spanish territory from Roussillon. In Italy, Louis XIV sought to increase the strength of the troops of the garrison of Casale and to tighten an offensive alliance with Victor Amadeus II, duke of Savoy, in order to threaten the Spanish possessions in Lombardy and to immobilize significant troops there.

Spanish Front (Iberian Peninsula-Catalonia)

Once again, as in the past, in the event of war with France, the Catalan front was the one that suffered the greatest attacks in peninsular Spain[261]. In June 1689, when Madrid joined the Grand Alliance, the total number of troops that Spain

---

261 The narrative of the progress of the war on the Spanish front is based in many parts on the text of the doctoral thesis by **Antonio Espino Lopez** ("*El Frente Catalan en la Guerra de los Nueve Años, 1689-1697*" Universitat Autonoma de Barcelona 1994; published in 1999 with the title "*Catalunya durante el Reinado de Carlos II. Politica y guerra en la frontera catalana, 1679-1697.*" Universitat Autonoma de Barcelona, Bellaterra 1999). The correspondence of the Nuncio from Madrid also provides many elements and the text of contemporary reports, just as in the National Library of Madrid there are numerous accounts of clashes and feats of arms, narrated from the Spanish point of view. Finally, the "Gazettes" of the time, especially those published in the territories under the influence of the Crown of Spain or in allied countries, often add news and information on these events. The majority of "modern" sources are instead based on the narration of the facts from the French point of view [first and foremost Quincy's *Military History of Louis XIV* and the memoirs of the

had in Catalonia was officially calculated at 10,356 foot and about 4,000 horse, under the command of the viceroy duke of Villahermosa[262].

The main objective of the French throughout the war was to first occupy the cities and strongholds that commanded the border crossing towards Roussillon and French Cerdania, to avoid Spanish invasions of French territory, then to occupy as much of the Catalan territory as possible and in particular the capital Barcelona, and finally to threaten the coastal cities with naval actions in order to "nail" the greatest possible number of troops into the garrisons, which might otherwise have found deployment on other fronts, particularly in Flanders.

On the Spanish side, the behaviour during the campaigns was characterized by an essentially defensive attitude with little propensity for initiative, especially for risks (Madrid would have remained exposed and defenceless in the event of a serious defeat of the field army), blocking of the troops in the garrisons due to the threat of the French fleet: financial and logistical problems, chronic insufficiency of the staff, also linked to the previous reasons; absence of the fleet in the Mediterranean, little support from the allies, all the resources were dedicated to America and the arrival of the galleons with the cargo of gold and silver !!!

▲ Francisco Antonio de Agurto, Marqués de Gastañaga

The conduct of military operations in Catalonia during the War of the League of Augsburg was characterized by many repetitive circumstances. Due to the nature of the country and the disposition of the forces there was a preference for sieges rather than open field operations and a considerable part of the war activities on the Spanish side consisted of continuous guerrilla operations. The inhabited centers had to succumb alternately to the besiegers of one side and then the other, as was the case of Gerona, Castelfollit, Roses, and finally Barcelona. The war campaigns in Catalonia were rarely signed by significant clashes in the open field. The low propensity of the Spanish generals to engage combat in the open field, the relatively low number of infantry and the profile of the country made sieges the only decisive form of warfare. Therefore the militia recruited from the cities and the countryside became an important aid for the defenses by providing a significant share of the garrisons that could oppose the besieging enemy forces, as well as the guerrilla warfare against the French convoys by the much feared miquelets.

A great concern that held the Spanish Generals back from an offensive attitude was that if the army underwent a major defeat in the field, there would not be another sizeable force in the whole of Spain that could stop the enemies from reaching Madrid.

Even more than the problem of men, the procurement and availability of funds for the war, for the wages, equipment, food, weapons, ammunition and clothing of the soldiers and the poor capacity and attention to the preparation of warehouses and a planning of supplies of *ammunition for mouth and war*, as they said at the time; in essence the Intendancy of the army was totally absent, entrusted as it was to a plurality of authorities often in antagonism with each other; all this constituted a permanent obstacle to the war effort of the Spanish Monarchy [in all European theaters], since Catalonia had a budget with its own currency, for which reason most payments had to be made in silver. The peasant discontent of 1688 - the *Barretines* uprising - represented a serious obstacle to the stability of the Principality, since the population refused any payment in money. There is little doubt that the French could have taken Barcelona, but for the moment Louis XIV's attention was focused on the Rhineland and other theatres of northern Europe, where there were also numerous enemy armies, Minister Louvois preferring that Catalonia should disintegrate from within, rather than launch a costly campaign of conquest.

Unlike other theatres of war in Europe, such as Flanders and Northern Italy, on the Catalan front the concentration of troops on both sides was always small, and for most years the war developed according to the classic parameters of a

---

main French generals, Navailles, Noailles etc...] or of the main ally, Great Britain which, although narrating the facts, almost never have specific information on the actual participation of the "Spanish" troops in the events described.

262   D. Carlos Gurrea de Aragon y Borja, duke of Villahermosa, already Governor of the Spanish Low Countries between 1675 and 1677, Knight of the Golden Fleece since 1678, was Viceroy of Catalonia between 1688 and 1690.

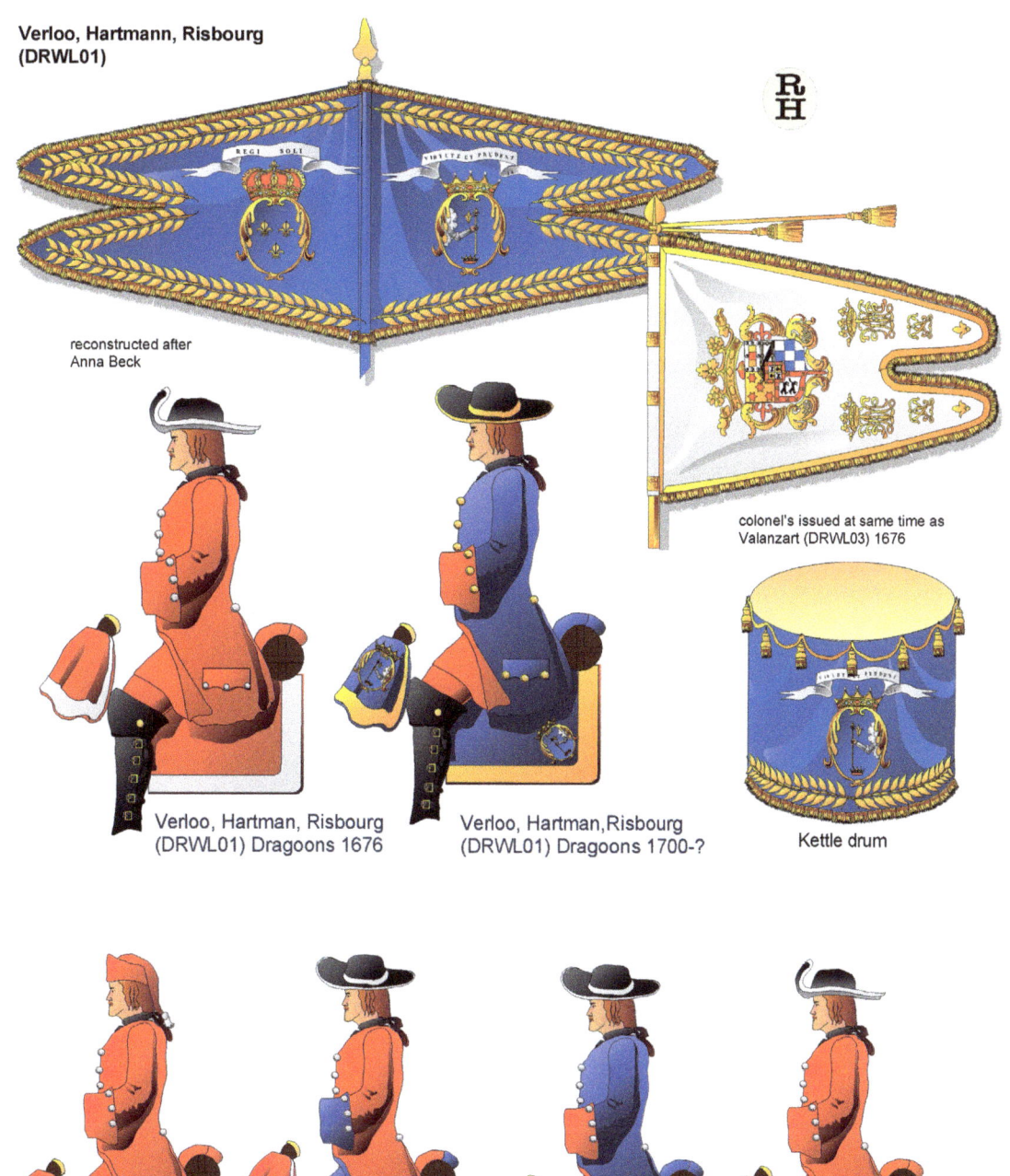

▲ *Plate 40 - 1676-1700 Tercios of Flanders Dragoons [Drawings by Robert Hall]*

▲ *Plate 41 - 1688-1697 Dragoons of Flanders and Catalonia [Drawings by Robert Hall]*

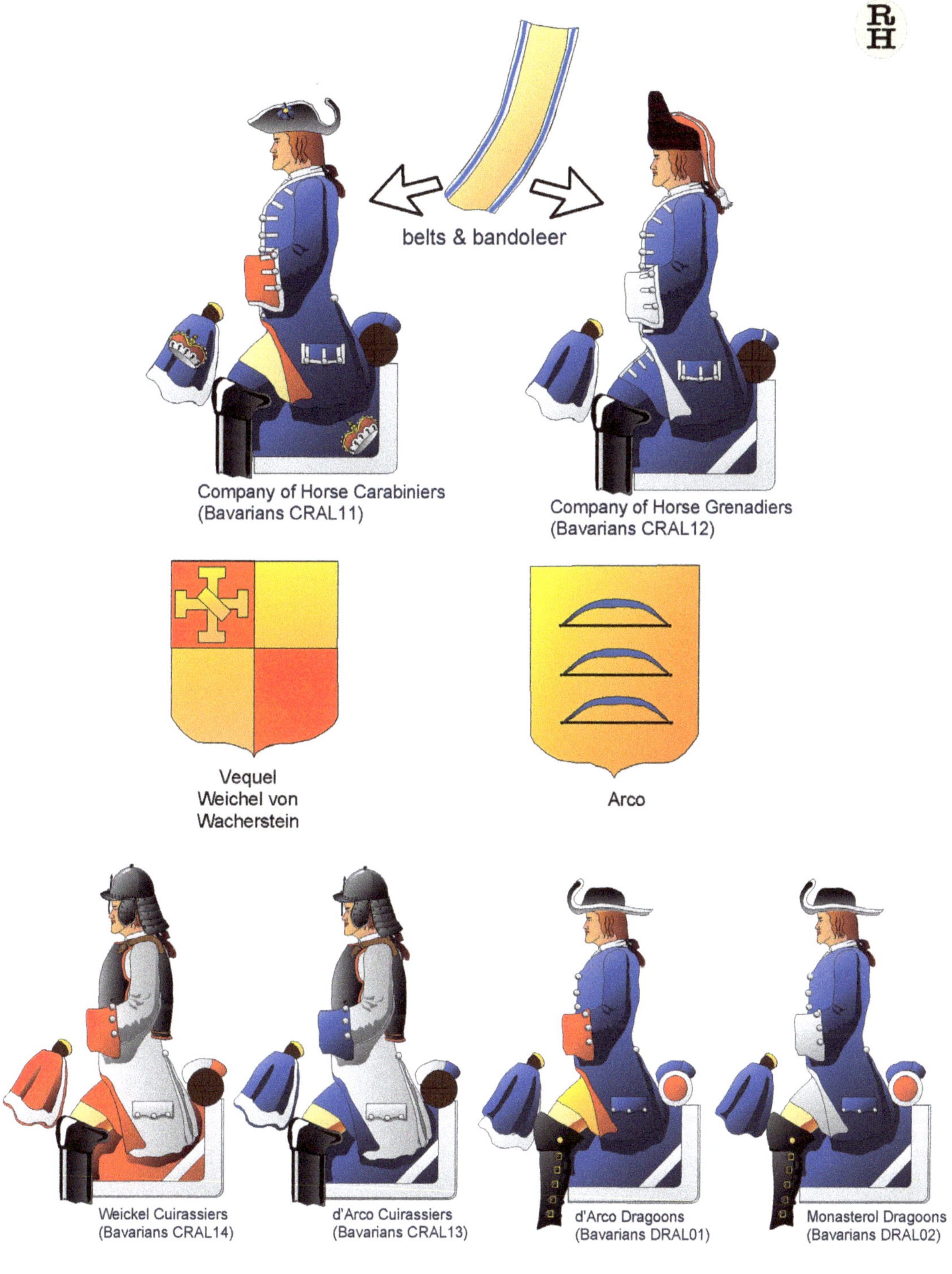

belts & bandoleer

Company of Horse Carabiniers
(Bavarians CRAL11)

Company of Horse Grenadiers
(Bavarians CRAL12)

Vequel
Weichel von
Wacherstein

Arco

Weickel Cuirassiers
(Bavarians CRAL14)

d'Arco Cuirassiers
(Bavarians CRAL13)

d'Arco Dragoons
(Bavarians DRAL01)

Monasterol Dragoons
(Bavarians DRAL02)

▲ *Plate 42 - German Auxiliary Cavalry [Drawings by Robert Hall]*

frontier war. The Spanish corps of troops available was almost always comparable in size to the not vastly superior French army, but a great part of it was immobilised in garrisons because the initiative was always with the French who made use of their superiority in artillery and cavalry as well as an incontestable supremacy at sea which allowed them to threaten the coastal cities at short notice and land troops behind the backs of their opponents. This volume of firepower exceeded enormously what the Spaniards could bring to bear and played a significant role in the fall of Barcelona in 1697.

A different temper was demonstrated by the Catalan people and also because of errors the French made in treating the conquered territory and its population. The people rose up in arms and hindered the march of the enemy troops, representing for a good portion of the duration of the war the major cause of disturbance and grave losses to the enemy (this fact is rarely acknowledged by official military sources).

It should also be noted that the maintenance of the possessions in Northern Africa represented for the Spanish crown throughout the war a constant need for supplies of men and equipment, in competition with the demands of the war against France, since the threat of the Moors (often fomented by the French) to take over the positions still held by the Spanish on the southern side of the Mediterranean always remained present.

Year 1689
France entrusted to the duke of Noailles[263] the direction of military operations on the Catalan border. Hostilities opened in Catalonia in May 1689 when a French army under the command of the duke of Noailles invaded the territory of the Spanish crown from the border of the Roussillon. The Royal Spanish army was commanded by the reigning viceroy, the Duke of Villahermosa, and he set out to face the enemy. The first action of the French consisted in laying siege to the place of Camprodón the 19th of May, the place, defended only by 125 regular soldiers and 200 irregulars, capitulated to the enemy the 23rd of May. The governor of its castle, don Diego Rodado, was accused of treason and hanged in a square of Barcelona by the duke of Villahermosa. The movements of the Spanish were hindered by the fact that they had to defend the places of Gerona and Barcelona with significant garrisons because of the threat represented by the French fleet, against which the Spanish had no effective answer (a situation which lasted for the duration of the war). Only at the end of June could the viceroy disposed of 4,000 foot and 2,000 horse to employ in field operations. Once the danger of an invasion by the French was aknowledged, the Principality raised people for its defence, and the Madrid Court sent reinforcements of troops under the command of the marquis of Conflans[264]. Once gathered together the twenty thousand men of the army Villahermosa decided to recover the place of Camprodón. Noailles hurried to its relief, but neither desired to engage in a field battle, only cannonading each other. The place was abandoned by the French the night between 25th and 26th of August, not without blowing up the two fortresses before leaving.

Year 1690
In this year there were no actions of relevance, the duke of Noailles limiting himself to the pursuit of the squads of miquelets[265] that disturbed French movements in the mountains; to empower himself of some fortified positions and of San Juan de las Abadesas (with the capture of the *tercio de la Diputacion*, maestro de campo Joan de Marimon [**IRSP12**]) and of Ripoll in May; to raise a redoubt on the mount that was between Camprodon and the Ampurdan; and to harvest the plane of Vich to mantain his troops at the expense of the Catalans. The war just started in Piedmont required that 5 infantry batallions and a regiment of cavalry and one of dragoons were withdrawn from the French army in Catalonia and this obliged Noailles to withdraw to its places beyond the border, leaving thus practically free Catalonia. The Spanish army just limited itself to controling the French movements during the remaining of the campaign.

Year 1691
This year there was a tentative offensive advance of the Spanish into the French Cerdanya towards Mont Louis; the duke of Medina Sidonia[266] replaced Villahermosa as Viceroy of Catalonia. When he took possession of his charge the French

---

263 Anne Jules, count of Ayen, duke of Noailles, born in 1650, died in 1708. Between 1689 and 1694 commanded the French troops on the front of Catalonia.
264 **D. Jean Charles Watteville** de Joux (1628-1698), II **Marqués de Conflans** y I de Usiès, Conde de Bussolino y de Comières, Señor de Château-Vilaine, Chargey-Les-Gray y les Foncines, Cabº del Toisón de Oro (1653); Sargento General de Batalla (1667), Gobº Interino de Namur (1675-75) y Luxemburgo (1676), Gobº Armas de Galicia (1682-84) Maestre de Campo General De Cataluña y Gobº Armas del Principado (1695), Virrey de Navarra (1698)
265 From the Catalan *Miquelet*. Name that in the principality of Catalonia received the mountain fusiliers (*fusileros de montaña*), a term that came into use for designating the men of volunteers corps raised in war time. They derived their name from one of their first chiefs: **Miquelot de Prats**.
266 Juan Alonso Pérez de Guzmán, duke of Medina Sidonia. Viceroy of Catalonia between 1690 and 1693.

had just started to besiege the town of Urgel with 7,000 infantry and 2,000 cavalry, defended by about 1,000 men (among them the *tercio* of *Madrid* [**IRSP05**] and that of *Burgos* [**IRSP02**]), which, notwithstanding the efforts of its governor don José de Agullo, surrendered the 12th of June, the entire garrison becoming prisoner of war. Noailles fortified Bellver, where Medina Sidonia arrived the 15th of August, but in consideration of the advancement of the works of Noailles, the Spaniards marched to the East in order to set siege to Prats de Mollo, ending the siege soon because the French were at their rear. At the same time a corps of French troops at the orders of Chaseron succeeded in reaching the neighbourhood of the same town of Barcelona.

This same year a French squadron of 40 sails, under the orders of Count de Estrées, showed-up in front of the harbour of Barcelona, bombing the city for two days (the tenth and the eleventh of July), although with little damage. Afterwards they sailed towards Alicante, where they shelled once more the town, until the Spanish fleet of Count de Aguilar was discovered. These actions created a deep hatred in the souls of the Catalans against the French. The Court ordered Medina-Sidonia to take Bellver, but instead he turned his troops towards Prats de Mollò, and in sight of the place he made the troops take winter quarters, causing a great distrust among the Catalans, who blamed the indetermination of the Viceroy.

Year 1692

In this year French operations concentrated in Flanders; this implied a reduction of the available forces in Catalonia and Piedmont. Spaniards entrenched at Pont de Molins. Medina Sidonia did not show himself very active during the campaign of this year, leaving Noailles able to camp and move freely in the Principality even if the French counted on very inferior resources. Louis XIV ordered Noailles to transfer part of his battalions to the army of the Marshal of Catinat in the Delphinate. Medina-Sidonia fortified the pass of Pertus, and with his army descended to Maurellas in the Rosellon; Noailles, who was regrouping his troops at Le Boulou, turned around the Spaniards, making it difficult to forrage, and obliged them to withdraw. Following this the French entered Catalonia by la Junquera, while the Spaniards entrenched at Figueras. At this moment the orders of Louis XIV arrived asking Noailles for the transfer of the battalions, there not being any other action worth mentioning during the rest of the campaign. Armies faced each other with continuous encounters among patrols and cavalry and ambushes by the miquelets against French convoys.

Year 1693

For the campaign of this year, Louis XIV ordered an intensification of the activities in Catalonia with the objective of taking the town of Roses, the main naval base of Catalonia. The newly nominated Marshall of Noailles with 14.000 foot and 5.000 horse and dragoons, 20 siege guns, 16 fiend pieces and 5 mortars, laid siege to the town the first of June, protected by the squadron of Count d'Estrées (35 galleys), moved for this purpose from the harbour of Toulon. The place was defended by about 1,400 infantry and 200 dragoons with 15 pieces of artillery in bad shape, with very bad conditions of the defensive works. The 8th of June D. Pere Rubì, the brave governor of the place was mortally wounded and the breach was opened on June 10th, his replacement, D. Gabriel Quiñones, faced with the impossibility of receiving reinforcements from the Duke of Medina Sidonia, had to surrender the place on the 13th of the same month. Facing the impossibility of receiving reinforcements from the duke of Medina Sidonia, the place surrendered the 13th of the same month. The French started also the siege of Gerona, after that the fall of Roses, opened on 10th June, then the opening of the breach and the death of the governor. At the end of July a cavalry battle forced San Jordì with losses to the French. The French fleet remained in front of the harbour of Barcelona for some time menacing the town as a diversionary move against the Spanish. After this Noailles adopted a defensive attitude, having to transfer 5 battalions and 12 squadrons to Marshal of Catinat's army in Piedmont, returned to its original bases and prepared for winter quarters leaving the conquered place of Roses well garrisoned by his troops.

Year 1694

The army of Catalonia was reinforced by the new provincial tercios raised in Spain, but the majority of the soldiers were completely inexperienced. The Court replaced the Viceroy, the Duke of Medina Sidonia, with the duke of Escalona, who did not show more resolution than the former. In the months of April and May, many royal troops arrived in the Principality: six *tercios* from Castile of those newly formed, by sea two *tercios* of the city (*Casco*, **IRSP07**) and the kingdom of *Granada* (*Costa*, **IRSP08**) who landed at Palamos, a Neapolitan *tercio* of 1,000 men [maestro de campo D. *Domenico Caracciolo*, **IRIT03**] and other 3,000 men on May 15th. In total, an army of 20,000 infantry and 5,000 horses could be counted on, although the quality of the men in many cases was extremely poor, often being recent recruits and without military training or preparation. On the other side, the French army of Roussillon was reinforced with 15,000 infantry and 6,000 horses. Noailles had entered Ampurdan the 17th of May, placing his place of arms at La Jonquera. According to various Spanish sources, the enemy army consisted of 22,000 to 30,000 infantry and 5,000 to 6,000 cavalry, the lowest figures probably being the closest to reality. Noailles moved from Santa Llogaia to Sant Pere Pescador, while Escalona-Villena passed from Foxà to Verges, near the fords of the Ter River, which he hoped to be able to dispute with the French. The French admiral Tourville dominated the coast with a fleet of 45 ships and in the Strait of Gibraltar there was another French fleet of 60 vessels. The Council of State had requested, through the ambassador in the Hague, the dispatch of a more powerful allied fleet. The Spanish and allied fleet in the Mediterranean currently consisted of 36 vessels - 14 Spanish, 14 English and 8 Dutch - and 13 auxiliaries, mounting 1,440 pieces of artillery with a crew of 7,781 men.

The campaign of 1694 was marked by a terrible defeat of the Spanish army: on May 27th, the Iberian troops were defeated in a bloody battle near the Ter river, not far from the Pont Mayor near Girona. According to the viceroy's report, on May 21st, he was in Girona in command of 12 *tercios* and two regiments of [German] infantry, expecting four more, seven *trozos* of cavalry, another 300 horses expected, with 12 field guns[267]. The French were between Borrassà and Santa Llogaia with 34 squadrons and 20 field guns. The expected reinforcements having arrived on the 23rd, the Spanish army moved to Foxà; the following day the ford of Verges was covered with several cavalry units and a battery of five cannons. On the 25th the remaining fords were covered with other troops, but not adequately because there were many of them and there was not a sufficient number of men available. The following day the enemy approached and the viceroy's army divided into three corps to defend the fords of Verges, Ullà and that of Torroella.

According to the viceroy, "*our entire army consisted of 11,900 infantry and 4,000 horses, which in total amount to 16,300 (including 400 miquelets), most of them inexperienced people who had never taken up arms in their entire lives, and enlisted by force so much so that it was necessary to take them as prisoners, and a large part of the cavalry without pistols and*

---

[267] *According to a contemporary engraving by Etinger, made in Paris immediately after the battle, the corps that made up the infantry of the Spanish army were the tercio of Granada (Casco) and that of la Costa, of Villaroel, of Encio, Porres, Pimienta, Aragon, Morados, Napoles, Olalla, Burgos, Torres, Velez, Venegas, Pignatelli, Papagalidos (=los amarillos), Valencia, Mastrotuccio, Verdes, Diputacion, Ciudad, Colorados, Amarillos, Azules, Cabries (=rgto Cabrera), Beck; the cavalry was composed of the companies of the Guards of Conflans, Guards of Catalonia, Guards of the Viceroy, Mounted Arquebusiers Guards, Dragoons, and the trozos of Ordenes, Milan, Extremadura, Valones, Alemanes, Osuna, Rosellon.*

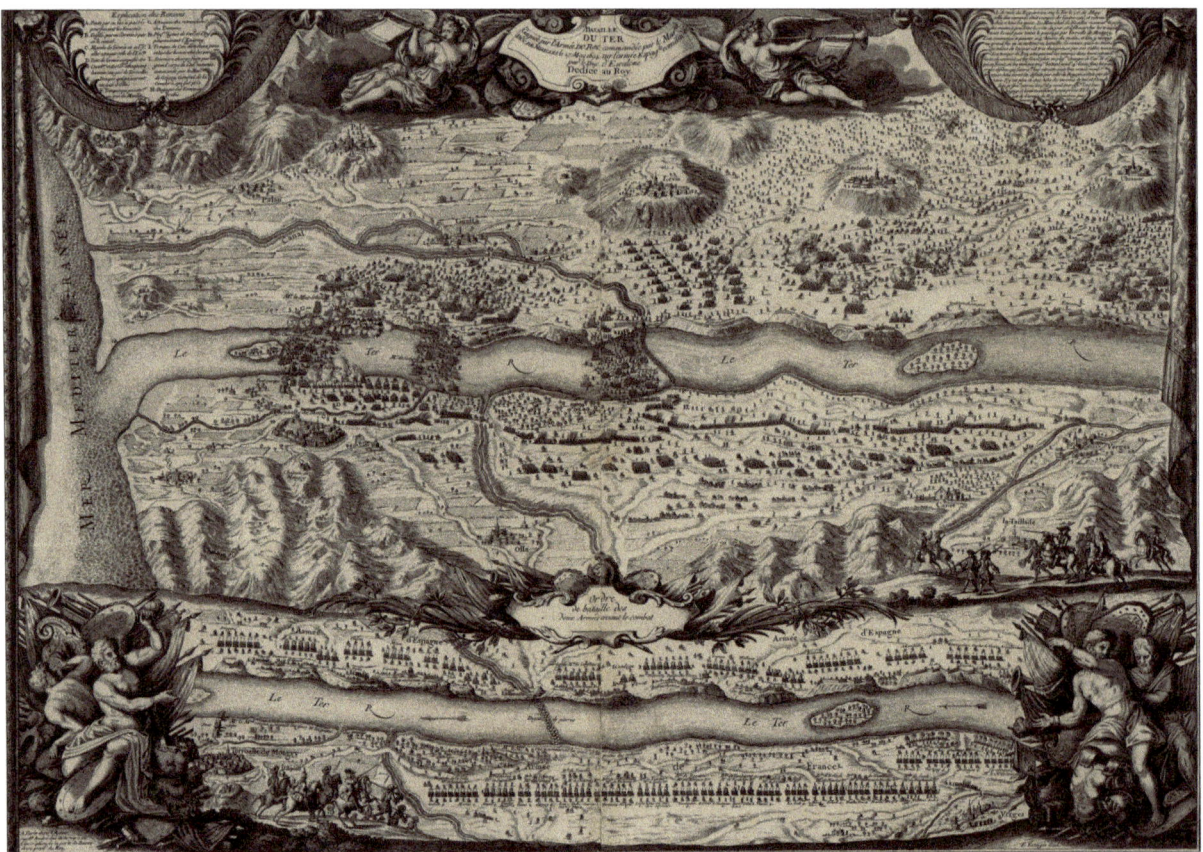

▲ *Battle of Rio Ter, 27 May 1694. Contemporary engraving by Etinger, made in Paris immediately after the battle.*

Tercio Madrid · (IRSP05) los colorados viejos

Tercio Burgos-Valladolid (IRSP02) los amararillos viejos

Tercio Cordova (IRSP03) 1693 los verdes viejos

Tercio Sevilla (IRSP04) los morados viejos

Tercio Toledo · (IRSP01) los azules viejos

Tercio new Burgos ·(IRSP16) 1694

2nd Tercio Valladolid · (IRSP17) grenadier

los verdes nuevos man

▲ *Plate 43 - 1691-1698 Army of Catalonia: Spanish provincial tercios (old and new) [Drawings by Robert Hall]*

Tercio Leon ·(IRSP19) los amararillos nuevos

Tercio Murcia · (IRSP20) los azules nuevos

man 1691

man 1694-95

Tercio Costa de Granada (IRSp08)

2nd Tercio Toledo (IRSp24)

Tercio de la Ciudad de Barcelona · (IRSp11)

Tercio Segovia · (IRSp25) de los plateados

Tercio Gibraltar (IRSp22) los colorados nuevos

▲ *Plate 44 - 1691-1696 Army of Catalonia: Spanish provincial and royal tercios [Drawings by Robert Hall]*

▲ Plate 45 - 1694-1703 Army of Catalonia: Spanish and Walloon provincial tercios [Drawings by Robert Hall]

Tercio Cuenca · (IRSP18)

Tercio Casco de la Ciudad de Granada (IRSP07)

Tercio del Reino de Valencia (IRSP10)

Tercio Henry Gage (IRSC01) 1677-91

Tercio (1673) O'Berny, (1689) O'Neil (IRIR01)

Tercio Diego Porter (IREN01)

Tercio del Conde de Grajal (1680-1684)

▲ *Plate 46 - 1673-1690 Armies of Flanders and Catalonia: Spanish and British tercios [Drawings by Robert Hall]*

man 1684-1685   drummer 1687   Tercio deVexar (Bejar) (IRSP31)
Tercio de Moncada y Aragon (IRSP36)   man 1685   drummer 1685

captain   sergeant   man

Tercio de Mariño / Amezaga (IRSP32) 1701

▲ *Plate 47 - 1684-1701 Army of Flanders: Spanish tercios [Drawings by Robert Hall]*

▲ Plate 48 - 1698-1701 Army of Flanders: Spanish tercios [Drawings by Robert Hall]

▲ *Plate 49 - 1687-1701 Army of Flanders: Spanish and Walloon tercios [Drawings by Robert Hall]*

▲ Plate 50 - 1690-1701 Army of Flanders: Walloon tercios [Drawings by Robert Hall]

▲ *Plate 51 - 1687-1701 Army of Flanders: Walloon and Italian tercios [Drawings by Robert Hall]*

▲ Plate 52 - 1684-1701 Army of Flanders: German regiments; Tercio fixo (Naples) [Drawings by Robert Hall]

the dragoons without muskets ..." The army of the Marquis of Escalona-Villena even lacked the wagons, the contract for the availability of which arrived in Girona, only after the battle. The enemy tried in vain to force the passage at the ford of Verges, and then marched to Ullà and Torroella. On the 27th the French cavalry, aided by a thick fog, forded the river and charged the Spanish infantry: in particular the *tercios* of *los Amarillos* (=*Burgos*, **IRSP02**), of the *Casco of Granada* (**IRSP07**), of *PeñaRubia* (=*Toledo*, **IRSP01**), of *Pimienta* (=*Valladolid nuevo*, **IRSP17**) and of D. *Juan de Nuero* (=*Aragon*, **IRSP09**) were almost completely destroyed. Only one squadron (*trozo*) of Spanish cavalry, commanded by D. *Fernando of Toledo* [= *Rosellon*, **CRSP41**] tried to stop the enemy, while the rest of the cavalry fled, leaving the infantry exposed. Faced with the news of the defeat, the Spanish army fell into confusion and the cavalry fled with the rearguard of the infantry to Girona. D. Josep Boneu, field master of the tercio of the *Generality* [= *Diputacion*, **IRSP12**], kept calm and, placing himself at the head of his tercio and that known as the *morados* [= *Sevilla*, **IRSP04**], he tried to put them in battle formation and face the French cavalry, thus saving many people who, disbanded, were heading towards Girona. D. Josep Boneu, maestro de campo of the *tercio* of the *Generality* [= *Diputacion*, **IRSP12**], kept calm and, placing himself at the head of his *tercio* and that known as the *morados* [= *Sevilla*, **IRSP04**], tried to put them in order of battle and face the French cavalry, thus saving many people who, disbanded, were heading towards Girona. According to the official version, the Spanish lost 2,931 infantry and 324 horses, including dead, wounded and deserters. According to the French, the Spanish losses were over 9,000 men. Among the dead were the cavalry commander [commissary general of the *trozo de Rossellon*] D. Fernando de Toledo, D. Alonso de Granada maestro de campo of the *tercio* of the *Casco de Granada*, the count of Peñarubia and D. Giulio Pignatelli. In this situation the viceroy had no other option than to allocate troops to garrison Girona and marched with the bulk of his army towards Barcelona, where he remained throughout the month of June.

This information is confirmed by a report sent by the Papal Nuncio in Madrid to the Secretariat of State in Rome.

June 10th 1694 <u>Madrid</u>. *From the news that was later received of the encounter of the two Armies in Catalonia, it was learned that under the cover of a thick fog, 2,000 French Dragoons had crossed the river Ter at the ford that was guarded by some Spanish infantry troops. After the first discharge, these troops, not having any defence from trenches, nor supported by cavalry, were forced to flee and, not being able to be repaired by the Viceroy and the other leaders, put the corps of battle in disorder, nor was the opposition of D. Ferdinand of Toledo with his Regiment of Horse* [=Trozo de Rosellon] *availed, who had rushed there to resist the enemy, who had crossed the river with all his forces. Where he remained dead, and the Regiment defeated, after which charging the 4 Tercios of* Granada [Tercio del Casco and de la Costa de Granada], Amarillo [Burgos] *and* Pimienta [Tercio nuevo de Valladolid], *given the aforementioned disorder, received the major charge. The Marquis of Conflans was on the right wing and seeing things in that state he marched the artillery with his Tercios towards Girona, covering them with some Cavalry, which was on his side, with which everything was brought to safety in that Place. It is said that about 2,800 soldiers and about 300 horses were missing from the Spanish army with the loss of the greater part of the baggage, and ammunitions both for mouth (=food) and for war, the mortality of the enemies not being known, which is deduced not to have been less from having seen the river run stained with blood for a long space, where they had the greatest charge. The General of the Spanish Cavalry* [Grigny] *remained prisoner, and among the dead are la Carrera, Toledo, Pegna Rubia* [Toledo], Colon [Trozo de Alemanes], Granata [Don Alonso de Granada] *and D. Giulio Pignatelli. In the heat of victory, nine lands were burned by the French with every kind of hostility and now they are under Palamos besieged by land by the entire army and by sea by galleys and vessels. However, it is defended up to now bravely by the garrison of 4,000 soldiers, although it is a fortress of little consideration, with Mr. D. Ferdinando Pignatelli having governed it pro interim*[268].

Two days after his victory, the 29th of May, the French laid siege to Palamos both by sea and by land. The twelve vessels of the squadron of the Marshal de Tournville blocked any relief. The fortress was defended by a small force of 3,000 men. The breach was opened in the walls on 5th of June. The governor had to capitulate the 10th of June, 3,000 men more remaining prisoners of war (among the defenders the *Tercio de la Costa de Granada* – **IRSP08** - distinguished itself).

The 17th of June Noailles invested the town of Gerona, surrendered over to the French by the Sergeant General Carlos Sucre the 29th of the same month. The garrison was allowed to retire to Aragon under parole of not taking part in any war operations for the rest of the year. Louis XIV rewarded the successes of Noailles naming him Viceroy of Catalonia, of which charge he took possession with great pomp and ceremonies the 9th of July.

A generalized panic caught Escalona and his troops, a situation from which the French profited by attacking Hostalrich the 18th of July, the castle of Corbera and investing Castellfollit the 4th of September, the town was surrendered the 8th of September. The town of Hostalrich had to surrender after the powder magazine was blown up by a cannonball. From this position the French were able to press forward to within 4 miles of Barcelona. Rising popular resistance to the French and on the other hand the actions of the Catalan guerrillas became more intense forcing the French to strongly protect their own convoys. At the end of September the Spanish in their turn attacked Hostalrique, but the pressure from the French from Castelfollit forced them to desist.

---

268   A.A.Vat. Segreteria di Stato (Nunziatura) Spagna 175

Year 1695

During the winter and in the early months of the year the guerrilla activities of the Catalans against the French patrols and convoys intensified and became a cause of losses the French could not ignore. As an example in a skirmish with miquelets and peasant militia near Sant Esteve (in the area of Castelfollit) on the first of March the French lost good 500 men in an ambush and 500 others (killed, wounded and prisoners) in the following pursuit. The repetition of such events caused the French to abandon several minor garrisons. On the 19th of May an expedition of 8,000 French infantry and 3,000 cavalry succeeded in bringing help to Hostalrique which had been besieged in a leisurely way by the Spaniards. On its return the column was attacked by the Spanish cavalry. The Spaniards thereafter put Castelfollit under siege. The strongplace was then demolished and, soon after, that of Hostalrique too, and a large part of the force reached Gerona.

The court of Madrid, faced with the constant requests of troops by Escalona, and the complaints about the feeble help he received from the Catalans, decided to substitute him by sending to Barcelona as viceroy the Marquis of Gastañaga. The new viceroy did not want to expose his regular troops, entrusting the defence of the principality to peasants and miquelets, who turned to their customary hostility without mercy to the French, intercepting and taking his convoys, eliminating his stragglers, taking some small fortifications, and formally blockading Castelfollit and Hostalrich, forcing the French to demolish their fortifications in order to avoid them falling into the hands of the miquelets who could use them as a defense against them.

In the course of the year the prince George of Hessen-Darmstadt[269], relative of the queen[270], arrived in the Principality with a large number of German, Italian and Walloon reinforcements, and clashed with the viceroy and the main military commanders. In August there came a combined operation with the allied fleet (Anglo-Dutch, which had been present in the Mediterranean since 1695, blocking the maritime actions of the French) and the Spanish army was to attempt to force the place of Palamos. Two English infantry regiments and one Dutch infantry regiment participated in the operation, disembarking from the allied fleet. After a few combats the fleet abandoned the operation withdrawing the troops, and the siege was ended without conquering the place. Anyway, at the end of the campaign the French also razed this place.

The duke of Noailles retired to France, ill and laden with glory, was substituted in the command of the troops by the duke of Vendôme[271].

The marquis of Gastañaga, notwithstanding the reinforcements received, and the support of the allied fleet under the orders of Admiral Russell, was unable to recover Palamos. He achieved only that Vendôme demolished his fortifications and retired to Gerona. The only result for the Spaniards this year was the recovery of Hostalrich, although desmantled.

Year 1696

This year saw no major actions, besides multiple encounters and skirmishes, in which the Spaniards often had the worst part. In one of these at the mouth of the river Tordera all the Walloon cavalry *trozo* with its Commisary General, Count de Tilly, commanding it, was badly defeated. Since April the French were quartered at Toroella de Montgri, where they regularly received convoys, that regularly the same were ambushed by Spanish forces, in particular by the Catalan miquelets. On the 1st of May the Marquis de Gastañaga ordered the Landgrave of Hessen-Darmstadt, now bearing the office of general of the cavalry, to bring most of the cavalry to Hostalrique to fortify the town and from there hinder the enemy movements. A significant portion of the infantry supported the cavalry. The French army was clearly superior in number to the Spanish, and furthermore they employed the whole campaign in the demolition of forts, exacting contributions from the peasants, and

---

269 Prince **George Louis of Hesse-Darmstadt** (1669 – September 13, 1705) was the third son of Louis VI, Landgrave of Hesse-Darmstadt. First he fought against the Turks under Prince Eugene of Savoy. He was present at the Battle of Mohacs. Then he joined William III of Orange in the Irish campaign. After his return he converted to Catholicism and became *Generalfeldwachtmeister* (Major-General) in the Austrian Army in 1692, at the age of 23. In 1695 he was sent by the Emperor to Spain at the head of an army-unit of 2,000 German soldiers to help defend Catalonia against superior French army and navy forces. After the war he was honoured in Spain and made a knight in 1697 of the Order of the Golden Fleece. After the withdrawal of the French, he became Viceroy of Catalonia. He learned some Catalan and initiated some reforms, making him quite popular in the region. In 1699 he was appointed General of Cavalry. Prince George Louis was replaced in 1701 by a pro-Bourbon Viceroy: Luis Antonio Tomás Fernández de Portocarrero, and he returned to Austria. There, he was ordered by the Emperor Leopold to negotiate an alliance with England and Portugal to support the claims to the Spanish throne of Leopold's son, the Archduke Charles. After the start of the War of the Spanish Succession he was appointed the head of the Austrian troops supporting Archduke Charles's cause in Spain. In 1704, under his command, 1,800 Dutch and English Marines were landed near Gibraltar, took the fortress and defended it successfully against a Spanish-French siege, holding off repeated attacks. When the siege was abandoned in 1705, he left Gibraltar and took command of the conquest on Barcelona. He was killed on September 13, storming the citadel of Montjuich

270 **Mary Anne of Palatinate-Neuburg.**

271 **Louis Joseph, duke of Vendôme**, de Mercoeur, de Estampes, Penthievre, pair of France, prince of Martingues, knight of the orders of the King and of the Golden Fleece, senescal major, governor of Provence, and general of the galleys, son of Louis duc de Vendôme and Laura Mancini. Born in the year 1654, and died at Vinaroz 11th June 1712.

living off the country, utilizing as a base of operations the town of Gerona. All this caused such a number of complaints by the Catalans against the viceroy Gastañaga and against the Maestre de Campo General marquis de Villadarias, that the Court at Madrid resolved to replace both. The charge of viceroy was provided to Don Francisco de Velasco, and as Maestre de Campo General the count de Corzana was nominated in his place. On the 1st of June the French cavalry, supported by 6.000 infantry, moved against Hessen-Darmstadt between Masanes and Hostalric. The Landgrave, surrounded by the enemy, had to open his way sword in hand. The losses were equal on both sides, but some of the retreating cavalry diffused panic in Barcelona. Vendôme attacked Castellciutat with 1,500 men, the place being defended by the marquis de Preu. Gastañaga did not want to risk his troops before the arrival of the new viceroy. This inactivity originated many a protest from the Catalans. A review of the army exposed a force similar to that of the enemy. On the 17th of June D. Francisco de Velasco took over as the new viceroy. He did not change the defensive attitude of the Spanish army, leaving free the way to the French incursions. On the 8th of August the *Trozo de Estremadura* [**CRSP11**] and miquelets tried an ambush against the enemies, with no result. The campaign ended with the French harassing the small villages and the country, sometimes encountered by the regular troops, always suffering from the miquelets and the countrymen, who in turn suffered actions of reprisal.

Year 1697 The siege of Barcelona and the end of the War

At the beginning of 1697 it was clear that France would conduct that campaign by attacking Catalonia hard, Vendôme's army having been reinforced with part of Marshal Catinat's troops, freed from the Piedmontese theatre. For the Empire and for the Elector of Bavaria it was essential that Charles II did not accept the neutrality of Catalonia, because this would

▲ *Contemporary engraving of the Plànol, depicting the siege of Barcelona in 1697.*

have meant a greater French presence on the Rhine and Flanders front. For the Maritime Powers, without a doubt, the prolongation of the war was no longer essential, and therefore there was no presence of the allied fleet in the Mediterranean to protect the Catalan coasts. In fact the allies could accept peace counting on the fact that Louis XIV could keep Strasbourg and Luxembourg, what happened on the Savoy-Piedmont and Catalonia frontier did not matter to them in the least. For some court ministers, peace was necessary without prolonging useless war actions in Catalonia. Viceroy Velasco came to believe that Barcelona would not be besieged, but that the enemy would only attempt demonstrations of force to obtain peace, especially considering that England and Holland were working to end hostilities. The author of the Annals Consulars explains that it was the imperial envoy, Count Harrach, who convinced the Spanish court to prolong the war in Catalonia. Two parties were created: for the Francophile party, to which Viceroy Velasco is usually associated, only the surrender of Barcelona would allow peace. However, at the same level, the Austrian party believed that it was necessary to prolong the war while avoiding the fall of the city.

Viceroy Velasco sounded out the Councilors to see what efforts the city could make to complete its system of fortifications. According to Velasco, if Barcelona were to present its defenses to the enemy in good order, the enemy would have to field an enormous army for the siege, which, if it were to last, would force him to withdraw due to lack of aid. The city granted 128,000 reales to build a bastion in front of the Tallers gate. The Council of One Hundred, in return, asked the king for the means necessary to keep the French as far away from Barcelona as possible. Although the Court apparently took the threat seriously and began raising funds, only 320,000 reales arrived in Velasco, an amount insufficient to maintain the troops, especially the veterans and foreign ones.

Louis XIV, having already started negotiations for peace, and in order to be able to negotiate with Spain from a stronger position, ordered Vendôme to besiege Barcelona with an army of 24,000 men. The siege started on the 12th of June, at the same time that count d'Estrées blocked the town by the sea with the fleets of Toulon and Marseille. The viceroy Velasco left within its walls 11,000 men from the regular army under the command of Count de Corzana and of prince George of Darmstadt supported by 4,000 militiamen, and retired to his head-quarters at Molins de Rey. The cavalry kept to the hills to disturb French movements as far as possible. All the same Vendôme won an encounter with the Spanish forces on the 14th of July near that village, capturing even the trunks, the baton and the money of the Spanish viceroy, who was not up to the situation.

The defence of Barcelona was carried out with exceptional zeal by the militia formations, with some of their chiefs (Agullo, Boneu) at their head, and with some discredit of Count de Corzana and the guarrison of regular troops. The higher volume of heavy fire by the French army at last overcame the resistance of the Spanish troops, which contested every single foot of terrain to their enemies, but had ultimately to capitulate.

The city of Barcelona agreed to raise a new *tercio* of 1,000 men and the Generalitat did the same with one of 500 men, asking for help in money and men from several cities of the Principality. In mid-April the Prince of Hesse-Darmstadt asked the Viceroy Velasco to draw up a defense plan. Hesse-Darmstadt said that the French had 14,000 or 15,000 men and would reach a maximum of 22,000 or 23,000. The Spanish army at that time had 10,000 infantry and 4,000 horses, awaiting the arrival of the *tercios* of **Granada** [**IRSP 07-08**], and of **Navarre**. Thus with similar forces Hesse-Darmstadt recommended that his positions be advanced to Girona, so that the cavalry could consume the fodder that the enemy would need, repairing the cordon of Hostalric or fortifying themselves at Maçanet. With these measures, Barcelona would first be preserved, the conservation of which was to be the main objective of the campaign, as well as the entrance into the Valley. If the French reached Granollers - argued Hesse-Darmstadt - they could reach Vic, Lluçanés, Berga, Cardona, Solsona and Manresa and, once in possession of this territory, they could move against Barcelona. Ultimately, the prince asked to give battle to the enemy at Hostalric, as had been decided in 1696, since it was certain that an army arranged for battle behind a well-fortified defensive cordon, even if it was less strong by a third than the enemy, could not be routed. Velasco communicated to the War Council in Madrid that all the news indicated the imminence of the siege of Barcelona; he posed the question of whether he should remain in the city, where there were many capable officers garrisoned who were able to direct the defense of a siege, or leave it to organize the preparation of men and food. Likewise, part of the infantry could be taken to the mountain, leaving 1,500 cavalry men in Barcelona. Velasco was in favor of abandoning Hostalric and demolishing the defenses to avoid having to leave a fortification that could be taken by the enemy, without exposing the garrison to certain loss given the superiority of the French. In exchange he proposed to leave 2,500 cavalry men in Montmeló so that they could reach Vilobì, burning the forage, while the bulk of the garrison of Hostalric would march to Barcelona.

The entire War Council voted in favour of abandoning the defensive line of Hostalric. Strategically, since the Catalan army was inferior to the French, it was better to retreat without suffering losses and give battle in the siege of Barcelona. Evidently the Council of *the One Hundred* could not agree and allowed itself to be influenced by those, including Hesse-Darmstadt, who wanted to give battle by contesting the enemy's passage to the city.

Velasco estimated the strength of the French army at 23,000 men, and, in the event of its retreat, he foresaw that with the miquelets and the militia it would be possible to cause them much damage. For the time being he had sent 1,000 horses, 500 infantry and miquelets to the mountainous areas around Barcelona with the task of guarding that area. In the end, the solution adopted by Velasco was to also accept the formation of the *Coronella* of the city of Barcelona, composed of 4,000 men, who would take care of the defenses of the walls. Velasco brought 10,000 infantry and 1,300 horses into the city, in addition to the 4,000 men of the Tercio de la Coronela. The viceroy moved with the rest of the campaign army to Martorell, a position from which he could immediately reach Barcelona by means of the Royal Road and, at the same time, guard the interior of the territory in case of a French attack up to Vic, Cardona or Lleida. Vendôme had 18,000 infantry, 6,000 horses and a fleet of 14 vessels, 30 galleys, 3 palandres and 80 auxiliary vessels. His artillery train consisted of 56 cannons and 18 mortars.

In Barcelona, the Maestro de campo general, Count de la Corzana, remained as Governor-in-Chief, with the Prince of Hesse-Darmstadt, general of the cavalry, as his assistant, the Count de la Rosa, governor of the place, and also the generals Pignatelli, Gondolfo, Corada, Acuña, the Count of Peñarrubia, Salinas, Don Josep Agullò, the Marquis of Preu, and, as a volunteer, the Marquis of Aytona. In the first week of June 1697 the enemy attacked the city's defenses. The invader's fleet operated by sea. The French camped on the mountain range of Besòs, from Sant Adrià to Badalona, where they made fascines; their right wing passed through Esplugues and they had their main warehouse in San Martì. On the 7th the *tercio del Casco* [**IRSP07**] and the *tercio della Costa de Granada* [**IRSP08**] arrived to reinforce the army, so that the garrison was reinforced by 1,700 men. On the 11th the viceroy Velasco returned to Barcelona holding a war council and ordering the printing of a proclamation in which the general call-up of the Popular Militia was called for the 18th of June. The Maestro de Campo Marimon went down with 500 men to reinforce the garrison of Montjuic, but on the 12th Vendôme decided to concentrate his attack between the Portal Nou and the Portal de l'Angel. The French occupied and fortified the convent of the Capuchins and the convent of Jesus, approaching the walls. On the 15th Vendôme moved his right wing from Esplugues to Sants, garrisoning the Sarrià neighborhood, where the bread ovens were. His quarters were set up in the convent of Gracia. With their cavalry they foraged from Hospitalet to Sarrià and Collserola, devastating a vast portion of the land. Between the two armies they eliminated all the grain that was in the surrounding area, leaving behind the French neither doors nor windows of the houses of the villages through which they passed. The miquelets in the service of France controlled the roads leading to Barcelona, plundering anyone who ventured there, but despite the presence of the enemy, 70 Majorcan artillerymen managed to enter Barcelona. On the night between the 15th and the 16th the French began to build trenches up to the Capuchins Convent, making two branches in which 800 and 1,200 men worked respectively. On the 16th the bombardment continued until midday by two boats and a dismasted ship. The besieged responded by firing on the batteries installed by the enemy in the Convent of Jesus and that of the Capuchins, complaining a lot that Velasco had not demolished both buildings, especially after the experience of Girona in 1694. On the 27th, the land bombardment began at 5 a.m. from the Capuchins battery with two mortars and 10 cannons. Among the first victims were 4 quartermasters who had gone to get bread for the troops from a place where a bomb had fallen. The French placed another battery of 12 40-pound cannons each to pound the walls at the indicated point. On this day, someone from the garrison was shot for the first time: two Germans caught while stealing from the houses destroyed by the bombs. On the 18th the first sortie from the besieged place was made. About 800 men went out and reached the enemy's batteries without being able to silence them due to the lack of tools to nail the pieces. On the 19th a new sortie was attempted from the place. In all this the mountains and the passes from Montcada to Llobregat remained in Spanish hands, after the arrival of the Catalan Militia. All these militia troops were commanded by reformed Catalan field masters, officers who had directed the *tercios* of Barcelona or the Generalitat in previous years, such as E. Llobet, J Copons, B. Bru or J. Boneu. The sergeant general of battle Agullò and the lieutenant general of the cavalry Otaza commanded other detachments. D. Francisco Vila and the Marquis of Grigny were at the front with the cavalry that blocked the enemy's passage on the side of Llobregat.

On the 20th there was a lot of shooting from both sides. From the city side it was fired from 7 batteries installed on the bastions and at the gates towards the French attack lines. The French, for their part, could not use the fleet due to bad weather. On the 22nd the third sortie was made from the place, but it too was wrecked by the crossing over to the enemy of two Granadian soldiers who revealed the plan, with Spanish losses of 200 men and six captains. On the nights of the 22nd and 23rd of June the enemy bombardment was more intense because a French boat had approached the coast and caused serious damage by shelling from the sea. The Catalan militia and the cavalry made several sorties trying to dislodge from their positions the miquelets in the pay of the French and other enemy troops entrenched in the farmhouses near Barcelona. On the 25th the micheletti and the mountain militia tried to attack a French detachment of 600 infantry, who were however supported by another 2,000 infantry and 3,000 horses. On the 26th the French advanced their artillery towards the bastion of Sant Pere, making the defenders of the square an earthen trench within pistol shot of them. From there they attempted a general advance with 42 dead, 99 wounded and 35 captured on the Spanish side. On the night of the 27th to the 28th Vendôme ordered three attacks towards the convent of Jesus with 200 dead and 80 wounded on the Spanish side and between 2,000 and 3,000 Frenchmen, the artillery of the square having been loaded with musket balls, decimating the enemy at the moment they assaulted the exposed road.

On the 28th, the number of mortars firing at the city increased to 16. The attackers' trenches already reached the fence, hitting the ridge of the walls between the bastion of Portal Nou and that of Sant Pere. Between the 30th of June and the 3rd of July, the number of cannons - thirty - hitting the bastion of Portal Nou increased. At Portal de Santa Clara, two mortars fired, causing great damage to the city. The enemy's rate of fire was calculated at 120 balls per hour.

On the night of July 4th to the 5th, the French made three advances to the barricade of Portal Nou with 400-500 casualties on the Spanish side and 2,000 on their own. Twice they were driven back from the barricade despite having partially blown it up and fortifying themselves at the corners of the bastions of Sant Pere and Portal Nou. On the 6th they attempted another advance with 8,000 men, 300 of whom managed to enter the covered street, being massacred by the walls. The Spanish losses that day were only 19 men. On the 7th a reinforcement of 1,400 men from Ceuta and Andalusia entered Barcelona. Between the 8th and 9th of July the enemy erected a battery of 20 guns in the ditches near the attached bastions, with another 9 in other nearby places, all firing at the bastions and to cause damage to the City. Vendôme's main problem was the loss of people. On the 10th, a sortie from the place was planned to attack the French Navy quarters with 300 infantry and 800 horses under the command of the Prince of Hesse-Darmstadt. On the 11th, Hesse-Darmstadt left in the morning and achieved the objective of destroying the Marina quarters, but on the way back they got too close to the sea and a broadside was fired at them from the French galleys, killing 30 men. The losses suffered by the enemy were estimated at 300 dead and 60 prisoners. On the 13th, the enemy's batteries caused a large part of the Sant Pere bastion and the walls to fall, and the French reached the ditch of the Portal Nou bastion. On the same day, the 14th, the enemy blew a mine into the bastion of Sant Pere, but the work fell flat, destroying only one side. Instead, part of the walls collapsed, overwhelming 200 Frenchmen. However, the last actions and a reinforcement of 2,000 men gave the enemy new courage to continue the fight. On July 15th, Velasco sent 1,000 horses to Barcelona, but no new sortie was attempted from the place. The following day, the French made a gallery capable of holding three men in front in width by hammering away at the wall of the bastion of the Portal Nou, but they set it on fire from the walls.

On the 19th Velasco withdrew the cavalry from Barcelona, which had just been brought in, because it had not made any sorties. The French continued to open the breach, as they did the following day. Cannons were brought to the traverse, which was widened with the work of 300 men, and planks with nails were placed on the outside to avoid the assault.

On the night of the 22nd the French fleet approached and bombarded Barcelona at the same time as two mines were blown into the bastions of Sant Pere and Portal Nou, the French attacking them three times, with the loss of 2,000 men on their part and 200 of the Spanish, but the former managed to fortify themselves in the ruins of Portal Nou. At six o'clock in the morning of the 23rd the Germans of Hesse-Darmstadt recovered the bastion that had been lost, but it was not possible to drive the French out, until Don Joan Marimon, field master of the *tercio de la Generalitat* [**IRSP12**], counterattacked by coming out of the traverse and driving out the French who were in the bastion.

But at three in the morning the French blew up another mine in the said bastion and returned to occupy it, since Marimon and his men could not retreat or obtain reinforcements, due to the order given by the Count of Peñarrubia, who that day had command of the Portal Nou, to block the small door of the bastion, arguing because of the danger represented by the possible entry of the enemy from that side.

On the 24th the French attempted to take the bastion of Sant Pere again, but were repelled by the Germans, who caused them 200 deaths. On the following days, the 25th and 26th, the French continued operations at the bastion of Sant Pere. From the batteries of Santa Clara and the other nearby tower they fired at the attackers who were in the Portal Nou. On this last day, 1,700 men arrived to reinforce the enemy. In Barcelona, more than 2,000 men arrived, including troops from Ceuta, the Armada (marine infantry), Neapolitans and 600 Catalans from the mountains. A defensive cordon was also organized to cover the mine of the Sant Pere bastion, placing two cannons and a mortar. On the 27th, the French finished installing a battery in the Portal Nou to hit the crosspiece. On the 28th the French breached the two bastions they had taken, placing another battery in the bastion of Sant Pere. On the 29th those in the place flew a countermine into the bastion of Sant Pere destroying a crescent and killing more than 300 French. On the 30th and 31st of July the French continued to perfect the paths they had opened in the defenses leveling the ground for the final assault. They attempted to land people in Castelldefels and Sitges with 20 galleys and 5 vessels, but were prevented by two squadrons of Spanish cavalry. On August 1st and 2nd the attackers continued to hammer the crossings that protected the open breach. There were fears in the place that they had laid mines - with the danger that the French would launch an assault through the breach opened when they exploded - or that a considerable reinforcement of troops was arriving. On the 5th the French made a call for capitulation.

However, on August 4th, the City, in a letter addressed to the king, accused Viceroy Velasco and Lieutenant General Otaza of having prevented any action against the enemy from the mountains surrounding Barcelona. On the 5th, the French made a call for capitulation. The Count of Corzana obtained a three-day truce to be able to inform Viceroy Velasco who was in Esparreguera. According to the engineer J. Chafrion, in the bastions of Sant Pere and in that of Portal Nou the enemy had lodged 500 reserve infantry and in the ditch and in the breach another 800, with an opening in the walls capable of letting two paired squadrons pass.

There was also a mine in the bastion of Sant Pere, capable of four furnaces, which could have destroyed all the walls with an easy climb for the attacker, and another mine in the bastion of Portal Nou which was very deep.

In view of this information, the Count of Corzana had arguments to accelerate the capitulation, opposed by the Prince of Hesse-Darmstadt, who maintained that the mines were imaginary. In addition to reporting the mines, the French occupied the Portal de Sant Antoni on the 10th and signed the pacts for the surrender on the 11th, the garrison leaving on the 15th, with full military honours and 30 cannons with ammunition for 30 shots. According to some sources, 9,128 infantry and 1,837 horses left the city. The French suffered 15,000 losses and of the 52 engineers who had brought there only 12 remained in service, the rest being dead or wounded. Of the garrison there were 4,500 dead and 800 wounded.

The 7th of August from Madrid arrived the nomination of the new Viceroy and Captain General in favour of Count de Corzana, who in three days, on the 10th of August, surrendered the place, notwithstanding the opposition of Darmstadt and of all the Catalans who did not want to give up the fight. The garrison marched out through the breach with full honours, and from the first days of September a truce began, the river Llobregat separating the two rival armies. The truce concluded, Vendôme once more surprised Corzana, who, in his hastened flight, left in his camp his own coach. This fact practically ended the war on this front, and induced the Allies to come to general terms for the peace. The last triumph of the French on the Catalan front before the conclusion of the peace was the capture of Vich.

Hesse-Darmstadt stationed himself in Berga, with the intention of controlling Cardona, Seu d'Urgell and Berga itself. The rest of the army, with the count of la Corzana, remained in Igualada. In the Penedès there was another detachment that covered that territory. Then the count of la Corzana passed towards the area of Tarragona to control the movements of the enemy who, in turn, intended to head towards those places. According to Corzana Vendôme had 12,000 men in that area and another 9,000 in the vicinity of Manresa. On September 20th, the peace of Rjiswik was signed. The news reached the Court the following day to the great pleasure of the king and the jubilation of the population. News of the agreements reached Vendôme on October 4th, who wrote to la Corzana informing him that he would withdraw beyond the Rio Llobregat to remove the garrisons from the occupied places.

Carlos II exiled Velasco in his lands, naming as General in chief of the army of Catalonia the prince of Darmstadt, who gathered in Martorell the remainder of the garrison of Barcelona. For his part Louis XIV rewarded Vendôme by increasing his revenues.

The French occupied Barcelona until January 4th, 1698 and withdrew from Catalan territory until the completion of the surrender of the places, including Bellver, whose fortifications they destroyed.

Garrisons in Northern Africa

With the rise to power of sultan Muley Ismail the Spanish garrisons in North Africa began experiencing continual harassment, sometimes as sieges and other times as surprise attacks. The most important events that concerned these places were the following.

Melilla

In September 1687 the Moors conquered the fort of San Pedro de Albarreda and started the formal siege of the place[272]. The 5th of October the governor Francisco López Moreno, led a strong sortie against the besiegers that destroyed most of the camp of the moors, even if at the cost of severe losses and the death of the governor. The siege was converted into a blockade, the hardest times being those of the years 1689, 1694, 1695 and 1697. In this last year a well equipped army commanded by Mohamed, son of the sultan, was repulsed.

Ceuta

The first serious attempt was carried out by the bey of Tetuan and Tangier Alí ben Abdallah, who tried to empower himself of the place leading an army 40,000 men and a good train of artillery. The place was defended by the marques of Valparaiso with a garrison composed of just a thousand men able to serve. The garrison was reinforced and in April 1695 it could

---

272 The garrison of Melilla was constituted of four companies of Spanish infantry of the standing establishment of the place, the *tercio viejo de infantería napolitana de la armada* and the *tercio of the casco de la ciudad de Granada*.

count on the Castillan companies of the fixed garrison, four Spanish *tercios* of the armada (*Marín, Barrientos, Canales* and *Villalonga*), a Neapolitan one of the armada, two of Portuguese infantry (*Gomes* and *Mascarenhas*) and one of militia from Extremadura (*Espinola*), supported by two mounted troops. Total 5462 occupants. The moment of greatest danger happened the 30th of July 1695, when the Moors surprised the garrison and came very near to taking the town. The town remained under a near permanent siege until 1727.

Larache
This was the only place that was lost during this period. In 1689 the moors surrounded the place with a strong army with French advisors. In October the Spaniards succeeded in introducing reinforcements into the place, composed of the *tercio* of Neapolitan infantry "*de la armada*" (maestro de campo *Antonio Domínguez Dura*) and a group of artillery-men, evacuating all the women and children that it was possible. The governor of the place was the maestro de campo Fernando de Villorias Medrano, who conducted an honourable defense. The garrison, extenuated and much reduced, capitulated on the 11th of November after defending the place with great valour. Nothwithstanding having agreed that they should have been free to pass into Spain they were taken prisoners and lead to Mequinez, only a hunderd men receiving permission to be ransomed of the 1,300 who composed the garrison.

Oran and Mazalquivir
Oran and Mazalquivir, that depended on it, lived in a state of continuous siege so that they had to be continuously reinforced especially with militia units from the kingdom of Murcia and Andalusia and with the *tercios* of the armada. In July 1689 the garrison was composed by a *tercio* of the town, of which *Diego Merino* was maestro de campo, formed of 17 companies, the *tercio* of Spanish infantry of the *armada* of *Pedro Fernández Navarrete* and the companies of the garrison of the castles. The mounted troops were composed by two companies, the total of the garrison never exceeding 2,000 men.

Spanish Low Countries (Flanders)[273]
In the Spanish Netherlands, the royal army acted in concert with the allied troops (Great Britain, Holland, the Empire and the German princes). The infantry had a role in defending the places (and was therefore involved in their sieges), while practically only the mounted troops were employed in the offensive marches and thrusts. The dragoons in particular also carried out raiding actions in enemy territory or against their lines.

Campaign of the Year 1689
In May 1689, Great Britain declared war on France and sent an expeditionary force to the Netherlands to honour the Anglo-Dutch mutual defence treaty. At the start of the campaign, the forces of the Grand Alliance were numerically superior to those of France; however, there was the problem of their coordination since they had never operated together and never in such proportions. The French army in Flanders was under the command of Marshal d'Humieres[274], who in the middle of May gathered his forces around Boussières. In Spanish Flanders, D. Francisco Antonio de Agurto, Marquis of Gastañaga, governor of those states, and Charles Henri de Loraine, prince of Vaudemont, *maestro de campo general* of the Spanish army, were ready to go into action with their troops; they had established a camp of observation at Arche; Prince Georg Friedrich von Waldeck, generalissimo of the army of the United Provinces of Holland and of all the allied troops, was also ready to move towards Brabant with a Dutch army of 35,000 men, while the German princes and the Empire fielded three separate armies.

The prince of Waldeck commanded the allied army assembled near Tirlemont. Throughout the summer the opposing armies manoeuvred catiously, employed in foraging and skirmishing. The 25th of August there was a battle at the ancient fortified city of **Walcourt**, near Charleoi and at 10 km from Philippeville in the province of Namur. The French (just over 30,000) were repulsed by the Allies (about 29,000), commanded by Waldeck. The battle incurred some 2,000 French casualties against the Allied losses of less than 300.[275] The action brought to a close summer of uneventful

---

273 For the narration of the progress of the war in the Low Countries (Flanders and Holland) we used as a guide the text of the thesis of **Etienne Rooms** on the Army of the Spanish Low Countries, particolarly the part not published "*De operatie van de troepen van de Troepen van de Spaans-Habsburgse Monarchie in de Zuidelijke Nederlanden (1659-1700)*", as well as the text by **John Childs** "*The Nine Years' War and the British Army 1688-1697. The operations in the Low Countries.*" Manchester University Press 1991, which provides an "allied" (essentially British) version of the progress of events, integrating it with data relating to the Spanish army in the Low Countries, taken from various sources.

274 Louis de Crevant.

275 **August 29th 1689** Brusells *The Marquis Governor having heard that General Calvo had sent a detachment of 2000 horses to support Marshal Humieres, he immediately sent General Count Valsassines with 2500 reinforcements to the Prince of Waldeck; and then the aforementioned Calvo removed all his camp, and went to join Humieres, leaving the country open to our men, who can now live there as they please.*

marching, manoeuvring, and foraging. The battle resulted in a success for the Great Alliance – the only significant action in the theatre during the campaign of 1689. It had been an auspicious opening of the war for king William and the Alliance, but for Humières, his military reputation received a fatal blow; in the following campaign of 1690, Humières was replaced by the duc de Luxembourg.. Humières had been humiliated, but due to health problems (an epidemy among the troops) and administrative ones, Waldeck made little attempt to follow up his success. For a few days the two armies remained face to

Having then on the 25th of this month gone to forage a good number of cavalry of the Dutch Army, the Prince of Waldeck received notice that Humieres was on the march with his Army; whereupon he immediately gave the warning signal to the foragers with some cannon shots: in the meantime the village of Forge was attacked by the French Vanguard, in which 800 infantry had been positioned, under the English Colonel Mr. Hodges, to cover the foragers themselves; the attack lasted 2 hours, and the Dutch defended themselves bravely, until Major Roo came to their aid with some cavalry, who was sent to lead the foragers back to the camp; but as the whole French Army came upon them, they all retreated from the village fighting, up to an eminence near the small town of Walcourt, which was garrisoned by a battalion of Lüneburgers, and then reinforced by another. The French vigorously attacked that town with many battalions, and with cannon, which lasted 2 and a half hours. Meanwhile, the Dutch Lieutenant General Alva advanced with 3 Regiments; followed by Lieutenant General Malburry with the Body Guards, and with 2 English Regiments on one side of the town, while on the other side Major General Slangenburg advanced with a detachment of infantry: whereupon the French became confused, and retreated, leaving behind, in addition to the guns, and ammunition, a great number of dead, and wounded, among whom 3 Captains of the Guards, and Mr. d'Artignan, commander of the same, and many others were taken prisoner. While retreating, two French Drummers came to ask for an armistice, in order to kill their dead; and they said that 6 Battalions of the Guards were almost ruined. Among the Dutch, Lieutenant Colonel Grim of the English, and the Major of the Dragoons of Zell, and a Lieutenant Captain remained dead; another Captain, and some few Foragers remained prisoners; and in the town there are a few wounded and dead. The French retreated to their Camp, but the Dutch stopped there until night; and a greater advantage could have been hoped for, if the mountainous situation of the country had permitted them to pursue the enemy. The Marshal Count of Nassau, and all the other Generals, Officers, and common Soldiers, even the English, have distinguished themselves in these actions: and more than 2000 French are believed to have died. [**Avvisi italiani di Vienna**]

Settember 2nd 1689 <u>Brusells</u>... *Of the written action between the Prince of Waldeck and the Marshal of Humieres we still have the following particulars: they had hidden themselves in a forest during the night, 2 to 3000 English infantry, to cover the foragers, who on the morning of the 25th of last at 6 o'clock came out under the escort of 2000 horses, and began to forage on the left of Walcourt, extending up to half an hour from Philipville. At 8 o'clock some French squadrons appeared, to recognize ours: whereupon Waldeck put the rest of his army in order, and it was known shortly after, that the greater part of the French army, was on the march, and their first squadrons began to remove the foragers, and attack their escort, driving it as far as a hill near Walcourt, where it stopped. A battalion of English ambushers defended itself so bravely in a small wood near the village of Forgé, that there was time to second it, although it was attacked by more than 1000 French Dragoons supported by their cavalry drawn up in battle formation, which had to be broken up and separated by cannon fire, to facilitate the retreat of the battalion, and of the foragers, of whom 180 were captured, with a major and 2 captains. The French, wishing to mark the day of St. Louis with more remarkable actions, came to attack with all their forces on the hill of Walcourt our aforementioned escort, which not being yet reinforced by more than a few squadrons and battalions, was obliged to retreat (though in good order) to the Lazaretto near the said Walcourt; and the French put their cavalry into battle there, while ours crossed the bottom, and did the same on the opposite eminence, under the wise and prudent conduct of the Prince of Waldeck, and cannon fire was fired from both sides, with little effect, and only a few were killed on each side; and the French could up to that time boast of having put our foragers to flight, although with great loss; but not content with this they attacked Walcourt at one o'clock after midday in our sight, believing to overcome with sword in hand that small town surrounded by simple walls. There were two Battalions inside, which were immediately reinforced by our men with another, and subsequently with more; accordingly the heat of the attack increased, which was very fierce and lasted 4 hours, while also outside they fought to drive out the French, who were finally forced to retreat with loss, and confusion, towards 6 o'clock in the evening, & to leave to our men the Victory together with the Battlefield, & some small cannons, with 7 Standards. Ours lost there a Colonel of the troops of Zell, an English Lieutenant Colonel, and some Captains, over 900 men, dead and wounded, including the 180 foragers taken prisoners; and it is certain that the French left there more than 2000 dead. Having then received word from Mauberge, that 320 wounded were taken there, and 550 to Philippeville, with a list of how many they lost in the first skirmishes before the attack of Walcourt, which is the following: the Marquis of St. Golay, Field Marshal, the Lord of Chafferon, Exempt from the Guards, and Governor of Brest; the Lords of May-Tiercelin, and of Tibergeon, Commissioners of Artillery; the Knight Colbert, Commander of Vaillapont, Brigadier General and Colonel of Ciampagna; the Horseman of the Count of Soissons; Lagée, Chamillac, Roinville, and d'Aurignac, all 4 Captains of the Guards; Lusac, Donsu, Lusansy, Gayan, du Gassé, and Bineville, all Majors, Captains, Lieutenants, & Ensigns: all these above-mentioned were killed. The wounded are the following: the Counts d'Artagnan, Choiseul, Champlatreuse, Jonsac, Guion, Fonlibon, Boisi, Meure, Nosse, Jouy, Renansac, the Cavalier Salian, Vitry, Mongeorge, la Tur de Champ, Contat, and du Vivier; 8 Officers of the Swiss Regiment of Greder; and 24 of that of Ciampagna, among whom Mr. Vasse Captain, with his Lieutenant, and his Sargent; Borgé Captain with his Lieutenant; Giacomo Maggiore; Clement Captain of the Grenadiers with his Lieutenant; Bourgiron Captain, with his Lieutenant. There are also among the dead and wounded 600 Soldiers of the Guards, 300 of the Swiss Regiment of Greder, 200 of the Swiss Guards, and many of the Regiment of Ciampagna. Of the Cavalry: Ruelle, Captain of Vilpion, wounded, and Condé, his Cornet, killed; a Lieutenant, and a Cornet of Beson, killed; the Knight of Salendre, Major of the Pralin Regiment, wounded; Couvesson, wounded, and about 30 Reitteers* [=troopers], *not including the dead; an Adjutant of the Camp, relative of Humieres, killed; Chevanche, Master of the Camp, wounded; the Messrs. of Chitille, Brothers, Captains of the Guards, killed; Terrasse, also a Captain, wounded, and 26 subalterns, killed and wounded. The list of their losses at the attack of Walcourt will be given, as is hoped, with the next one. The French themselves confess to having more than 2,000 dead, and that their Army, with the wounded and deserted, has been reduced by 5,000 men.* [**Avvisi italiani di Vienna**]

face, cannonading one another at intervals, but no further fighting occurred. Humières returned to the region of the Scheldt fortresses, and Waldeck to Brussels. With the year 1690, the main war theatre once again became Flanders.

Campaign of the year 1690. Battle of Fleurus (1st of July 1690)

In 1690 one of the major efforts of the French was in Flanders, with a strong army led by marshal Luxembourg. The French soon started major foraging actions towards Ghent. After some manoeuvring the Franch army camped at Bossu at the end of June and prepared to cross the Sambre, which they crossed on the 30th of June. Preceded by an inconclusive cavalry encounter the day before on the 1st of July 1690 the two armies met in a battle at Fleurus, that ended in a triumph fot the French at a heavy cost for both armies (6,000 dead, 5,000 wounded and 8,000 prisoners the Allies, 3,000 dead and 3,000 wounded the French). Among the Spanish troops there were the Spanish infantry *tercios* of *Zuñiga* (**IRSP31**), and of *Antonio Mariño de Andrade y Sotomayor* (**IRSP32**), of *Joseph de Moncada y Aragon* (**IRSP36**) and *Gaspar de Rocaful y Rocaberti* (**IRSP33**), the *tercio* of Spanish horse of *Gabriel de Buendia* (who died in the battle; C**RSP25**), the *tercio* of Italian horse of *Brancaccio* (**CRIT01**), who distinguished himself and captured a French standard and a battery of 10 pieces of artillery, the *tercio* of Walloon horse of *Severin de Betencourt* (**CRWL03**), the regiment of German horse of *François Dumont* (**CRAL01**) and the *tercios* of dragoons of *du Puis* (**DRWL0**), *Theodore Valenzart* (**DRWL03**) and of the *Prince of Steenhuise* (**DRWL06**), all under the orders of the General of the Cavalry *marquis of Grigny*[276]. The Allied army retired to Brussels and rebuilt its force, and the French did not pursue. The remainder of the campaign was uneventful.

Campaign of the year 1691 Mons taken by the French (8th of April 1691) and battle of Leuze (19th of September 1691)

In 1691 France fielded a strong army, headed by Louis XIV himself. The first objective was Mons, the main town of Hainaut, that the French army, 46000 men strong, besieged starting on 17th of March and conquering the place on the 8th of April[277], because the allied army led by William of Orange could not bring relief in time. The blow was hard for the Allies, who were not able to react in a decisive way for the remainder of the campaign. Continuing their operations, the French subsequently took possession of the town of Hal, but avoided the siege of Brussels, protected by the troops of William III. The French shelled Liège at the beginning of June. The prince of Waldeck encircled the French army with the cavalry, forcing it to withdraw. On the 19th of September there was a cavalry encounter near **Leuze** (in Hainaut), where the French "*Maison du Roi*" gained a minor victory over the enemies.

The 13th of December 1691 the Elector Maximilian Emanuel, duke of Bavaria, was nominated Governor of the Spanish Low Countries. He brought with him a consistent body of his own troops to act as auxiliary forces of the Spanish crown (and substitute some of those capitulated with other German princes).

Campaign of the year 1692. Siege of Namur (March-June 1692). Battle of Steenkerque (3rd of August 1692)

The 1692 campaign was opened by the French with the ambitious enterprise of the siege of Namur, considered one of the most formidable places of Flanders (25th of March – first of July), by 60,000 troops, after taking Mons and Huy the previous year, key fortresses that guarded the access to Namur. Once more Louis XIV wanted to assist personally at the siege. The garrison, under the command of the prince of Barbançon, was composed, among others, by the *tercios* of Spanish infantry of *Zuñiga* (**IRSP31**), of *Manrique de Arana* (**IRSP35**), of *Diaz Pimienta* (**IRSP33,** the previous maestro de campo *Gaspar de Rocaful* died in the siege), the Walloon *tercios* of the *count of Thian* (**IRWL11**), on the *count of Grobendoncq* (**IRWL09**), and of the *count of Falais* (**IRWL08**). After the capture of the town, the Sun king returned to Paris, while the marshal of Luxembourg took the command of the French army of Flanders with orders not to risk any great engagement. William of Orange led the Allied troops under his command against the enemies and on the 3rd of August a battle was fought at **Steenkerque**, 6 km from Enghien in the province of Hainaut. The fight was very hard. At the end the French won the day, capturing most the the artillery of the enemies. The losses were extremely high on both sides: nearly 10,000 each. The Spanish army at the battle was represented by the Spanish infantry tercios of *Zuñiga* (**IRSP31**), *Diaz Pimienta* (**IRSP33**), the cavalry tercios of *Bettencourt* (**CRWL03**) and *Dupuis* (**CRWL04**), as well as the dragoons tercios of *Valensart* (**DRWL03**) and of the *prince of Steenhuise* (**DRWL06**).

---

276   **Juan Bauptista de Bassecourt, Sr de Huby**, then [since 1691 **marquis of Grigny**.
277   The garrison of Mons included 67 foot companies from the *tercios* of Antonio Mariño de Andrade (**IRSP31**), of Luis de Aguiar (**IRSP33**) and Juan Francisco Manrique de Arana (**IRSP34**), the tercio of horse of Severin de Betencourt (**CRWL03**) and the tercio of dragoons of the baron d'Ourges (**DRWL02**), besides 1,000 militiamen [**Etienne Rooms**]. Among the troops which tried to support the garrison there was also the tercio of Spanish horse of count of Mastaing (**CRSP23**).

▲ Plate 53 - 1685-1701 Army of Flanders: German regiments; Tercio Bonesana (Milan) [Drawings by Robert Hall]

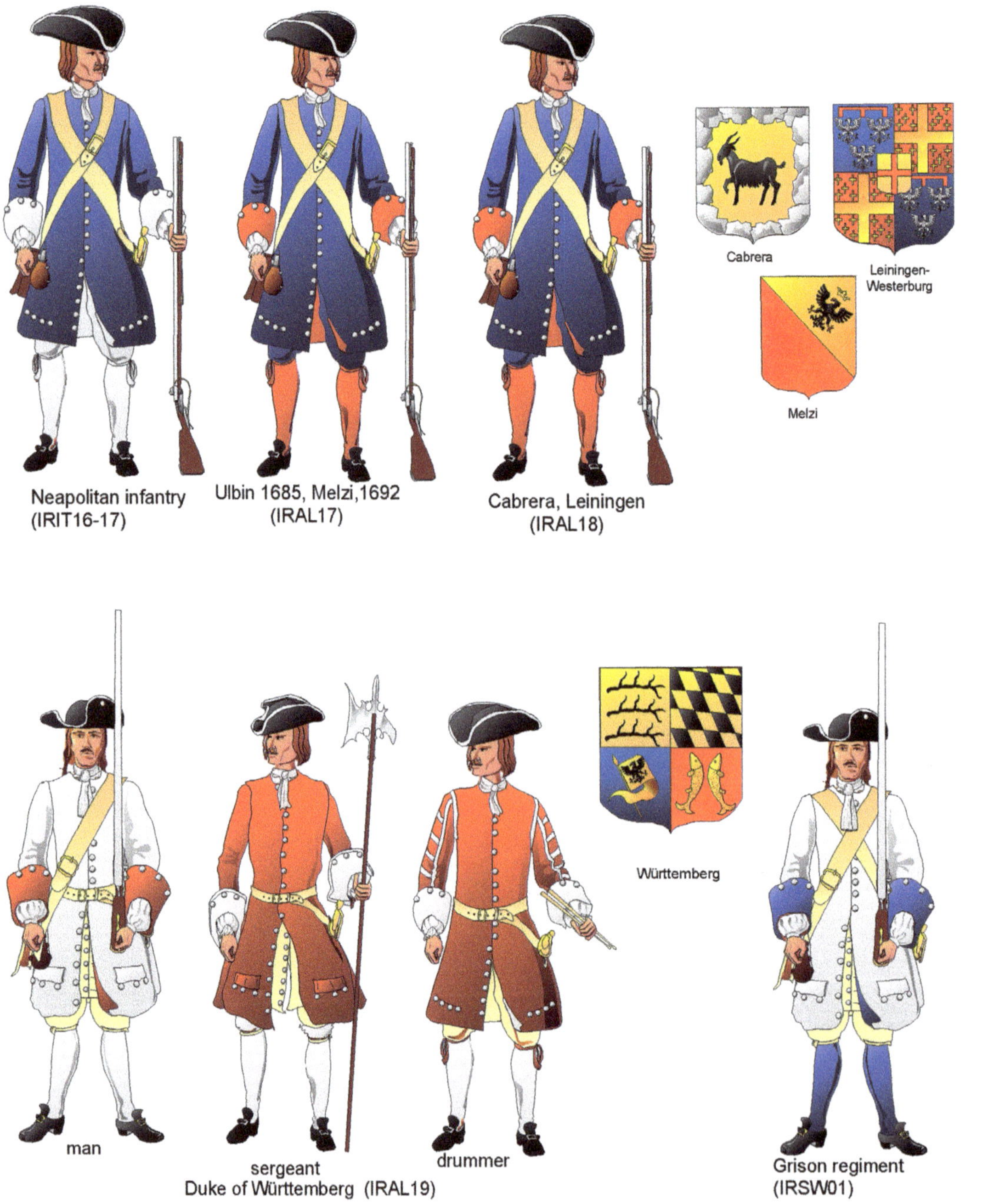

▲ *Plate 54 - 1685-1694 Army of Milan. Neapolitan Tercio and German and Grison regiments [Drawings by Robert Hall]*

▲ Plate 55 - 1690-1695 Tercio de Aragon; Tercio de las Ciudades and of the Gremios de Madrid [Drawings by Robert Hall]

▲ Plate 56 - 1690-1702 Tercios of the Armada (Fleet) and Neapolitan infantry [Drawings by Robert Hall]

▲ *Plate 57 - 1690-1698 German and Neapolitan infantry in Catalonia [Drawings by Robert Hall]*

Company colour

Colonel's colour, (reconstructed)

Bavarian I.R.
Gds of His Electoral Highness
(IRAL14)

▲ *Plate 58 - 1690-1693 German (Bavarian) Auxiliary Infantry Regiment Guards of S.A.E. of Bavaria (IRAL 14 Milan) [Drawings by Robert Hall]*

Company colour, Tattenbach

Colonel's colour, Tattenbach

drummer Coburg (IRAL04)

sergeant Coburg (IRAL04)

Bavarian I.R. Tattenbach (IRAL05)

Austrian I.R. Zweibrücken Deux Ponts (IRAL03)

Austrian I.R. Coburg (IRAL04)

Austrian I.R. Coburg (IRAL04)

▲ *Plate 59 - 1695-1698 German auxiliary infantry regiments in Catalonia (IRAL03-04-05) [Drawings by Robert Hall]*

Grenadier 1698   Grenadier officer 1698   Musketeer 1698

▲ *Plate 60 - 1699 Grenadiers and infantrymen, according to the illustrations by Fernando de Medrano in El perfecto artificial Bombardero y Granadero, 1698. [Drawings by Robert Hall]*

Campaign of the year 1693. Battle of Neerwinden (Landen – 29th of July 1693). Loss of Huy and Charleoy (October 1693)

During this year's campaign the French started to besiege Lieges, and the Allied decide to contrast this. At the beginning of July the French succeeded in conquering the fortress of Huy on the Meuse[278]. On the 29th of July the two armies joined in a battle at **Neerwinden** (**Landen**), near the Geete and near the village of Romsdorf on a small watercourse named *Landen*. William of Orange was encamped with his army between Neerwinden and Romsdorf and knowing that the enemy was approaching had his lines fortified. The French succeeded in breaking the lines of the Allies, after being repulsed three times from Neerwinden. The result was a heavy defeat. In trying to hastily cross the Geete many were drowned. The losses of the Allies were 18,000 among dead, wounded and prisoners. Among the Spanish troops there were the *tercios* of Spanish infantry of *Mariño* (**IRSP32**), *Juan Claros de Guzman* (**IRSP36**), *Zuñiga* (**IRSP31**), *Diaz Pimienta* (**IRSP33**), *Chacon* (**IRSP34**), *Manrique de Arana* (**IRSP35**), the *tercios* of horse of *Luis Borja* (**CRSP23**), *Phelipe Gourdin* (**CRWL04**), *Ignace de Fourneau* (**CRWL03**) and the *tercios* of dragoons of *Valenzart* (**DRWL03**) and *prince of Steenhuise* (**DRWL06**). French losses had not been low either and the marshal of Luxembourg decided not to pursue the enemies, but instead invested **Charleroi** on the river Sambre, that had to capitulate on the 11th of October. This achievement of the French marked the end of the campaign that year.

---

[278] Due to its military importance, Huy was exposed to numerous sieges during the wars of the 16th and 17th centuries: in 1595 it was taken by the Dutch and retaken by the Spanish. Taken by the French in 1675 and 1693, retaken by the Spanish in 1694, it was occupied by the French and then by the Allies in 1701, 1703 and then again in 1705.

Campaign of the year 1694   Huy reconquered (27th of September 1694)
The campaign of 1694 in Flanders was uneventful. The French remained on the defensive, starting the operations late in the season. Throughout the summer the opposing armies marched and countermarched without any major clashes. Armies changed camps to shadow their foes and to ensure new supplies of fodder. For three months the French manoeuvred to protect their system of entrenched lines and to hinder the allied thrusts towards Courtrai and Ypres. In Autumn, anyhow, the Allies gained some success: 2,000 men were introduced into Dixmunde, where the French had failed to put a garrison and they succeded in retaking Huy from the French. The place was invested on the 17th of September, trenches opened the night of 18-19 September and the French governor capitulated on the 27th of September.

Campaign of the year 1695. Siege of Namur (by the Allies). Bombing of Brusels
The campaign of this year was more favourable for the Allies. Marshal François de Neufville, duke of Villeroi replaced in command of the army of Flanders the duke of Luxembourg, who had died in January. The first act of the campaign was carried out by the French, who had been ordered by their king to construct new fortified lines between the Lys at Courtrai and the Scheldt at Avelghem; 20,000 men were to cover 20,000 workers during this project, that was carried out in about a week. During this time the Elector of Bavaria came out of Brussels and assembled an army of 24,000 troops at Ninove, but upon reconnoitring the French lines, he withdrew. Louis XIV ordered his troops to defend the lines as opposed to taking an offensive attitude. The Allied army under William III started the siege of Namur, defended by 13,000 men. The town surrendered on the 4th of August, but the fortress carried its defence till the 1st of September. In the meanwhile from the 13th to the 16th of August the French shelled Brussels, as a revenge against the move upon Namur and perhaps hoping to divert troops from the siege. Among the Spanish troops engaged in the siege of Namur there were the infantry *tercios* of D. *Gaspar de Zuñiga* (**IRSP31**), D. *Antonio Mariño de Andrade y Sotomayor* (**IRSP32**), D. *Juan Claros de Guzman* (**IRSP36**), D. *Juan Diaz Pimienta* (**IRSP32**), D. *Gonzalo Chacon de Orellana* (**IRSP33**), D. *Juan Francisco Manrique de Arana* (**IRSP35**) and the dragoons *tercios* of *Ignace de Fourneau* (**DRWL01**) and *Theodore de Valenzart* (**DRWL03**).

Campaign of the year 1696
Operations in 1696 were reduced on both sides to fruitless manoeuvres, the contenders having exhausted most of their human and financial resources and reserves during the previous campaign, and therefore not wishing or being impossibilitated to risk engage them in doutful confrontations. The French had two army corps under the command of Villeroi and Boufflers, with 60,000 and 35,000 men respectively, while the Allies had a total of 130,000 men. The army corps in Flanders was given the task of preventing the French from detaching substantial reinforcements to the German theatres. Allies disposed so of a slight numerical majority, but the French under Villeroi started acting from Valenciennes in order to break communications between Bruges and Ghent, being confronted by the army corps of Prince of Vaudemont. He was entrenched along the canal from Bruges to Ghent and from this position he discouraged any attempt of the enemies. Another French corps under Boufflers had gathered around Mauberge towards Fleurus. William III with 70,000 men was around the Sambre and blocked the pass to Boufflers. At mid October both armies started taking winter quarters.

Campaign of the year 1697. Siege of Ath. Peace of Risjswisk
In 1697, the command of the French in Flanders had passed to Marshal Nicolas de Catinat, who had arrived in Flanders with a large force of troops, now free from the campaigns in Italy after Victor Amadeus of Savoy had demanded and obtained Italy's neutrality. Despite the signs that the war was about to end, the French marshal with 40,000 men advanced into Hainaut to besiege ***Ath***, a small town, but built with great regularity, which allowed for a good defensive capacity (whose defenses had been designed by Vauban after the town had been taken by the French in 1667). The fortress had a garrison of about 3,600 men, among which the tercios of Walloon infantry of ***Philippe Emanuel count of*** *Hornes* (**IRWL07**), of the marquis of *Merode-Westerloo* (**IRWL04**), quello ***di Thian-Lede*** (**IRWL11**) and the tercio of Italian infantry commanded by ***Domenico Acquaviva e Aragona*** [**IRIT08**]; furthermore there were two regiments from Brandenburg and a Dutch one[279], also assisting in the defense of the square were the tercio of dragoons of the Marquis of Risbourg (DrWL01), of 400 men[280]. The first parallel around the place was opened by the French on the night from the 22nd to the 23th of May (1697) at a distance of less than 700 paces from the covered street on the east side of the place. This was followed on the night of the 24th to the 25th by the digging of the second parallel, 300 paces nearer the fortress. The next two days were spent in advancing the artillery, and on the 27th the French opened fire with 36 guns, divided into five batteries. These batteries were arranged in an unusual manner for the times, as they embraced the whole front under attack, providing enfilade and transverse fire on

---

279   The garrison [of Ath], about 3,700 men strong, was commanded by Gaston Lamoral de Croy, sixth Count of Roeulx, who would later die in the capture of Ceuta. There were, alongside the Walloons, who were in the majority, a hodgepodge of disparate allied regiments, including about 150 Spanish ones, remnants of the poorly formed tercios. ... [*"Recuerdos españoles en Flandes: Bélgica, zona valona con región alemana* "**Antonio Bermejo Herreros** 2008]
280   **Thesis Etienne Rooms.**

the bastions, ravelins and covered streets. Vauban fired the cannons with reduced charges, so that the balls bounced inside the parapets and ramps. In this way in less than six hours the ramps were swept of defenders. On May 28th, mortars were added to the concert and the following night Vauban placed batteries to open a breach in front of the bastions of Limburg, Brabançon and Namur. The inevitable capitulation was signed by the governor *Ferdinand-Gaston Lamoral de Croy, count of Roeux* on June 5th 1697, the French having suffered only 53 dead and 106 wounded.

After this success the French did not move any further. The capture of the city was however exploited by the French as a strong point in the peace negotiations, since the Allied army, encamped near Nivelles and Ath in French hands, left the door to Brussels open to the enemy. Therefore the negotiations went on until the treaty of Riswijk that was finally signed in September of that year, after the surrender of Barcelona, thus ending the long war that found all contendents exhausted.

▲ Nicolas Catinat de la Fauconieres (1637-1712)

Italy

There are not many classical sources for the treatment of the events linked to the conduct of the campaigns in Italy (essentially in Piedmont) during the War of the League of Augsburg, perhaps because this has been considered a secondary front by historians of the past, and above all among the foreign sources there are French historians and memoirists (but they treat the events from the French point of view, and almost never provide detailed information on the adversaries). We believe that among those most worthy of mention are **Amoretti**, **Guido**. "*The Duchy of Savoy from 1659 to 1713*" 4 Vols. Ed. Piazza Torino 1984-1988 (based on mostly French sources) and the "*Campagne del Principe Eugenio*" (essentially Austrian sources and, in the Italian edition, partly Piedmontese) and for the first three years the Special Issue Accademia San Marciano "*La Guerra della Lega di Augusta fino alla Battaglia di Orbassano*", Turin 1993. Information from "Spanish" sources can be found only in the dispatches of the Apostolic Nuncio in Madrid and Turin [Vatican Apostolic Archives], and in contemporary notices and gazettes. Of course in the various collections of the Archivo General de Simancas, scattered among the papers, reports of notable documentary value can be found.

Year 1690 – Battle of Staffarda

On the 8th of June 1690 a treaty was signed between the duke Vittorio Amedeo II of Savoy and the king of Spain (also in the name of the other Allies) for the war against the French, who held the fortresses and towns of Pinerolo and Casale. By this treaty a Milanese army was immediately to join Savoy's army, to be followed as soon as possible by Imperial troops and other reinforcements and subsidies by the Allies (particularly by the so-named Maritime Powers, Great Britain and Holland).

For the entire duration of the war in Italy (1690-1696) the French tried to bring consistent reinforcements to Casale, with which to threaten Milanese territory directly. The French won two great field battles [Staffarda and Marsaglia or Orbassano], but suffered continuous heavy losses through the guerilla warfare of Piedmontese peasants and militia and particularly from the Vaudois in their valleys and mountains.

The body of troops of the Duchy of Milan that went on campaign in 1690, under the command of the maestro de campo general of the army, the Walloon D. *Christian Carlos Christian de Landas, count of Louvignies*[281], was made up of five *tercios* of the Spanish infantry of *Lombardy* (maestro de campo the *Marquis of Solera*, son of the Viceroy of Naples[282] **IRSP41**),

281 **(Jean) Charles Christian de Landas Comte de Louvignies** (30th of October 1603???-20th of October 1696 Milan) Lord of Feignies, Fréhart, Florival, la Hutte, Baron of Graincourt, Prevostle Count at Valenciennes, of the King's War Council, General of Battle of his Armies, Governor and Captain General of the Duchy of Luxembourg and County of Chiny. (April 4th, 1675) created Grand Bailiff of Mons after the death of the Marquis of Risbourg, did not take possession of the city being besieged (from March 15 to April 10th, 1691), and he having died in Milan before the conclusion of peace. **8th of November 1681** Nomination of *Juan Christian de Landas, conde de Louvigny*, maestro de campo general of the army of Milán. **A.H.N. Estado Libro 376.** In March 1682 Louvigny set out, passing through Naples to Milan, having until then held the position of Governor of Arms in Messina. In 1691 Louvigny had been appointed Maestro de Campo General of the army of Catalonia; but then, also due to the protests of the Allies and the good offices of the duke of Savoy, he remained at his post in Milan. He died in October 1696 in Milan, at the age of 92. **A.A.Vat. Segreteria di Stato. Savoia 119.**

282 D. **Diego de Benavides y Aragon, marquis of Solera, Conde del Risco**

of *Savoy* (maestro de campo Don *Manuel Velasco* **IRSP42**), of *Naples* [=*Mar de Napoles*] (maestro de campo Don *Francisco Fernandez de Cordova* **IRSP43**), of the maestro de campo D. *Francesco Maria Spinola, Duke of San Pietro* (**IRSP44**), and of two *tercios* of the maestros de campo Don *Manuel de Orozco* and Don *Manuel de Velasco*, formed with Spanish infantry sent by the viceroys of Naples and Sicily to which had been added the infantry of the *tercio* that the maestro de campo Don *Francisco de Villalonga* had raised at his own expense in Majorca the previous year for service in the State of Milan. The Italian infantry was represented by the tercio of Neapolitans of the maestro de campo D. *Marco Antonio Colonna* (**IRIT16**), who was joined by the new tercio of Neapolitan infantry of the maestro de campo D. Domenico Dentice (**IRIT17**), and by the Lombard *tercios* of the maestro de campo count *Francesco Bonesana* (**IRIT09**), of the *Marquis of Porlezza* of the House of Este (**IRIT11**), of the *Marquis Pompeo Litta* (**IRIT12**) and of the *Marquis Benedetto Ali* of Cremona (**IRIT10**).

The two German infantry regiments in the pay of Milan, commanded by colonels *Michele Ulbin* (**IRAL17**) and *Simon Enriquez de Cabrera*, (**IRAL18**) also took part in the expedition, as did the Grisons regiment of colonels *Sprecher* and *Capuol* (**IRSw01**) and later joined by the two Swiss infantry regiments of *Besler* (**IRSw02**) and *Mayer* (**IRSw03**), which had already capitulated in 1690 in anticipation of the war with the French.[283]

The contingent of troops of the Duke of Württemberg [in Italian and Spanish documents of the time it was often written *Virtemberg*], hired with the capitulation of June 1690 for the service of the duchy, included an infantry regiment, a cavalry regiment (cuirasses) and a dragoon regiment. The nominal colonel of the infantry regiment was Prince Charles Alexander, son of the Duke, who was then very young and therefore unable to exercise command, so in his place a lieutenant colonel was sent who had the effective command of the unit. Duke Charles was the colonel of the dragoon regiment, and in this case too, for operational needs, command was entrusted to a lieutenant colonel. These troops began to arrive in Piedmont towards the end of July.

The cavalry of the field army, all under the command of its general D. Giuseppe d'Azza, was composed of almost all the companies of men-at-arms and light horses of the State cavalry (Spanish and Milanese), five companies of Neapolitan cuirassed horses united in trozo, six companies of foreign cavalry (German-speaking), similarly organized and under the command of the general commissioner Artung, and the regiment of State dragoons, commanded, at the time of entering the campaign, by Colonel Crivelli. To these were added the two regiments of the Duke of Württemberg (dragoons and cuirasses) and a regiment of Bavarian cuirasses, commanded by the *Count of Arco*, also paid by the Milanese treasury. As with the infantry, these troops also arrived in Piedmont between July and early August.

The artillery, as per the treaty concluded with the Duke of Savoy, was composed of 12 pieces served by a large train. The imperial aid that was being collected with troops coming from the Rhine, would have required even more time to be able to reach the theatre of the campaign.

The year 1690 was characterized by the battle around the abbey of **Staffarda** (**18th August 1690**) in the vicinity of Saluzzo, where the French army led by Catinat defeated the Allied army [Savoy and Spain, Huguenots in British pay and some Imperial Cavalry], commanded by the Duke of Savoy. In the battle the Spanish units – practically all the field army of the State - together with the Vadois and Huguenots suffered the greatest losses.
On July 1st, the Allied army moved from Turin to form a camp at Lingotto, then three miles outside the city walls, while in the following days, mainly by the Spaniards, the place of Casale was underwent a blockade. The French garrison of Casale had immediately begun to demand war contributions from the neighboring lands, both on the Piedmontese side (Vercelli and Trino) as in the Alessandria and Novara areas. The Spanards then decided to set up a camp of troops, at Candia in front of Casale, to counter the action of the French patrols and armed the forensic militia of the entire area for the defense of the inhabited centers and to free the greatest possible number of line troops from garrison duties.

Catinat attempted to cross the Po south of Carignano, but was once again repulsed. Recalling Feuquiéres on the

---

283 **7th of June 1690** Milan. (**Avvisi italiani di Vienna**) On Thursday the Pay Officers were sent from here to Pavia and Vigevano to review the troops, which were found in very good condition; and on Saturday the Count Governor passed through Pavia itself to see them, ordering the march, as followed, towards Novara, and returned the same day to Milan. Not far from Binasco he received an express dispatch from the Duke of Savoy carried by a gentleman, which His Excellency immediately stopped to read; and immediately sent the order to the Maestro de Campo General Count of Louvigny, to speed up the march of the aforementioned troops towards Novara, and then towards Vercelli; arriving on Sunday after lunch their vanguard, consisting of 24 cavalry companies, in the vicinity of Borgo Vercelli, to continue the march towards Turin, in order to serve the Duke of Savoy, who had openly declared himself an enemy of France, because he wanted to force the Duke to hand over the Citadel of Turin, the Piazza di Verrua, 3,000 men, and one million lire as a pledge of the security of remaining neutral. ... On the same day of Sunday, the review was given in Abbiategrasso to the Forensic Militia of this Duchy, and of the Provinces of Cremona, and Lodi; and from them 300 men were chosen, to send them to guard the Fort newly erected on the Ticino; and the others will be distributed in the Places, to take the paid people, and use them in the Campaign. The Troops that march in the service of Savoy consist of 6,000 Infantry, and 2,000 horses, and shortly 4,000 more fighters will be sent there. On Friday an express arrived here from Genoa with the news that the Galleys of Naples, and of Tursis had arrived there with 2,500 Soldiers, and good sums of cash; so some Officers were immediately sent to receive them; and the German Dragoons arrive daily in this State, as well as the Swiss, and Grisons. ...

7th of August he launched an attack on the small village of Cavour, which was defended by a company of Piedmontese infantry and the Waldensians, and after capturing the place, the small garrison retreating to the mountain, he had all those who fell into his power put to death (to provide a warning to any town that dared to resist, all the inhabitants of any age and sex were put to the sword, about 600 people including civilians and soldiers), then moving on the 17th of August with 12,000 infantry, 5,000 cavalry (almost all veteran troops and with good and well-led artillery) and 16 pieces of cannon, divided into three columns, preceded by 400 horses, to advance on Saluzzo. Three battalions (Feuquières) were detached against the hill overlooking Saluzzo, defended by the Marquis Marignano, forcing him to shut himself up in the city, whose walls were immediately undermined by the French.

The opening of the breach was however suspended as soon as Montgomery reported having made contact with the enemy in the Staffarda area, reached by 16,000 ducal and Spanish troops who had left Villafranca Piemontese, passing on the left bank of the Po. Vittorio Amedeo, in vain advised against this by Prince Eugene, who had just arrived from Austria preceding a reinforcement of 7 imperial cavalry regiments, advanced with 15,000 infantry, 4,500 cavalry and 12 cannons of the two Savoyard and Spanish armies up to the abbey of Santa Maria di Staffarda, where the two armies clashed the following day (18th of August 1690). The Allies lost the battle and with it almost all the ducal artillery in the field, they had 4,000 dead, 1,500 wounded and 1,200 prisoners (the majority of the losses were sustained by the troops of the Spanish/Milanese army)[284] and had to retreat to Moncalieri. Catinat left a thousand men on the ground, sacked and devastated Saluzzo, Savigliano, Fossano and the nearby villages, then headed towards the mountains; but in the meantime the reinforcements of the imperial troops had arrived at the allied camp,

▲ King Charles III in armour (Prado Museum, Madrid)

re-establishing parity of forces; the French were therefore unable to fully exploit the victory and were unable to join up with the garrison of Casale, given that the Allies managed to block all the fords on the Po, having also placed a strong garrison in Carmagnola. The Governor of Milan, Count of Fuensalida, despite the grave mourning he suffered for the death of his wife, left Milan with reinforcements for the allied army.

Year 1691

At the beginning of the campaign season the Milanese army was engaged in an expedition against Mantua and Casalmaggiore in order to oblige the duke of Mantua (who was also sovereign of Monferrat, Casale being its principal town and fortress and formally a fief of the Holy Roman Empire) to abandon the French side and order his subjects not to assist the French in Casale any further and to demolish the fortifications that he, helped by French engineers, had raised at Casalmaggiore near the Po River on the Eastern side on the duchy of Milan. After some weeks of blockade and a few engagements, the duke of Mantua gave up, accepting the Allies' conditions. By the end of May the Spanish expeditionary corps has reached Piedmont, where the French were besieging the town of Cuneo, that resisted their efforts. In October the Spanish troops

---

284 **August 23rd 1690** Milan. (**Gazzetta di Bologna**) We have received news from Como that 600 horses have been disembarked and are passing through Turin for Prince Eugene, and 1,500 German infantry from Vittembergh have arrived at the Camp della Motta, and the day before yesterday His Excellency had a review given to all the Swiss and Grisons who are in the Places of the State. Then on Sunday General Santa Croce of the German Cavalry arrived here from Germany, who, having received the orders of the Count Governor, set out yesterday by post towards Turin, and at the same time General Heuscien of the German Infantry arrived, who will also shortly leave for the Camp. Yesterday evening sent from H.R.H. also arrived Mr. count Filippo Archinto and immediately went to dismount at the Palace to inform the count Governor of all the success achieved in the battle against the French last Friday at the Turin Camp, that will have been bloody while in our Army among the dead are counted the Sergeant Major Mercurio Gattinara, the Captains D. Felice Giaconi, Bedoia and Gustamante, D. Antonio Agudo, the Sergeant Major Coniglio, the Ensign of the Prince Picco, the Quartermaster Marazani, the Lieutenant Colonel of the Dragoons, and of the State Cavalry there are several dead Soldiers and many horses, among the wounded there are also the Sergeant Major Cignudo, D. Francesco di Cordua, D. Marc'Antonio Colonna, the Captain D. Giuseppe Cordua, Cavalier Besozzi, D. Francesco Altamira, & other reformed Spanish Officers, Captain Gio. Morauo, General Commissioner Judge, General of the State Cavalry d'Azza, a Page of the General of the Cavalry, & the Master of the Camp Count of Louvigni in one leg and D. Giovanni Stoppani prisoner. The Count Governor, although troubled by the death of his wife, the Countess, which occurred on Friday evening, intends to send 4,000 men to the aid of the Duke, and as many horses as he can get from the Nobility.

▲ Battle of Staffarda in Piedmont, 18 August 1690, from a slightly later engraving.

led a successful attack against the place of Carmagnola, that the French had captured in June. The duke of Savoy with the help of Spanish troops tried then to send a relief by the valley of Aosta to the Fortress of Montmellian, that had been under siege for over a year, but the fort had to capitulate before.

Year 1692
In July the Allies, who could now count on an army of about 50,000 men while the French concentrated their efforts in Flanders, after making a feeble effort to besiege Casale that was sustained essentially by Spanish regular and militia troops, mounted an expedition against the French Delphinate. The French territory was entered by three different columns: the third column was formed by about 7,000 men of the Spanish army, while another 1,500 went in the valley of Aosta for guarding it against enemy attempts from Savoy. The towns of Guillestre, Embrun and Gap were taken and burnt and Grenoble threatened, and then in September retiring again into Savoy and Piedmont, after an epidemic of smallpox exploded among the troops and affected duke Vittorio Amedeo himself. Spanish and Imperial troops distinguished themselves in the attacks on the French towns. In one of these actions the commissary general of the Neapolitan cavalry [**CRIT08**], D. *Giuseppe Giudice*, was killed by enemy fire.

Spanish Troops
Spanish Infantry
Tercio of Lombardy   650
    of Savoy   650
    of Naples   650
    of Lisbon   650
    of St. Pietro   650
        tot.   3250
Lombard Infantry
Il Terzo di Alì   700
    di Bonesana   700
Il Terzo di Napolitani   600
German Infantry
Il Reggimento di Cabrera   700
        di Ulbino   500
            di Wittembergh   400
Grisons   600
2 Swiss Regiments   1200
        tot.   8650

Cavalry
Guardie del Sig. Marchese di Leganes	200	
Cavalleria dello Stato		900
Cavalleria Napolitana		400
Cavalleria Straniera	700	
Wittembergh di Corazze		300
Dragoni d'Urse		600
Wittembergh		300
tot.		3400

The Allies moved along three lines, divided into three columns and crossed the Alps with 29,000 men. The first column, with an advance guard led by the Marquis of Parella composed of Savoyards and Imperials, from Saluzzo gathered on 23rd of July under the walls of Cuneo, camped the following day at Demonte and, through the Stura valley, descended into the Vicariate of Barcelonnette and entered the Durance valley in the French Dauphiné; the second column, formed by about 7,000 men of the Spanish troops, through Saluzzo and Casteldelfino and the third, formed by about 4,000 Religionaires [=Huguenots][285] led by the Duke of Schomberg, through Luserna and Queyras. Almost all the allied cavalry remained initially in Piedmont, in addition to two infantry regiments and, between Cuneo and Demonte, two companies for each infantry regiment engaged in the expedition beyond the Alps, in total from 15,000 to 16,000 men, under the command of the Imperial general Palfi, to guard the main places and keep the valley of Susa, Pinerolo and Casale under pressure.

▲ Ferdinando Carlo Gonzaga Nevers (1652-1708)

Through the Vars hill, the main column reached Guillestre where it joined up with that of Schomberg without having encountered up to that moment much opposition from the French troops under the command of Catinat.

The allied troops, after a short siege, took Guillestre, a fortified city with old walls flanked by towers, at the end of July, Embrun[286] and Gap in August and threatened Grenoble, treating the Dauphiné as the French had done with the Palatinate and Piedmont: everywhere the squadrons of Imperial and Spanish cavalry spread terror and desolation; Sisteron, the gateway to Provence, was taken and burned. Cities, towns, villages were set on fire, the population forced to flee to the rugged places, the allied troops collected an enormous booty and imposed heavy contributions. In the meantime, General Palfy, with a large body deployed in front of Pinerolo, protected the supply lines of the expeditionary corps in the Dauphiné and the territory of Piedmont from the incursions of the French, blocking them in their garrisons.

Year 1693

The 1693 campaign opened with the Allied bombardment of Pinerolo and the capture of Fort Santa Brigida near the city. However, on October 4th, French forces reinforced by armies from Catalonia and the Rhine defeated the Allied army in a pitched battle at Marsaglia near Orbassano village (called "La Marsaille" by the French after a nearby abbey), capturing numerous standards and about 30 artillery pieces. The blow was severe - with approximately 8,000 Allied casualties (dead and wounded) - forcing their retreat to fortified positions to regroup[287].

The Spanish army, ... *at the head of which was the Marquis of Leganes Governor of Milan, the Count of Louvigni their Maestre de Campo General, the Duke del Sesto General of the Foreign Cavalry of the same State, and other Chiefs and Officers of consideration by birth and military experience*, bore the brunt of the fiercest French attacks (only Huguenot troops,

---

285 This was the name given to the French Protestants who fled their country and were welcomed in the Northern states, who fought against the troops of Louis XIV, who had persecuted them and forced them to abandon their homes because they had refused to convert (forcibly) to Catholicism.

286 For the siege of Embrun (from the French point of view) see also "*Historiques du 84e* régiment d›infanterie de ligne ..." 1905

287 *Three times the French attempted to break through the right wing of the Allies, where the German cavalry was, and as many times they were repelled with great courage from the infantry that supported it, and with the slaughter of the aggressors, who, not being able to gain any final advantage from that side, set out with all their forces to attempt the other, where with the help of the cannon they penetrated into the Spanish camp and, forcing their cavalry to yield, also disorganized the infantry. To restore both, their leaders gave the last proofs of the most distinguished valour, but without giving the French any time to do so, who promptly took advantage of the opportunity, a large part of the infantry with almost all their officers remained prisoners or dead on the field and the remainder were saved by flight. The right wing maintained itself in much better order, in which General Palfi, who commanded it, highly distinguished himself, ordering the march and the volleys so appropriately, that he clearly showed how experienced he is, not having disturbed him at all to see his own son on foot hit by a musket shot at the first encounters with the enemy.* **AA.Vat. Segreteria di Stato - Savoia Year 1693**

under the command of Mons. of Schombergh[288], received harsher treatment). This is clearly evidenced by the casualty list, which includes some of the most distinguished names from the Allied ranks. Among the dead were:
- Maestre de Campo Don Emanuel Velasco of the Spanish Tercio of *Savoy* [**IRSP42**]
- Don Sebastian Pimentel of the Tercio of *Lisbon* [**IRSP45**]
- The Marquis of Solera, governor of Novara and maestre de campo of the Tercio of *Lombardy* [**IRSP41**]
- Don Fadrique de Cabrera, colonel of a German regiment [**IRAL17**] (missing in action)

Notable wounded and prisoners included:
- Don Francisco Colmenero of the Tercio of *Naples* [**IRSP43**] (whose ten captains fell in battle)
- Marquis Melzi, colonel of another German regiment [**IRAL18**] (later died of wounds)
- Count Bonesana, Maestre de Campo of a Lombard tercio [**IRIT09**]
- Prince Trivulzio, Commissary General of the Foreign Cavalry [**CRAL15**]
- Don Ambrogio Fiorenza, Commissary General of the Neapolitan Cavalry [**CRIT08**]
- Count d'Ursel, wounded commander of dragoons
- Don Antonio di Francia, Maestre de Campo of Neapolitan infantry [**IRIT16**] [289]

Though the French, after the battle, promptly torched surrounding villages, they couldn't pursue the retreating Allies due to strained supply lines and their own substantial casualties. Their only strategic gain was managing to slip minor reinforcements into Casale, before taking winter quarters.

"*A secret council was held between the Duke, Marshal Caprara and the Marquis of Leganes, who will go to Milan for ten or twelve days to put things in order and then return. It was decided to provide for Cuneo, the French could apply for its conquest if they do not have sufficient opposition in the countryside and with the troops already reorganized by the Germans and the Country* [=State of Milan], *the countryside around Turin is beaten, where they are encamped. The Duke has sent orders to all the militias of Piedmont to take up arms and has offered exemption from taxes for four years to all those communities that will distinguish themselves most in the expedition of the aforementioned militias by serving their Sovereign by infesting the French army in small parties and in large bodies. In addition with the troops that by express sent to them have been removed from the blockade of Casale, and have arrived here, and with the recruits, who are already seen arriving from Germany, it is thought to reorganize things throughout this week in such a way as to be able to keep the French at bay, and prevent greater advances, which they could make. The latter in the meantime yesterday set fire to the large Terra di Giaveno located between Pinerolo and Susa and have threatened others with similar massacres.*"[290]

Year 1694

This year, the Allies initiated a blockade and preliminary siege of the fortress of Casale, deploying among their forces Brandenburg auxiliary troops (4 infantry battalions largely composed of French Huguenots) that had arrived as reinforcements. The Spanish contingent included the Lombard infantry tercio of *Porlezza* [**IRIT11**], the *State Dragoon Regiment* [**DRIT01**], and the *State Cavalry* [**CRIT07-08-15**], later joined by three Spanish infantry tercios. On August 28th, they successfully recaptured Fort San Giorgio once again. However, considerations for a greater military effort were hindered by severe supply shortages, resulting from years of devastation in Piedmontese and Montferrat countryside by warring armies. Additionally, the French had chosen to concentrate their main effort in Catalonia. Despite this, the Spanish army managed to repel several French sorties from Pinerolo.

In December 1694, the Duke of Württemberg's regiments serving in the Milanese army - whose numbers had dwindled due to casualties and desertions, with insufficient recruits to compensate - underwent reorganization. The two mounted regiments (cuirassiers and dragoons) were consolidated into a single cavalry regiment, while the infantry regiment maintained its existing strength.

Year 1695

After suffering several delays due to unusually severe weather conditions, in the late spring of 1695 the Allied Army - consisting of a strong contingent of the Spanish-Milanese forces (which deployed, besides troops including the notable Tercio of *Lombardia* [**IRSP41**], 40 cannons and 24 mortars) and Imperial troops, assisted by English engineers and artillerymen - once again began the formal siege of the city and fortress of Casale. The encirclement was completed in June 1695, while maintaining the blockade around Pinerolo as well. On July 9th, the city and fortress of Casale surrendered after offering relatively determined resistance. All the principal allied leaders were present at the siege, which had been preceded by a blockade maintained throughout the winter by the Spanish and Imperial troops quartered in Monferrato. Among them were the Marquis of Leganés, Governor of the State of Milan in the name of the King of Spain; Prince Eugene for the Imperial forces; Lord Galloway for the British; Margrave Charles of Brandenburg (brother of the Elector), who later died of an illness con-

---

288 **Charles Schomberg, 2nd Duke of Schomberg** ('s-Hertogenbosch, 5th August 1645 – Turin, 17th October 1693)
289 **AA.Vat. Segreteria di Stato - Savoia Year 1693**
290 **AA.Vat. Segreteria di Stato - Savoia Year 1693**

tracted during the siege; as well as Victor Amadeus, Duke of Savoy himself, and his leading generals.

The French surrendered, yielding the city and its fortifications, which were demolished (in reality, there was a secret agreement between Louis XIV and the Duke of Savoy to end the war in Italy). The Duke compelled the allies to accept the capitulation proposed by the French—already agreed upon by him—despite them deeming it too generous for the defenders. The besiegers' losses had not been insignificant. Seventy cannons were captured in the city, 28 cannons and one mortar in the castle, and 120 cannons plus 10 in the citadel. The French troops, around 3,000 men, were allowed to leave Casale and head partly to Pinerolo and partly to France. The city, with its walls and fortifications dismantled, was returned to its rightful owner, the Duke of Mantua—a decision displeasing to the Habsburgs, though they ultimately had to accept it.

The outcome was far worse for the Montferrat defenders found inside the fortifications. They were considered rebellious subjects of the Emperor (Casale was still an imperial fiefdom), and except for a few noblemen, all were strangled by the executioner (three executioners were needed, working for three full days, to complete the punishment, as recorded in numerous chronicles of the time).

Year 1696

This year, Duke Victor Amadeus of Savoy abruptly signed a peace treaty with France, bringing the war on the Italian front to an end. In exchange, the Duke received from France the city and fortress of Pinerolo, most of the occupied strongholds in Piedmont, the cities of Nice and Susa, and all the ducal territories seized by the French during the war—including Savoy. Meanwhile, Spanish, British, and Imperial troops were forced to evacuate Piedmont.

The Spanish also had to endure a brief siege at the city of Valenza Po, located on the border of the Duchy of Milan, which was defended by the troops of the State as well as their Imperial and German allies. The siege was carried out by French and Savoyard forces before hostilities ceased and Italy's neutrality was finally established.

Once the armistice with France—which stipulated Italy's neutralization—was reached, the Spanish, British, Imperial, and auxiliary troops had to evacuate Piedmont without delay. The Duke of Savoy, now effectively aligned with the French camp, ordered them to retreat beyond the old borders. To pressure Madrid and Vienna, he even besieged the stronghold of Valenza Po with his own troops, joined by the French. This border city in the Duchy of Milan was defended by the Spanish and Imperial forces[291] until the two Habsburg courts finally accepted the peace terms. For their defense of the stronghold, several officers were rewarded for their tenacity during the siege being appointed Sergeants Generals of Battle (Sergente generale di battaglia) for the vigor with which they and their *tercios* had held out. D. Francisco Colmenero, who already served as governor of Mortara, was forced to relinquish command of his *tercio*. D. Joseph Arteaga and Count Francesco Bonesana, however, retained command of their respective units.

The war between France and the allies of the League continued on other fronts and at sea, but Spain no longer had to commit all the troops of the State of Milan to Italy (after all, there were no longer French garrisons in either Casale or Pinerolo). Each of the belligerents was thus able to redeploy troops where they were most needed. The Spaniards concentrated theirs in Catalonia (nevertheless, Barcelona was taken by the French in 1697).

---

291   **12 September 1696, Milan (Avvisi Italiani di Vienna)** In addition to the previously reported four regiments, a Regiment of Huguenots and another Danish(?) one - exceptionally fine troops - have reinforced Alessandria. They have encamped at Borgoglio, while others remain in the city in field formation. Work on the fortifications continues unabated, with fascines being used to cover the countryside. At Valenza, construction began last Thursday near the Santa Caterina convent on a new citadel, which will reinforce the weakest sector of that stronghold. Numerous labourers have been dispatched from Milan for this purpose. A flying camp of allied forces is forming at Candia, from where they can support Mortara, Novara, Valenza, and Alessandria. The Bonesana Tercio, a German regiment, and 500 Grisons have arrived as reinforcements at Valenza. The French are finally in Casale, behaving as good friends and even paying for forage.
22 September 1696 (A.A.Vat, Segreteria di Stato Savoia) For the defense of the Valenza stronghold, two *Lorraine* battalions have entered, along with: 2 from *Stanau's* Regiment, 2 from *Vittembergh's*, 2 Spanish, and 3 Italian battalions. A certain Spanish gentleman, Mr. Colmenero, has been appointed Governor.
13 October 1696, Turin (Avvisi Italiani di Vienna). By the grace of God, the neutrality of Italy has at last been established, to last for three years—or until a universal peace is achieved—with the simultaneous withdrawal of all foreign troops from Italy. The withdrawal is to begin immediately, with proportional numbers: for every three French soldiers, one German shall depart, and so on until all have left. In the meantime, all hostilities are suspended.
The siege of Valenza was lifted on the 9th. There, the French had advanced their trenches nearly to the counterscarp and had seized an outer ravelin, which they had previously assaulted multiple times in vain, suffering heavy casualties.
The neutrality agreement was signed:
- **In the name of His Imperial Majesty (Caesar)**: Counts Mansfelt and Breiner, and His Serene Highness Prince Eugene.
- **In the name of Spain**: The Governor of Milan, Legañez, and the Catholic Resident in this city.
- **In the name of France**: A Marshal.
- **In the name of Savoy**: The Marquis of San Tommaso.

Negotiations are now underway with the Italian princes regarding the funds to be contributed for the Germans' departure. His Royal Highness [the Duke of Savoy] had already informed them in advance to expedite matters and prevent any delays in the German withdrawal. The infantry will march through Swiss territory toward the Tyrol, while the cavalry will pass through Venetian lands toward Trent. Meanwhile, the French army has suffered considerable losses, reportedly diminished by around 10,000 men—dead, wounded, or scattered through desertion. However, based on available accounts, the number is estimated to be at least 8,000.

BIBLIOGRAPHY AND SOURCES

Archivo General de Simancas
  Secreteria de Guerra (Guerra Antigua - Tierra)
      Estado
      España
      Flandes
      Napoles
      Milan
 Secretarias Provinciales
      Napoles
       Milan

Archivo Historico Nacional Madrid
      Estado

Biblioteca Nacional Madrid
      Ms de Villahermosa
      Francisco Antonio de Agurto, marques de Gastañaga *"Tratado y Reglas Militares de Francisco Antonio de Agurto, marques de Gastañaga, gobernador y capitan general de Flandes"* R/9773

Archivo de la Corona de Aragon (Barcelona)
      Consejo de Aragon

Archivo Historico Ciudad de Barcelona
      Manual del Consell de Cent
      Deliberacions del Consell de Cent
      Manual Concordias i Contracts

Biblioteca de Catalunya
      Arxiu Històric de l'Hospital de la Santa Creu i Sant Pau

Archives Generales du Royaume Bruxelles
      Secretariat d'Etat et de Guerre
      Contadorie et Pagadorie des Gens de Guerre
      Audience
      Secretairie d'Allemagne

Archivio di Stato di Napoli
      Scrivania di Razione
      Reali Ordini
      Tesoreria Antica. Cassa Militare
      Giunta dell'Arsenale

Società Napoletana di Storia Patria

Biblioteca Nazionale di Napoli

Archivio di Stato di Milano
      Militare P.A.

Archivio Storico Comunale di Milano

Archivio Apostolico Vaticano
>Segreteria di Stato
>"Avvisi" 1660 to 1700
>Nunziatura di Spagna,
>di Napoli,
>di Fiandra,
>di Portogallo,
>di Savoia,
>di Spagna,
>di Germania dal 1688 al 1700

Archivio di Stato di Torino
>Sez. I & II,
>Materie Militari - Imprese militari.

Archivio di Stato di Palermo
>Segreteria di Stato

Service Historique de l'Armée de Terre Vincennes
>Series A1

Bibliothèque Nationale de France, Paris «*Les Triomphes de Louis XIV et de Louis XV*», Id 42, Id 43, Id 44, Id 45, Id 46, Id 47

"*A List of Our Army as it was drawn up at Tillroy Camp*" 1689, as recorded by Rev. Percy Sumner, [***Tillroy list***]

"*An Exact List of the Royal Confederate Army in Flanders Commanded by the K. of Great Britain in Four Lines as it was drawn up at Gerpines-Camp, July 27. 1691*", London 1691, [***Gerpines list***]

„*Schlachtordnung der Engländer und Alliirten, Ath 1696*" Marburg Archive HStaM WHK 9/235/a [***Ath Camp list***]

TEXTS

ACCADEMIA DI S. MARCIANO. "*La guerra della Lega di Augusta fino alla battaglia di Orbassano*" in Armi Antiche 1992 Torino 1993

ANDUJAR CASTILLO, Francisco. "*El Sonido del Dinero. Monarquia, ejercito y venalidad en la Espana del siglo XVIII*" Marcial Pons Historia Madrid 2004

BELAUBRE, Jean. «*Les Triomphes de Louis XIV*» Paris 1971 (Ed. Terrana)

BELLOSO MARTIN, Carlos. "*La Antemuralla de la Monarquia. Los Tercios Españoles en el Reino de Sicilia en el Siglo XVI*" Coleccion ADALID Ministerio Defensa Madrid Dicembre 2010

BOERI, Gian Carlo; PEIRCE, Guglielmo. "*Origine delle uniformi nel Regno di Napoli*" in Studi Storico-Militari 1991 Uff. Storico S.M.E. Roma 1993

BOERI, Gian Carlo; PEIRCE, Guglielmo."*Origines de la uniformidad militar en el Reino de Napoles*" in "Researching and Dragona" Vol. II n° 4, Vol. V n° 12, Vol. VI n° 13, n° 14 & n° 15 Madrid, 1994-1997

BOERI, GianCarlo. "*El Ejército del Ducado de Milan en 1693*" in Dragona n. 2 Madrid, 1993

BOERI. Gian Carlo. "*Württemberg Regiments serving in the Army of the State of Milan 1690-1698*" Academia Letters, 2021

BOERI, GianCarlo; MIRECKI QUINTERO, José Luis; PALAU CUÑAT, José. "*The Spanish Armies in the War of the League of Augburg (Nine Years' War 1688-1697)*" (en CD) Dan Schorr USA 2001

BOERI, GianCarlo; MIRECKI QUINTERO, José Luis; PALAU CUÑAT, José. "*The Spanish Armies in the War of the League of Augburg (Nine Years' War 1688-1697)*" (Revised Edition) The Pike and Shot Society London, 2011

BOERI, GianCarlo; MIRECKI QUINTERO, José Luis; PALAU CUÑAT, José. "*Los tercios de Carlos II durante la Guerra de los Nueve Años (1689-1697). Tomo I : España y Africa*" La Espada y la Pluma Madrid 2006

BOERI, Gian Carlo; ILARI, Virgilio; PAOLETTI, Ciro. "*Tra i Borboni e gli Asburgo*" Casa Editrice Nuove Ricerche Ancona 1996

BOERI, Gian Carlo. "*El vestuario : de los tercios a los regimientos (1550-1748)*" In "*Caminos Legendarios. Los Tercios y el Regimiento Soria en la Historia y la Cultura.*" Las Palmas Diciembre 2009

Borreguero Beltran, Cristina; Retortillo Atienza, Asuncion. "*La sua professione fu di soldato. Italianos en los ejercitos de los Austrias*" in Studium, Magisterium et Amicitia Ediciones Eunate 2018

Bueno Carrera, José M.a. "*Soldados de España. El Uniforme militar español desde los Reyes catolicos hasta Juan Carlos I*" Grafica Summa Oviedo, Malaga, 1978

Bulifon, Antonio. "*Giornali di Napoli dal 1547 al 1706. Vol. 1: 1547-1691*" Società Napoletana di Storia Patria, Napoli, 1932

Buono, Alessandro. "*Esercito, istituzioni, territorio, Aloggiamenti militari, e Case Herme nello stato di Milano*" Firenze University Press, 2009

Calvo Perez, José Luis; Gravalos Gonzales, Luis. "*Banderas de España*" Silex Vitoria, 1983

Cardenas Piera De, Emilio. "*Forjadores del Imperio Español. Flandes*" Ed. Dyckinson Madrid 2001

Cheiron (Rivista A.A.V.V.). "*L'Italia degli Austrias. Monarchia cattolica e domini italiani nei secoli XVI e XVII*" Edizioni Centro Federico Odorici Mantova 1993

Childs, John. "*The Nine Years' War and the British Army 1688-1697. The Operations in the Low Countries*" Manchester University Press 1991

Clonard, Serafino de Sotto y Montes, conde de. "*Historia Organica de la Infanteria e Caballeria Española*" 16 Voll. Madrid ,1853-1856

Comines, Pedro de. "*Relacion diaria de lo sucedido en el ataque, y defensa de la ciudad de Barcelona, cabeza del principado de Cataluña, antemural de toda España; Escrivela Pedro de Comines, consagrala a la Magestad de Guillermo III. Rey de la Gran Bretaña*" Haya 1759

Coniglio, Giuseppe. "*I Vicerè spagnoli di Napoli*" F. Fiorentino ed. Napoli, 1967

Contreras Gay, José. "*La reorganizacion militar en la epoca de la decadencia española (1640-1700)*" Millars XXVI Any 2003 pp 130-154

Correa de Franca, Alejandro. "*Historia de la mui nobil y fidelissima ciudad de Ceuta*" Ciudad Autonoma de Ceuta, 1999

Dalla Rosa, Enrico. "*Le Milizie del Seicento nello Stato di Milano*" Università Cattolica Milano, Settembre 1991

De Mesa, Eduardo. "*Los Tercios en las Campañas del Mediterraneo s. XVI (Italia)*" Almena Madrid, 2000

Echeveria Bragado, Javier. "*El servicio mercenario suizo en los ejércitos de los Austrias : las ordenanzas militares de Suizos de 1589.*" in Ruiz Molina, L.; Ruíz Ibáñez, J.J.; Vincent, B. (eds.) La contribución de los extranjeros a la Monarquía Hispánica, 1500-1700. Yakka: Revista de estudios yeclanos, Nº 20, 2013-2014, pp. 229-242.

Elliot, John H. "*La Spagna Imperiale 1469-1716*" Il Mulino, Bologna, 1992

Espino Lopez, Antonio. "*Las tropas de Granada en las guerras de Cataluña, 1684-1697: una vision social*" Chronica Nova 20 Universidad de Granada, 1992

Espino Lopez, Antonio. "*Las tropas italianas en la defensa de Cataluña, 1665-1698*" Investigaciones Historicas 18 1998

Espino Lopez, Antonio. "*Las guerras en la frontera catalana durante el reinado de Carlos II 1679-1690*" III Congreso Internacional de Historia Militar Zaragoza Mayo 1994

Espino Lopez, Antonio. "*Los tercios catalanes durante el reinado de Carlos II 1665-1697. El funcionamiento interno de una institucion militar.*" Universidad de la Rioja Logroño BRIOCAR 22 1998

Espino Lopez, Antonio. "*Catalunya durante el reinado de Carlos II. Politica y guerra en la frontera catalana, 1679-1697*" Universitat Autonoma de Barcelona, Monografies Manuscrits 5 Bellaterra 1999

Espino Lopez, Antonio. "*El Esfuerzo de Guerra de la Corona de Aragon durante el Reinado de Carlos II, 1665-1700. Los servicios de tropas*" Revista de Historia Moderna Annales de la Universidad de Alicante n° 22 Alicante 2004

Espino Lopez, Antonio. "*La presion de la Armada francesa sobre los Reinos de la Corona de Aragon durante el reinado de Carlos II, 1665-1700*" Revista de Historia Naval Año XXII num. 86 pagg. 7-28 2004

Espino Lopez, Antonio. "*La formacion de milicias generales en los Reinos de la Corona de Aragon durante el reinado de Carlos II, 1665-1700.*" in Estudios humanísticos. Historia, Universidad de León, Nº 2, 2003, pp. 111-140

Feliu de La Peña y Farell, Narciso. "*Anales de Cataluña y Epilogo Breve de los Progressos, y Famosos Hechos de la Nación. Tomo Tercero, contiene los sucessos del año 1458, hasta el de 1709*" Barcelona por Juan Pablo Martí, 1709 (in particolare Tomo III)

Fernández de Medrano , Sebastian "*El Ingeniero Practico,*" Bruxelles 1687, II ed. id 1696

Fernández de Medrano , Sebastian "*El Perfecto Artificial, Bombardero Y Artillero*" Bruxelles 1699

Filamondo, Raffaele Maria. "*Il Genio Bellicoso di Napoli. Memorie Istoriche d'alcuni Capitani Celebri Napolitani*" Stampa di Antonio Parrino (2 Tomi) In Napoli 1694

Galante Gomez, Francisco [*director edicion*]. "*Caminos Legendarios. Los Tercios y el Regimiento de Soria en la Historia y la Cultura*" [vari contributi, tra cui **G.C. Boeri** "*Uniformes y banderas: de los Tercios a los Regimientos*"] Editorial Rueda Madrid Dicembre 2009

Galasso, Giuseppe. "*Napoli Spagnola dopo Masaniello*" Sansoni Editore, Firenze 1982
Garcia Martinez, Sebastian. "*Valencia bajo Carlos II*" Villena 1991
Guillame, Henri- Louis (baron de). «*Histoire de l'Infanterie Wallone sous la Maison d'Espagne (1500-1800)*» Academie des Sciences, XLII Bruxelles 1876
Hanlon, Gregory. "*The Twilight of a military Tradition. Italian Aristocrats and European Conflicts, 1560-1800*" University College of London Press London 1998
Hernandez F. Xavier. "*Historia Militar de Catalunya. Vol. III: la defensa de la Terra*" Rafael Dalmau Editor Barcelona 2003
Hernandez F. Xavier, Riart Francesc. "*Els Exèrcits de Catalunya (1713-1714) Uniformes, equipaments, organitzaciò*" Rafael Dalmau Editor Barcelona 2007
Hoffmann, Anton. "*Das Heer des Blaues König, die Soldaten des Kurfürsten Max II. Emanuel von Bayern, 1682-1726, geschildert in Wort und Bild von Anton Hoffmann*" Munchen 1909-1910 [rist. 1969]
Jeanmougin, Bertrand. "*Louis XIV à la Conquête des Pays-Bas Espagnols. La Guerre oubliée 1678-1684*" Editions Economica Paris 2005
Jennings, Brendan. [editor] "*Wild Geese in Spanish Fiandre 1582-1700*" Dublin Stationery Office for the Irish Manuscripts Commission 1964
Lierneux, Pierre. "*El Uniforme Militar en los Países Bajos Españoles: Mecanismos de un Nacimiento Esperado.*" Revista de Historia Militar Número 121 (2017), pp. 91-136
Lynn, John A. "*The Wars of Louis XIV 1667-1714*" Longmann 1999
Maffi, Davide. "*L'amministrazione della finanza militare nella Lombardia spagnola: i veedores e i contadores dell'esercito (1536-1700)*" in «Storia Economica», V (2002).
Maffi, Davide. "*Nobiltà e carriera delle armi nella Milano di Carlo II (1665-1700)*" Atti Seminario Border line: la società militare in età moderna tra società, economia e territorio" Milano 30 Giugno 2004
Maffi, Davide. "*Il baluardo della corona. Guerra, esercito, finanze e società nella Lombardia seicentesca (1630-1660)*" Edumond Le Monnier SpA, Firenze, 2007
Maffi, Davide. "*La Cittadella in Armi. Esercito, società e finanza nella Lombardia di Carlo II 1660-1700*" Franco Angeli Ed. Milano 2010.
Maffi, Davide. "*Los últimos tercios. El Ejército de Carlos II*" Desperta Ferro Ediciones, Madrid, 2020
Manzano Lahoz, Antonio. "*Las Banderas Historicas del Ejército Español*" Ministerio de Defensa Madrid 1996
Manzano Lahoz, Antonio. "*Las Banderas del Ejercito Español a lo largo de la Historia Siglos XVI a XXI*" Editorial Atenea, Madrid 2017
Manzano Lahoz, Antonio. "*Los estandartes del Ejército español a lo largo de la historia. Siglos XVI a XXI*" Ministerio de Defensa, Madrid 2023
Manzano Lahoz, Antonio. "*El militar viste como quiere 1500-1674*" Ministerio de Defensa, Madrid 2020
Manzano Lahoz, Antonio. "*Cada regimiento su uniforme. 1674-1788*" Ministerio de Defensa, Madrid 2022
Manzano Lahoz, Antonio. "*La uniformidad y las banderas*", en VV.AA., "*Historia de la Infantería Española. La infantería en torno al Siglo de Oro*", Madrid, Ediciones Ejército, pp. 369-416. (1993)
Martinez de Merlo, Jesùs. "*La Caballeria entre los Austria y los Borbones*" Revista de Historia Militar, Madrid 2017, pp 137-198
May De Romainmotier, M. "*Histoire Militaire de la Suisse et celle des Suisses dans les differens services de l'Europe*" Lausanne 1787
Mesa, Eduardo de. "*The Irish in the Spanish Armies in the Seventeenth Century*" Irish Historical Monographs 12, Boyden Press, Dublin 2014
Mesa Coronado, Maria del Pilar. "*Sicilia en la defensa del Mediterráneo en tiempos de Carlos II (1665-1700)*" Tesi Doctoral Universidad de Castilla-La Mancha Facultad de Letras Departamento de Historia, Ciudad Real 2012
Mesa Coronado, Maria del Pilar. "*Las Fuerzas terrestres del Reino de Sicilia (1665-1700)*" SISM Fucina di Marte, Roma 2022
Mirecki Quintero, José Luis. "*El Ejército de Flandes en tiempo de la paz de Rijswijk: un proyecto para su reforma*" Dragona an 1 num. 1 December 1992. Madrid
Montes Ramos, José. "*El Ejercito de Carlos II y Felipe V (1694-1727) El sitio de Ceuta*" Aqualarga, Madrid 1999
Nimwegen, Olaf van. "*De Veertigjarige Oorlog 1672-1712*" Prometheus, Amsterdam 2020
Palau, José; de Mirecki, José Luis. "*Rocroy. Cuando la Honra española se pagaba con sangre.*" STAR IBERICA S.A.. Madrid, 2016
Parker, Geoffrey. "*The Army of Fiandre and the Spanish Road 1567-1659*" Cambridge 1972
Parker, Geoffrey. "*La Rivoluzione Militare*" Il Mulino 1990

Parrino, Domenico Antonio. "*Teatro Eroico e Politico dei Governi de' Vicerè del Regno di Napoli dal tempo del Re Ferdinando il Cattolico fino all'anno 1675*" Napoli 1675

Perez Bustamante, Rogelio. "*El Gobierno del Imperio Español. Los Austrias (1517-1700)*" Comunidad de Madrid 2000

Piot, Charles. «*Les guerres en Belgique pendant le dernier quart du XVIIe siècle.*» In: Compte-rendu des séances de la commission royale d'histoire. Deuxième Série, Tome 8, Bruxelles 1880. pp. 31-126

Quatrefages, René. "*Los Tercios Españoles (1567-77)*" Fundacion Universitaria Española, Madrid 1979

Reina, Carlo Giuseppe. *L'origine, corso e fine del Po, con li nomi di tutti i fiumi & acque, che in esso concorrono; come anche delle città e luoghi insigni irrigati da detti fiumi ... Con l'aggiunta d'un breve Racconto historico dell'ultima guerra trà Collegati ... Imperiali, Spagnuoli, e Piemontesi contro i Francesi nel Piemonte, etc*, Milano 1700

Revista Internacional de Historia Militar. "*Presencia irlandesa en la milicia española*" n° 92 Ministerio Defensa, Madrid 2014

Revista Internacional de Historia Militar. "*Presencia germanica en la milicia española*" n° 93 Ministerio Defensa, Madrid 2015

Revista Internacional de Historia Militar. "*Presencia italiana en la milicia española*" n° 94 Ministerio Defensa, Madrid 2016

Revista Internacional de Historia Militar. "*Presencia suiza en la milicia española*" n° 95 Ministerio Defensa Madrid, 2017

Revista Internacional de Historia Militar. "*Presencia de flamencos y valones en la milicia española*" n° 96 Ministerio Defensa, Madrid 2018

Riart, Francesc; Hernandez F., Xavier. "*Soldats, Guerrers i Combatents de los Paisos Catalans*" Rafael Dalmau Editor, Barcelona 2014

Ribot Garcia, Luis Antonio. "*Historia de España*" Vol. XXVIII Madrid 1993

Ribot Garcia, Luis Antonio. "*La Revuelta Antiespañola de Mesina. Causas y antecedentes (1591-1674)*" Universidad de Valladolid "Estudios y Documentos" 1982

Ribot Garcia, Luis Antonio. "*Milano piazza d'armi della Monarchia spagnola*" in Claudio Donati (cur.), Eserciti e carriere militari nell'Italia moderna, Milano, Unicopli, 1998, pp. 41-61.

Ribot Garcia, Luis Antonio. "*El Ejercito de los Austrias. Aportaciones recientes y nuevas perspectivas.*" in Temas de Historia Militar (tomo I), Madrid 1983

Ribot Garcia, Luis Antonio. "*La Monarquia Española y la guerra de Mesina (1674-1678)*" Editorial Actas Madrid 2002

Rizzo, Mario. "*Alloggiamenti militari e riforme fiscali nella Lombardia spagnola fra Cinque e Seicento*", Milano, Unicopli, 2001.

Rodriguez Hernandez, Antonio José. "*De Galicia a Flandes: Reclutamiento y Servicio de Soldados Gallegos en el Ejercito de Flandes (1648-1700)*" Obradoiro de Historia Moderna n° 16 2007 pp 213-251

Rodriguez Hernandez, Antonio José. "*España, Flandes y la Guerra de Devolucion (1667-1668). Guerra, Reclutamiento y Movilizacion para el Mantenimiento de los Paises Bajos Españoles*" Coleccion ADALID Madrid Julio 2007

Rodriguez Hernandez, Antonio José. "*La Guerra de Restauración portuguesa en Extremadura.*" 2008 [articolo]

Rodriguez Hernandez, Antonio José. "*La presencia militar irlandesa en el ejército de Extremadura (1640-1668).*" In "Irlanda y el Atlantico Ibérico" 2010

Rodriguez Hernandez, Antonio José. "*Los Tambores de Marte. El Reclutamiento en Castilla durante la segunda mitad del siglo XVII (1648-1700).*" Universidad de Valladolid 2011

Rodriguez Hernandez, Antonio José. "*La Ciudad y la Guarnicion de Ceuta (1640-1700). Ejército, fidelidad e integracion de una ciudad portuguesa en la monarquia hispanica*" Instituto de Estudios Ceuties, Ceuta 2011 (CD)

Rodriguez Hernandez, Antonio José. "*Los Tercios de Flandes.*" Coleccion Breve Historia 2a edicion 2015

Rodríguez Hernández, Antonio José. "*La Evolución del Vestuario Militar y la Aparición de los primeros Uniformes en el Ejército de la Monarquía Hispánica, 1660-1680*" in Obradoiro de Historia Moderna, N.º 26, 179-206, 2017

Rooms, Etienne. Tesi Dottorale sull'Esercito dei Paesi Bassi Spagnoli nel secolo XVII., Bruselles 1999

Rooms, Etienne. "*De Organisatie van de Troepen van de Spaans-Habsburgse Monarchie in de Zuidelijke Nederlanden*" Musée Royal de l'Armée, Bruxelles 2003

Rooms, Etienne. "*Le operazioni dell'Esercito della Monarchia spagnola asburgica nei Paesi Bassi Meridionali (1659-1700)*" (Edito in proprio in Fiammingo) 2003

Col. Rouen, Charles-Auguste. "*Histoire de l'Armée Belge. ....*" Lyon-Claesen Ed., Bruxelles 1896

Rorive, Jean-Pierre. "*La guerre de siège sous Louis XIV. En Europe et à Huy*" Editions Racine, Bruxelles 1998

Sala y Abarca, Francisco Ventura, de. "*Despues de Dios la primera obligacion y glosa de ordenes militares*" por Geronimo Fasulo, en Napoles, 1681.

Samaniego, Juan Antonio. "*Disertacion sobre la antigüedad de los Regimientos de Infanteria, Caballeria y Dragones de España*" Madrid 1738 (Ed. Ministerio de Defensa Madrid 1992)
Sorando Muzás, Luis. *"Estandartes de Dragones (I)",* Memorial de Caballería nº 46, Valladolid 1998, pp. 17 - 25.
Sorando Muzás, Luis. *"Estandartes de Dragones (II)",* Memorial de Caballería nº 47, Valladolid 1999, pp. 21 - 25.
Sorando Muzás, Luis. (Illustrazioni **A. Manzano)** "*El Tercio de Aragon: Notas sobre su evolucion, indumentaria y emblematica (1678-1698)*" Emblemata n° 1 Diputacion de Zaragoza 1995, pp. 153 – 165.
Sorando Muzás, Luis. "*Bandera de compañía de un Tercio de Infantería española no identificado (siglo XVII)*", Banderas nº 60 (1996), p. 24.
Sorando Muzás, Luis; Manzano Lahoz, Antonio. "*La bandera del Tercio de Aragón*", Emblemata nº 3, Zaragoza (1997), pp. 475 - 477.
Sorando Muzás, Luis. "*Banderas, estandartes y trofeos del Museo del Ejército 1700-1843. Catalogo razonado*" Ministerio de Defensa Madrid 2000
(De) Sotto y Montes, Joaquin. "*Sintesis Historica de la Caballeria Española: Desde los primeros tiempos historicos hasta el siglo XX* " Madrid 1968
Staudinger, Karl. "*Geschichte des bayerischen Heeres.*" T. II 1680-1726, München 1904
Storrs, Christopher. "*The Resilience of the Spanish Monarchy 1665-1700*" Oxford Press 2006
Storrs, Christopher. "*The Army of Lombardy and the resilience of Spanish power in Italia in the Reign of Carlos II (1665-1700)*" War in History by Sage Publications Ltd 1997-1998
Storrs, Christopher. "*La pervivencia de la monarquia española bajo el reinado de Carlos II (1665-1700)*" pp 39-61 Manuscrits 21, 2003
Stradling, R.A. "*The Spanish Monarchy and Irish Mercenaries. The Wild Geese in Spain, 1618-68*" Irish Academic Press 1994.
Vegiano, Jean Charles Joseph de, Seigneur d'Hovel: «*Nobiliaire des Pays-Bas et du comté de Bourgogne*» Gand, 1865.
Vela Santiago, Francisco: Gravalos Gonzalez, Luis. "*Los Dragones en el Ejercito Español. (1635-1803/1805-1821/1885-1931)*" Madrid 2011
Wilson, Peter H. "*War, State and Society in Württemberg 1677-1793*" Cambridge University Press 1995
Winkler, Leonhard. "*Das kurbayerische Regiment zu Fuß Graf Tattenbach in Spanien 1695-1701*" Straub, München, 1890. Supplement-Heft zum Jahrbuch der Militärischen Gesellschaft München pro 1888-1890
AAA. "*Historia de la Infanteria Española*" 2 Voll. Madrid 1994
AAA. "*Los Austrias. Grabados de la Biblioteca Nacional*" Julio Ollero Editor Madrid 1993
AAA. "*Die Wildgänse. The Wild Geese. Irische Soldaten im Dienste der Habsburger*" (*Catalogo Mostra 2003-2004*) Heeresgeschichtliches Museum Vienna 2003
"*Wild Geese In Spanish Fiandre 1582-1700 Documents, Relating Chiefly To Irish Reggimenti, From The Archives Generales Du Royaume, Brussels, And Other Sources*". Edited by Brendan Jennings, O.F.M., D.Litt., M.R.I.A. Dublin: Stationery Office For The Irish Manuscripts Commission 1964

Magazines

Avvisi di Milano (varie annate)
Avvisi di Napoli (varie annate)
Avvisi italiani (di Vienna) (varie annate)
Foglio di Foligno (varie annate)
Gaceta de Madrid (varie annate)
Gazette de France (varie annate)
Gazzetta di Bologna (varie annate)
Gazzetta di Mantova (varie annate)
Mercure Galant (varie annate)
Theatrum Europaeum di Matthäus Merian (varie annate 1663-1738)

CONTENTS

Preface	3	Infantry	75
Introduction	5	Spanish Infantry	75
ARMIES OF THE KING OF SPAIN	9	Milan Infantry	75
Principality of Catalonia	11	Neapolitan Infantry	75
Infantry	12	German Infantry	76
Places in North Africa	16	Swiss Infantry	76
Cavalry and Dragoons	16	Cavalry	76
Flanders	18	Auxiliary Cavalry	78
Infantry	19	*Kingdom of Naples*	79
Cavalry	26	*Kingdom of Sicily*	80
Companies of Guards	28	**FLAGS AND STANDARDS**	81
Tercios and regiments	28	**CAMPAIGNS**	97
Italian possessions	33	*Catalonia*	97
Duchy of Milan	33	Year 1689	102
Infantry	33	Year 1690	102
Cavalry and Dragoons	37	Year 1691	102
Companies of Guards	37	Year 1692	103
Auxiliary Cavalry	38	Year 1693	103
Kingdom of Naples	38	Year 1694	104
Kingdom of Sicily	40	Year 1695	115
Artillery (Spain, Flanders, Italy)	46	Year 1696	116
Militia	49	Year 1697	117
UNIFORMS	51	*North-Africa Garrisons*	121
Catalonia	53	Melilla	121
Infantry	53	Ceuta	121
Old provincial Tercios	54	Larache	121
Tercios of the Kingdoms	56	Oran e Mazalquivir	121
Tercios 1694	56	*Flanders*	122
Catalan Tercios	65	Year 1689	122
Tercios de la Armada	65	Year 1690	123
Italian Infantry	65	Year 1691	123
Walloon Infantry	65	Year 1692	124
German Infantry	65	Year 1693	124
Cavalry and Dragoons	66	Year 1694	124
Cavalry	66	Year 1695	133
Flanders	67	Year 1696	133
Infantry	67	Year 1697	133
Spanish Infantry	67	**Italy**	134
Walloon Infantry	68	Year 1690	134
Italian Infantry	68	Year 1691	136
German Infantry	68	Year 1692	137
English, Irish, Scottish Infantry	72	Year 1693	138
German auxiliary Infantry	72	Year 1694	139
Cavalry	72	Year 1695	139
Dragoons	73	Year 1696	140
Auxiliary Cavalry	74		
State of Milan	74	**BIBLIOGRAPHY**	141

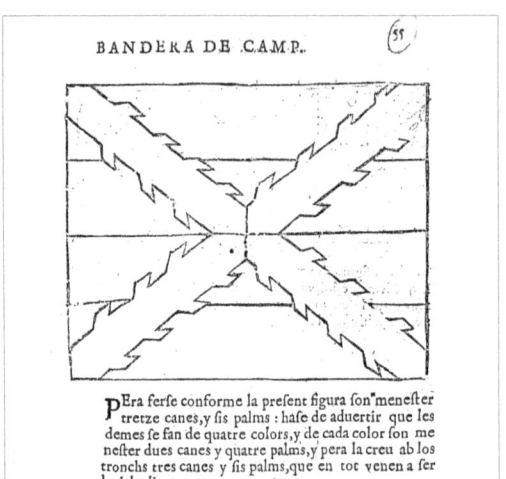
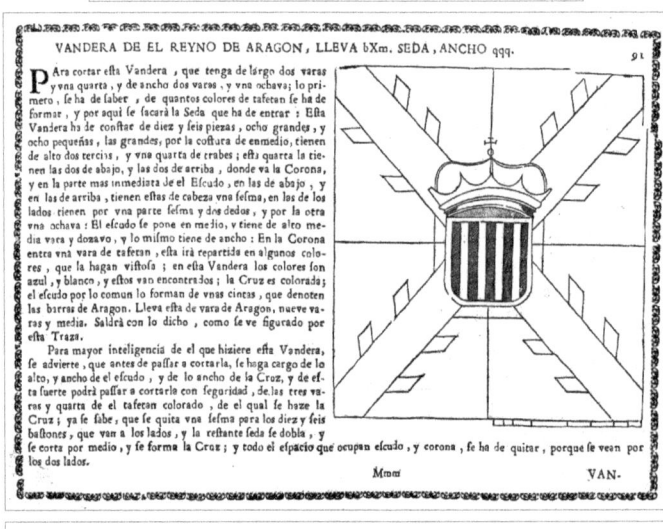
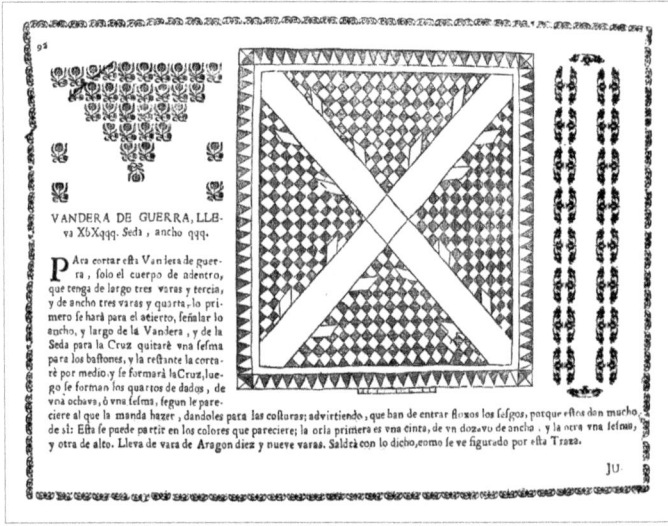

▲ *The first edition of the book (instructions for tailors) on how to make an infantry flag and some subsequent editions. (following page 91)*

ALREADY PUBLISHED

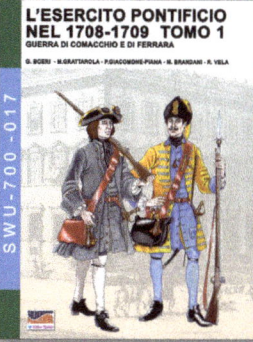
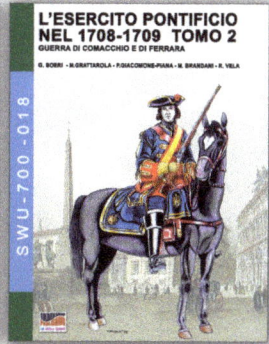

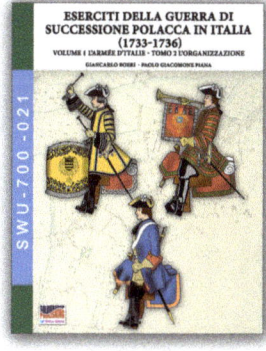
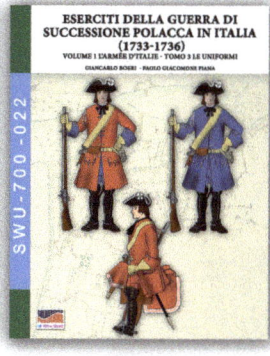

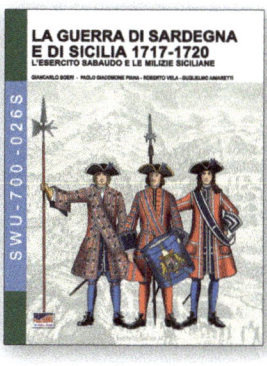

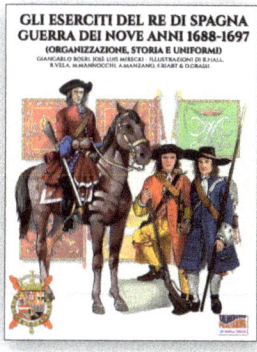

SWU-600-011 EN

www.ingramcontent.com/pod-product-compliance
Lightning Source LLC
LaVergne TN
LVHW072124060526
838201LV00069B/4965